100 American Horror Films

BFI Screen Guides

Barry Keith Grant

Dedication

For Dan Barnowski, Rob Macmorine, Ian Gordon – the Unholy Three
who in different ways helped in the writing of this book, and without
whom it might not have been possible.

THE BRITISH FILM INSTITUTE
Bloomsbury Publishing Plc
50 Bedford Square, London, WC1B 3DP, UK
1385 Broadway, New York, NY 10018, USA
29 Earlsfort Terrace, Dublin 2, Ireland

BLOOMSBURY is a trademark of Bloomsbury Publishing Plc

First published in Great Britain 2022 by Bloomsbury
on behalf of the
British Film Institute
21 Stephen Street, London W1T 1LN
www.bfi.org.uk

The BFI is the lead organisation for film in the UK and the distributor of Lottery
funds for film. Our mission is to ensure that film is central to our cultural life, in
particular by supporting and nurturing the next generation of filmmakers and
audiences. We serve a public role which covers the cultural, creative and economic
aspects of film in the UK.

Copyright © Barry Keith Grant, 2022

Barry Keith Grant has asserted his right under the Copyright, Designs and Patents
Act, 1988, to be identified as author of this work.

For legal purposes the Acknowledgements on p. vi constitute an extension of this
copyright page.

Cover design: Louise Dugdale
Cover image © Film, *Carrie*, (Brian De Palma, 1976), Courtesy of Everett/Mary Evans
Picture Library.

Bloomsbury Publishing Plc does not have any control over, or responsibility for, any
third-party websites referred to or in this book. All internet addresses given in this
book were correct at the time of going to press. The author and publisher regret any
inconvenience caused if addresses have changed or sites have ceased to exist, but
can accept no responsibility for any such changes.

A catalogue record for this book is available from the British Library.
A catalog record for this book is available from the Library of Congress.

ISBN: HB: 978–1–8390–2145-9
       PB: 978–1–8390–2146-6
       ePDF: 978–1–8390–2143-5
       eBook: 978–1–8390–2144-2

Series: BFI Screen Guides. Original text design by couch

Edited, typeset and colour produced by ketchup/Tom Cabot
Printed and bound in India

To find out more about our authors and books visit www.bloomsbury.com and
sign up for our newsletters.

Contents

Acknowledgements

I am grateful to the Department of Communication, Popular Culture and Film, Brock University, and to the Dean of the Faculty of Social Sciences, Dr. Ingrid Makus, for their continued support of my research. Rebecca Barden has been my steadfast editor once more, this time through the challenges of the Covid-19 pandemic. It was a pleasure to work again with Sophie Contento, who expertly sourced the images in this book. Tom Cabot of Ketchup Productions provided the excellent design and production during a difficult time. And last but certainly not least, I thank Genevieve for gracefully entertaining so many monsters during the last year.

Introduction

Writing on the horror film, S.S. Prawer describes terror as the 'principal ingredient' of horror, while James B. Twitchell claims that the source of horror 'is always in dreams, while the basis of terror is in actuality'.[1] Twitchell's distinction suggests that imagination is involved in horror, while terror is produced by empirical perception; but this is virtually the opposite of dictionary definitions, which tend to identify horror with an almost physical loathing and terror with the more imaginative and anticipatory sense of dread. Terror in the past was associated with the transcendent, the awesome, and the Romantic notion of the sublime, while horror was seen to involve mere loathing or repugnance.[2] Certainly, Stephen King distinguishes between the two in his book *Danse Macabre* when he remarks that 'I recognise terror as the finest emotion … and so I will try to terrorise the reader. But if I find I cannot terrify him/her, I will try to horrify; and if I find I cannot horrify, I'll go for the gross out. I'm not proud.'[3]

Yet whether we choose to define the kinds of responses sought by horror films as horror or terror – not to mention fear, suspense, disgust, revulsion – the horror film (the genre's very name points to its intended affect) addresses fears that are, on the one hand, both universal (torture, death) and, on the other, that respond to historically and culturally specific anxieties (for example, atomic radiation in the 1950s, environmental contamination in the 1970s and 1980s, and terrorism and digital technology in the new millennium). As King writes in *Danse Macabre*, horror 'is extremely limber, extremely adaptable, extremely *useful*'.[4] As is true of every genre, individual works of horror may endorse or undermine our conventional views – in this case, of what is monstrous, and what isn't – whether deliberately or unintentionally. But whatever the particular fears addressed by specific horror films, overall the genre provides viewers with vicarious but controlled thrills, pitting something we regard as monstrous against our sense of normalcy,[5] and in so doing offer a release, a catharsis, of our collective and individual fears.

Horror texts exist across a range of media – fiction, comic books, television, video and table games, popular music, and so on. But the medium of cinema is especially conducive to horror. If it is true that the sleep of reason produces monsters, it is also true that, as many have pointed out, the experience of film viewing is very much like dreaming. In the dark, images flicker by that speak to our inner self as well as to our collective psyche. And while some regard the act of film viewing as a sort of regression to a womblike, infantile state, it is perhaps more accurate to say that we watch movies both absorbed and detached, passive and active – as if in dreams awake, to quote Thoreau.[6]

Thus, it is not surprising that while other film genres have cycled in and out of popularity, horror has been consistently present in one form or another throughout film history. With roots in such pre-cinematic forms as medieval woodcuts, Grand Guignol theatre, and the Gothic novel, horror transitioned to film in the one-reelers of Georges Méliès, the first pioneer of fantastic cinema. By 1903 Méliès already had made films with monsters, ghosts, devils, and other assorted spirits – all creatures that were to become central to the horror film as it would develop over time.

Many countries have developed substantial and distinctive horror film styles. One thinks immediately of German expressionist cinema in the 1920s, Italian *giallo* in the postwar period, Hammer horror in the U.K. a decade later. There are also strong horror traditions in the national cinemas of Japan, Mexico, Spain, Australia, and New Zealand, among other countries. In recent years, horror films from around the world have become more familiar to international audiences due to the rise of global film distribution companies, increased multinational film financing, and streaming and other digital capabilities.

Nevertheless, the United States has been extraordinarily prolific in the production of horror films, and many have been successful and influential around the world. At the same time as horror addresses universal themes, the genre is also firmly rooted in the American national character – in its history, its values, its crises. Critics have long noted that horror and violence have been integral to the American experience and the American psyche ever since the first European settlers arrived and began to wrest the land away from the indigenous peoples, cloaked in the nationalist myths of the westward course of empire and Manifest Destiny. D. H. Lawrence was indeed accurate when, in his discussion of Fenimore Cooper's Hawkeye, the first American mythic hero, he famously speculated that 'the essential American soul is hard, isolate, stoic, and a killer'. Beginning with the Puritan settlers, Americans created a cultural myth – so pervasive in the American psyche that it has been termed the national 'monomyth' – of a communal Eden that must be redeemed by what Richard Slotkin has called a 'regeneration through violence'.[8]

Central to this national project has been the demonization of the Other, evident already in the Puritan captivity narratives in which the unfortunate narrators were forced to live unchristian lives while 'possessed' by their swarthy Native American abductors. This demonization is evident in the western's depiction of 'Indians' as savages – whether lustful or noble – and surfaces with equal vehemence in the cavalry officer of *The Burrowers** (2008) as it does in Ethan Edwards in *The Searchers* (1956). In his monumental study of American literature, Leslie Fiedler describes American fiction as 'essentially a gothic one … a tradition of dealing with the exaggerated and the grotesque, not as they are verifiable in any external landscape or sociological observation of manners and men, but as they correspond in quality to our deepest fears and guilts as projected in our dreams.'[9] Fiedler shows how American writers, beginning with Charles Brockden Brown, adapted the conventions of the gothic novel to the American context, replacing, for example, the lustful nobleman with the Indian and the castle with the forest.

Already the forest issues forth the monstrous, like the return of the repressed, in a remarkable passage in J. Hector St. John de Crèvecoeur's *Letters from an American Farmer* in 1782. Leisurely strolling through the woods in the South on his way to an acquaintance's home for dinner, the author, an astute French observer of the American character, suddenly comes across a black man hanging in a cage from a tree. 'The birds had already picked out his eyes, his cheek bones were bare', writes Crèvecoeur, anticipating the moment when Lydia Brenner discovers the body of her neighbour Dan Fawcett after an avian attack in *The Birds** (1963). Director Alfred Hitchcock's series of jump cuts to the man's hollowed-out eye sockets expresses a comparable shock to Crèvecoeur's sudden 'alarm'. But the scene also expresses the tensions of America's slave legacy and the racial fears expressed in horror films from *King Kong** (1933) to *Get Out** (2017). The link to *Candyman** (1992) is particularly striking given that after Crèvecoeur chases the birds away, 'swarms of insects covered the whole body of this unfortunate wretch, eager to feed on his mangled flesh and drink his blood.'[10]

Philip Freneau's 1779 poem 'The House of Night' is remembered today as prophetic in articulating American culture's embrace of the gothic:

> Let others draw from smiling skies their theme,
> And tell of climes that boast unfading light,
> I draw a darker scene, replete with gloom,
> I sing the horrors of the House of Night.[11]

This sense of lurking horror informs so much of American culture, at least since Jonathan Edwards preached that people were 'Sinners in the Hands of an Angry God' (1741), dangling precariously and at His whim 'Over the pit of hell, much as one holds a spider, or some loathsome insect over the fire.'[12] It informs the fiction of Washington Irving, Charles Brockden Brown, Edgar Allan Poe, Herman Melville, Nathaniel Hawthorne, Ambrose Bierce, H. P. Lovecraft, and many other writers. It is there along with the evocation of the sublime in the paintings of the Hudson River School, in the revels of the Jazz Age, in the contemporary drive to build a border wall. One sees 'a darker scene' in the haunted faces of the common folk photographed by Walker Evans and Weegee, or those collected by Michael Lesy in *Wisconsin Death Trip* (1973). For David J. Skal, Diane Arbus's photographs of odd-looking people revealed that '"monsters" were everywhere, that the whole of modern life [might be] viewed as a tawdry sideshow… America, it seemed, was nothing but a monster show.'[13] As Donald Barthelme writes in his short story 'The Policemen's Ball': 'The horrors waited outside patiently. Even policemen, the horrors thought. We get even policemen, in the end.'[14]

Many of the one hundred horror films discussed in this book explore those basic and universal fears alluded to above – bodily violation, loss of will, death – but most are also unmistakably American, speaking to the American experience in some way. They respond to the American landscape, both human and natural; to the nation's triumphs and travails; its cultural trends and tests; its ideological values and the perceived threats to them. Like science fiction, horror also speaks to social and technological innovation and change, translating our concerns into concrete bugaboos. Together, the films discussed in these pages offer a dark chronicle of American history and culture, a house of night to balance the shining city on the hill.

As with my previous *100 Science Fiction Films*, also published by the British Film Institute, in choosing the films to include here I have sought to be broadly inclusive on several levels. Chronologically, the titles range from the silent period to the contemporary. Their varied production contexts include major studio releases, B films, international co-productions, and independent features. The various subgenres and types of horror are represented: gothic horror, found-footage horror, folk horror, eco-horror, body horror, survival horror; torture porn; haunted houses and home invasions; parody and slapstick; and so on. As well, the various types of horror monsters are accounted for, including mummies, mutants, and mad scientists; serial killers, psychos, and Satanists; creatures and crazies; devils and demons; plants and poltergeists; ghosts and ghouls; vampires, werewolves, and zombies. I have also included significant and representative films by important directors and producers associated with the genre from Tod Browning and James Whale to Jordan Peele and Robert Eggers, films adapted from and by authors whose work has been important to horror from Bram Stoker and H.P. Lovecraft to Stephen King and Anne Rice, and iconic stars from Lon Chaney to Jamie Lee Curtis.

In most cases where a horror film has been sufficiently successful to generate sequels, series, or franchise, I have focused on the first film for being foundational (and almost always more interesting). Some films – *Phantom of the Paradise* (1974), for example, or *Fatal Attraction* (1987) – have been included in part because of the ways they stretch our conception of what a horror film is. The inclusion of films such as *The Frighteners* (1996) and *Let Me In* (2010), the former made outside of America and the latter an adaptation of a Swedish horror film, show American horror as a dynamic cultural site with influence flowing in both directions. Indeed, drawing so much from such traditions as German expressionist cinema and British and European literature, American horror, like the nation itself, is a vast melting pot – one always in danger of boiling over.

Some films that are widely considered as both horror and science fiction were included in *100 Science Fiction Films*, so I have not included them here: *Island of Lost Souls* (1932), *The Invisible Man* (1933), *Alien* (1979), *They Live* (1988*), Prince of Darkness* (1987), *The Cabin in the Woods* (2012), both versions of *The Thing* (1951, 1982). Because that earlier book contains an entry on *Invasion of the Body Snatchers* (1956), I have included here Philip Kaufman's 1978 remake; and because *Frankenstein* (1931) appears there, *The Bride of Frankenstein* (1935) does here. I regret the omission of some other important horror films, including some personal favourites, that, for one reason or another as I attempted to work out a representative balance, did not make it into the book, among them *The Most Dangerous Game* (1932), *The Black Cat* (1934), *Frankenstein Meets the Wolf Man* (1943), *Invisible Invaders* (1959), *Night Tide* (1961), *Dawn of the Dead* (1978), *Love at First Bite* (1979), *Dracula* (1979), *Dressed to Kill* (1980), *The-Funhouse* (1981), *Wolfen* (1981), *Cujo* (1983), *The Stuff* (1985), *The People under the Stairs* (1991), *The Sixth Sense* (1999), *Hellbenders* (2003), *Drag Me to Hell* (2009), *Hereditary* (2018), *Mandy* (2018), and *Us* (2019).

All of the above having been said, I do recognise that no list like this will satisfy everyone – especially in the case of horror, whose aficionados are intensely committed to a degree characteristic of no other genre. What other genres can boast of such a network of magazines and journals, games, blogs, conventions and social events like zombie walks? I have no doubt that readers will find omissions that seem grievous and inexplicable, but at the same time hope they will approve of the overall selection. The majority of films discussed are acknowledged as classics or as having had significantly influenced the genre's development (and my own thinking about the genre), although such lists are of course always in process.

Each entry in this guide considers why the specific film being discussed is a horror film, mentions relevant production information, discusses the importance of its place within the history of the genre, and offers some analysis of its most salient textual features and themes. Within the short space of each entry, I have sought to provide a sense of established critical opinion and original insight in accessible, succinct, and sometimes – I hope – witty prose. Where relevant, the film is also contextualised within American culture and history, as well as the director's, writer's, or featured actor's other work. I confess to auteurist and psychoanalytic inclinations. In some cases, plot descriptions involve spoilers, but these were unavoidable for any serious discussion about those films. References in entries to other films that are also included in the book are indicated with an asterisk (*), and each entry includes a list of up to five recommendations for further reading about that film, director, actor, subgenre, or theme.

Notes

1. S. S. Prawer, *Caligari's Children: The Film as Tale of Terror* (New York: Da Capo, 1980); James B. Twitchell, *Dreadful Pleasures: An Anatomy of Modern Horror* (New York: Oxford University Press, 1985), p. 14.
2. Will H. Rockett, *Devouring Whirlwind: Terror and Transcendence in the Cinema of Cruelty* (Westport, CT: Greenwood Press, 1988), p. 45.
3. Stephen King, *Danse Macabre* (New York: Everest House, 1981), p. 37.
4. Ibid., p. 138.
5. See Robin Wood, 'An Introduction to the American Horror Film', in *Robin Wood on the Horror Film: Collected Essays and Reviews*, ed. Barry Keith Grant (Detroit: Wayne State University Press, 2018), pp. 73–110.
6. Henry David Thoreau, *A Week on the Concord and Merrimac Rivers* (Mineola, NY: Dover, 2001), p. 192.
7. D. H. Lawrence, *Studies in American Literature* (New York: Penguin, 1970), p. 68.
8. Richard Slotkin, *Regeneration through Violence: The Mythology of the American Frontier*, 1600–1860 (Middletown, CT: Wesleyan University Press, 1973).
9. Leslie Fiedler, *Love and Death in the American Novel*, rev. edn. (New York: Delta, 1967), pp. 142, 155.
10. J. Hector St. John de Crévecoeur, *Letters from an American Farmer* (New York: Dutton, 1957), p. 167.
11. For a discussion of Freneau's poem in the context of the American gothic, see Gary D. Rhodes, *The Birth of the American Horror Film* (Edinburgh: Edinburgh University Press, 2018), Chap. 1.
12. Jonathan Edwards, 'Sinners in the Hands of an Angry God', in *Jonathan Edwards: Basic Writings*, ed. Ola Elizabeth Winslow (New York: Signet, 1966), p. 159
13. David J. Skal, *The Monster Show: A Cultural History of Horror* (New York: Norton, 1994), p. 18.
14. Donald Barthelme, 'The Policemen's Ball', in *City Life* (New York: Farrar, Straus & Giroux, 1970).

The Addiction
1995 – 82 mins
Abel Ferrara

The Addiction interprets vampirism as a metaphor for addiction (Ferrara himself has struggled with drug addiction) and its philosophical implications. A bold updating of the vampire film, *The Addiction* was written by Nicholas St. John, who has worked on the scripts of several other films directed by Abel Ferrara, including the rape-revenge film *Ms. 45* (1981), the gangster film *King of New York* (1990), and the director's two other horror films, *The Driller Killer* (1979) and *Body Snatchers* (1993), the third adaptation of Jack Finney's 1955 novel of the same name. Although *The Addiction* was shot in gritty black-and-white, the film blurs and problematises any clear distinction between good and evil.

Kathleen Conklin (Taylor) is a graduate student studying philosophy, specifically the question of evil and human nature, at New York University. After being attacked by a woman on the street (Sciorra) and bitten on the neck, she begins to turn into a vampire, her demeanor becoming more aggressive as her worldview regarding evil also begins to evolve. One night prowling the streets for a victim, she meets Peina (Ferrara favourite Walken), who tells her that he has learned to manage his vampirism so that he is almost human in behaviour. Peina refers to the urge to drink blood as a 'fix' and urges her to read *Naked Lunch* (1959), the controversial novel about drug addiction by William Burroughs (adapted to film in 1991 by David Cronenberg), an author who also was an addict, to help her learn to exert her will against her need.

Kathleen dismisses the study of philosophy as irrelevant and incapable of confronting the fundamental truth of human evil, realizing that now she cannot escape what Burroughs calls 'the algebra of need' – the unquenchable drive for a fix over any rational objection. Kathleen comes to view her bloodsucking as a co-dependency, a collaboration between vampire and victim, even inviting those she attacks first to insist that she leave (a twist on the traditional convention of the vampire having to be invited in). But they do not – an act she understands as her victims' need to connect with the human capacity for evil in a world in which it has been largely repressed and people are merely amusing themselves to death. Kathleen's irreducible vampirism even presents her with a way of understanding the previously incomprehensible evil of the Holocaust.

The dialogue is laden with philosophical snippets – Santayana on history, Kierkegaard's *Sickness unto Death*, Nietzsche's 'will to power', Sartre's *Being and Nothingness*, this last after Kathleen discovers she has no reflection in the mirror – shards of thought that float through the film like bits of cut-up text in the manner of Burroughs's writing. The black and white cinematography evokes the corrupt milieu of film noir, with garbage and graffiti marking the city streets and indicating the fallen world Kathleen contemplates. In the climax, after she finishes and defends her dissertation, Kathleen unleashes an orgy of vampiric bloodletting at the reception in her honor with the help of all her previous victims ('I'd like to share a little bit of what I learned through my long hard years of study', she announces) in a vivid demonstration of her disillusionment with the abstractions of philosophy in the face of real evil (in her words, 'essence is revealed through praxis'). Perhaps

DIRECTOR Abel Ferrara
PRODUCER Preston L. Holmes, Russell Simmons, Denis Hann, Fernando Sulichin
SCREENPLAY Nicholas St. John
CINEMATOGRAPHY Ken Kelsch
EDITOR Mayin Lo
MUSIC Joe Delia
PRODUCTION COMPANY October Films
MAIN CAST Lili Taylor, Christopher Walken, Annabella Sciorra, Edie Falco, Kathryn Erbe

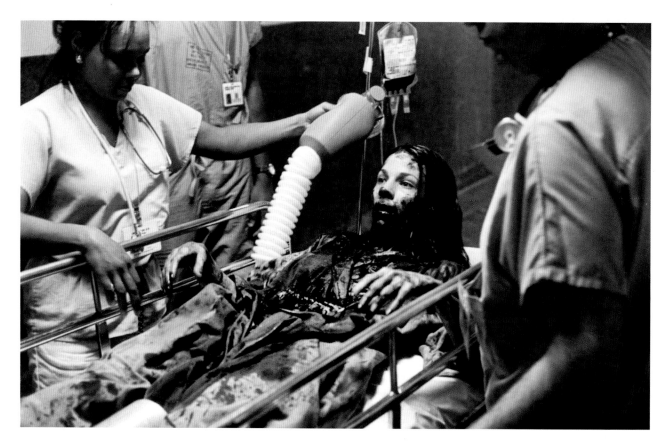

this scene was as cathartic for St John who, like Kathleen, attended NYU, but Kathleen seemingly overdoses during the bloodbath and attempts to commit suicide. She doesn't, and in the final scene she visits her own grave in broad daylight, apparently now able to control her urges like Peina, and giving the final word to Nietzsche, who in *Beyond Good and Evil* cautioned that those who fights monsters should beware of becoming monsters themselves.

Further Reading:

Brenez, Nicole. *Abel Ferrara*, trans. Adrian Martin. Urbana and Chicago: University of Illinois Press, 2007.

Burroughs, William S. *Naked Lunch*. New York: Grove Press, 1966.

Hawkins, Joan. '"No Worse Than You Were Before": Theory Economy and Power in Abel Ferrara's *The Addiction*'. In *Underground USA.: Filmmaking beyond the Hollywood Canon*, ed. Xavier Mendik and Steven Jay Schneider, pp. 1–12. London and New York: Wallflower Press, 2002.

Stevens, Brad. *Abel Ferrara: The Moral Vision*. Surrey, UK: FAB Press, 2004.

American Psycho
Canada/US, 2000 – 101 mins
Mary Harron

The films of Canadian director Mary Harron get inside the heads of murderous Americans, both female (*I Shot Andy Warhol* [1996], *Charlie Says* [2018]) and male (*American Psycho*). Brett Easton Ellis's satirical and controversial 1991 novel of the same name upon which *American Psycho* is based was attacked for its explicit misogynistic violence, a charge also levelled against the film adaptation. An entry in the serial killer cycle, the film, like the novel, is also a killer comedy of manners that targets the narcissism of the 'Me Generation' and the '80s culture of materialism. While Gordon Gekko may claim in *Wall Street* (1987) that 'Greed is good', in *American Psycho* it is, to the contrary, quite evil.

The plot follows Bateman, a wealthy New York investment banker who spends his time hanging out at fashionable bars and restaurants with his colleagues, all of whom seem interchangeable with similar hair-styles and tailored suits, and the same inane banter that consistently confuses each other's identities. One of

DIRECTOR Mary Harron
PRODUCER Edward R. Pressman, Chris Hanley, Christian Halsey Solomon
SCREENPLAY Mary Harron, Guinevere Turner
CINEMATOGRAPHY Andrzej Sekula
EDITOR Andrew Marcus
MUSIC John Cale
PRODUCTION COMPANY Edward R. Pressman Productions, Muse Productions, Lions Gate Films
MAIN CAST Christian Bale, Willem Dafoe, Jared Leto, Josh Lucas, Samantha Mathis, Matt Ross, Bill Sage, Chloë Sevigny

the film's jokes is that we never see him actually do any work, and there is never anything related to work on his office desk. As in the novel, Bateman provides lengthy monologues (voiceovers in the film) regarding the products he uses during his morning ablutions and reviews of pop rock of the period (Robert Palmer, Genesis), the latter often accompanying scenes of physical violence.

Bateman's killings and assaults of women are grotesquely graphic exaggerations, overtly monstrous depictions, of the treatment of women and fear of them within Bateman's overwhelmingly masculine culture. Like the money he supposedly manages at work, women are regarded merely as objects of exchange. The title of *American Psycho* obviously refers to Alfred Hitchcock's *Psycho** (1960) – it was Hitchcock, after all, who famously said that a sure way to create suspense was to 'torture the women!' – and the film contains the same kind of dark humour. Bateman quotes Ed Gein, the serial killer who partially inspired Robert Bloch's 1959 novel *Psycho*, on which Hitchcock's film was based, to the effect of imagining what a woman's head would be like on a stick, and later we glimpse several decapitated female heads in his refrigerator. It is hardly surprising that Bateman watches *The Texas Chainsaw Massacre** (1974) while working out.

It is only near the end of the film, when an ATM gives Bateman the message 'feed me a stray cat', that we realise that some or all of the violence we have witnessed may have been played out in Bateman's imagination rather than actuality. The wild shootout with police that follows, in which he manages to spectacularly explode two patrol cars with a pistol, even to his own surprise, and his secretary's discovery of a notebook in his office desk filled with drawings of sexual violence being done to women's bodies (no comparable scene exists in the novel) encourages such a reading. Willem Dafoe provides a perfect balance of mundanity and menace to his performance of detective Donald Kimball, who is investigating the death of the perceived rival Bateman murdered, that resonates with a similar ambiguity: like Bateman, we never know whether he knows more than he is saying, whether he is just odd or playing cat-and-mouse with Bateman, baiting him.

Bateman is the perfect example of the waning of affect and 'depthlessness' that is often said to characterise postmodern consciousness. Indeed, he describes himself as empty, a pure product of popular culture. But the film also makes its political implications clear when, in the final scene, Bateman and colleagues discuss whether President Reagan is a harmless old man or a secret psychopath. With the values of Reaganomics, and the wealth and privileges it can bring, the film's answer is clear. In a penthouse apartment, no one can hear you scream.

Further Reading:

Grant, Barry Keith. 'American Psychosis: The Pure Products of America Go Crazy'. In *Mythologies of Violence in Postmodern Media*, ed. Christopher Sharrett, pp. 23–40. Detroit: Wayne State University Press, 1999.

Knight, Deborah, and George McKnight. '*American Psycho*: Horror, Satire, Aesthetics, and Identification'. In *Dark Thoughts: Philosophic Reflections on Cinematic Horror*, eds. Steven Jay Schneider and Daniel Shaw, pp. 212–29. Lanham, MD: Scarecrow Press, 2003.

Lebeau, Vicky. *Lost Angels: Psychoanalysis and Cinema*. London and New York: Routledge, 1995.

Towlson, John. *Subversive Horror Cinema: Countercultural Messages of Films from Frankenstein to the Present*. Jefferson, NC: McFarland, 2014.

An American Werewolf in London
1981 – 97 mins
John Landis

John Landis has made box-office hits in both comedy (*National Lampoon's Animal House* [1978], *The Blues Brothers* [1980], *Three Amigos* [1986]) and horror (*Twilight Zone: The Movie* [1983], *Innocent Blood* [1992], and, of course, the extraordinarily influential music video *Michael Jackson: Thriller* [1983]), and both sensibilities are apparent in *An American Werewolf in London*. Released the same year as Joe Dante's *The Howling* and Michael Wadleigh's *Wolfen*, the film's title alludes to the 1951 Vincente Minnelli musical *An American in Paris* with Gene Kelly, but also to Henry James's 1877 novel *The American*. Indeed, the film invokes James's favourite theme of contrast between the Old World and the New, here cast in the form of a werewolf movie.

DIRECTOR John Landis
PRODUCER George Folsey, Jr.
SCREENPLAY John Landis
CINEMATOGRAPHY Robert Paynter
EDITOR Malcolm Campbell
MUSIC Elmer Bernstein
PRODUCTION COMPANY Polygram Pictures, The Guber-Peters Company
MAIN CAST David Naughton, Jenny Agutter, Griffin Dunne, John Woodvine

(A sequel, *An American Werewolf in Paris* [1997], involves another American tourist and the daughter of the couple in Landis' movie.) The corruption of the Old World takes the form of superstition, and like James's Christopher Newman, the American learns too late an unfortunate truth about evil.

Two young American men, David Kessler (Naughton) and Jack Goodman (Dunne), are backpacking across the Yorkshire moors when we first see them getting out of a farmer's truck filled with sheep – innocent but brash American lambs to the slaughter. They stop at a local pub, ominously named the Slaughtered Lamb, where the locals are strangely hostile, one making jokes about Americans and John Wayne in *The Alamo* (1960), at which everyone laughs – until Jack asks about the meaning of the pentagram on the wall. After the attack by the werewolf on the moors, when David is recovering in hospital, his nurse, Alex Price (Agutter), reads to him from Mark Twain's *A Connecticut Yankee in King Arthur's Court* (1889), another story about a brash American abroad. Throughout the film David's youthful exuberance is contrasted with British reserve, as when, trying to get arrested before he kills again, he shouts insults about the Queen in Trafalgar Square while a small crowd quietly watches and a policeman asks him politely to control himself.

Even as David's werewolf kills are gory, featuring dismembered hands and decapitated heads, the film plays with the genre's conventions, as in the requisite pub scene. Jack immediately recognises the pentagram in the pub as the same as the one in *The Wolf Man** (1941), and the two discuss 'The Hounds of the Baskervilles' as they trek across the moors. Yet the film doesn't hesitate to rewrite werewolf mythology, with the rotting souls of David's victims unable to rest in peace until David dies and the werewolf's bloodline is broken. In the climax, David terrorises Piccadilly Circus, the first monster to stalk there since *Gorgo* (1961). Jack's visitations to David as a ghost (each time in a more advanced state of decomposition), are presented in an appositely deadpan manner as he urges David to kill himself ('I'm not having any fun here'), as are the several suggestions for the best way to do it by the undead souls of David's victims, who gather in the porn theatre where he takes refuge.

And, of course, the film knowingly ups the ante on the transformation scenes, the money shots of the werewolf film, relying on pre-digital special effects by Rick Baker, whose many professional credits, beginning with *The Exorcist** (1973), include *The Frighteners** [1996] and the reboot of *The Wolf Man*, *The Wolfman* [2010]). Rather than a series of superimpositions with increasingly hirsute makeup on a mostly motionless actor's hand or face, David's transformations feature close-ups of limbs changing shape, snout thrusting forward, and fangs descending from a feral mouth, earning Baker an Academy Award for makeup.

Further Reading

de Blécourt, Willem, ed. *Werewolf Histories*. Basingstoke, UK and New York: Palgrave Macmillan, 2015.

Curran, Angela. 'Aristotelian Reflections on Horror and Tragedy in *An American Werewolf in London* and *The Sixth Sense*'. In *Dark Thoughts: Philosophical Reflections on Cinematic Horror*, ed. Steven J. Schneider and Daniel Shaw, pp. 47–63. Lanham, MD: Scarecrow Press, 2003.

Landis, John. *Monsters in the Movies: 100 Years of Cinematic Nightmares*. London: DK Publishers, 2016.

Mann, Craig Ian. *Phases of the Moon: A Cultural History of the Werewolf Film*. Edinburgh: Edinburgh University Press, 2020.

Walter, Brenda S. Gardenour. *Our Old Monsters: Witches, Werewolves and Vampires from Medieval Theology to Horror Cinema*. Jefferson, NC: McFarland, 2015.

The Avenging Conscience, or 'Thou Shalt Not Kill'
1914 – 78 mins
D. W. Griffith

Film pioneer D.W. Griffith came to the cinema from theatre, his sensibility more attuned to the mode of melodrama than Grand Guignol (although, among the literally hundreds of short films he directed was *One Exciting Night* in 1922, an entry in the 'old dark house' formula popular at the time, and the second version of *The Sorrows of Satan* in 1926). After leaving Biograph in 1913, Griffith moved to Mutual, which evolved into Reliance-Majestic, bringing many of his regular actors and crew with him. *The Avenging Conscience*, loosely based on Edgar Allan Poe's story 'The Tell-Tale Heart' (1843) and the poem 'Annabel Lee' (1849), is one of four films he made for the studio. Years earlier Griffith had directed *Edgar Allan Poe* (1909) for Biograph, a one-reeler made on the occasion of the centennial of Poe's birth that, taking historical liberties, shows the writer composing 'The Raven' while his young wife Virginia lay in bed nearby dying of tuberculosis. In *The Avenging Conscience* the director more ambitiously aspires to convey the abstract and overwhelming guilt of Poe's protagonist in visual terms.

In the plot a young man (Walthall) falls in love with a woman, 'she whom he calls Annabelle' (Sweet), but he is prevented from marrying her by his stern uncle (Aitken), who insists he spend his time working instead. The nephew's imagination grows morbid from reading Poe, and soon 'the plan of a fevered brain' begins to take shape. At first thinking to shoot his uncle, the obstacle to his happiness, he instead strangles him, choking off his voice, and seals his body behind the fireplace. The young man begins to grow increasingly mad, the ghost of his uncle emerging from the fireplace or through the open window in double exposure and pointing at him accusingly.

Griffith employs the stuff of cinema (he was only a year away from finishing *The Birth of a Nation* [1915]) to fine effect when the nephew descends into guilt and madness. We see the man's tormented visions of Jesus and Moses (bearing the commandment of the film's subtitle) and ghouls crawling in the steaming flames of hell. Griffith frames the long shots of the man in an iris in the lower right corner sur-rounded by black, a graphic representation of the mental darkness and isolation closing in on him. Earlier, when the man was reading, Griffith showed a close-up of the beginning of Poe's story in which the narrator describes his extreme acuteness of the senses, and now, when the man is being questioned by the police detective and is about to crack and confess, Griffith assembles a powerful montage of close-ups of the detective, the man, his fidgeting hands, the ticking clock, a tapping pencil, all at an increased tempo – a fever pitch, as it were.

The climax looks at first like one of Griffith's distinctive last-minute rescues, with the man, now desper-ate and holed up in a shack with a mob in pursuit, about to hang himself while 'Annabelle' runs to him to announce her undying love and save him. But, atypically, she arrives too late, and in despair she hurls herself off a cliff into the ocean, dying, in a sense, in a 'kingdom by the sea'. Griffith suggests that the man's mur-

DIRECTOR D. W. Griffith

PRODUCER D. W. Griffith

SCREENPLAY D. W. Griffith

CINEMATOGRAPHY
G. W. 'Billy' Bitzer

EDITOR James Smith,
Rose Smith

PRODUCTION COMPANY
Mutual Film Corporation

MAIN CAST Henry B. Walthall,
Blanche Sweet, Spottiswoode
Aitken, Ralph Lewis, Mae Marsh

derous inclination is an undeniable part of human nature, explaining in an intertitle that nature is 'one long system of murder' as the man sits on a park bench and sees a spider preying on a fly caught in its web in a scene that inevitably reminds one of the climactic scene in *The Fly** (1958). But Griffith's sentimentality triumphs in the end, and we discover that it's all been only a nightmare brought on by reading Poe. Uncle is alive and now happily blesses his nephew's union, and the film ends with images of the couple blissfully united while Pan and his wood nymphs frolic in images that might have been filmed by Ken Russell.

Further Reading:

Clarens, Carlos. *An Illustrated History of the Horror Film*. New York: Capricorn, 1967.

Jones, David Annwn. *Re-envisaging the First Age of Cinematic Horror, 1896–1934*. Cardiff: University of Wales Press, 2018.

Petric, Vlada. 'Griffith's *The Avenging Conscience*: An Early Dream Film'. *Film Criticism* 6, no. 2 (1982): 5–27.

Smith, Don G. *The Poe Cinema: A Critical Filmography of Theatrical Releases Based on the Works of Edgar Allan Poe*. Jefferson, NC: McFarland, 2003.

The Birds
1963 – 119 mins
Alfred Hitchcock

Loosely based on Daphne du Maurier's short story of the same name (Hitchcock had earlier filmed another of du Maurier's works, *Rebecca* [1940]), Hitchcock's follow-up to *Psycho** (1960) depicts a series of inexplicable and increasingly violent attacks by birds on the residents of a small California town. While the director's other horror films, *Psycho* and *Frenzy* (1972), focus on human monsters, *The Birds* uses the fantastic threat posed by these common winged creatures also to explore human nature in an early example of ecological horror. Well before CGI, *The Birds* posed enormous technical challenges, ultimately requiring hundreds of effects shots to make it seem as if actors and animals are occupying the same space and using an electronic score rather than conventional music to create the sound of the birds' chittering.

As the film begins, Melanie Daniels (Hedren) flirtatiously pursues lawyer Mitch Brenner (Taylor) from the San Francisco pet shop where they first meet to the small town of Bodega Bay, where he lives with his daughter, Cathy (Cartwright), and possessive mother, Lydia (Tandy). The scene introduces the film's elaborate motif of cages, traps, and entrapment, both physical and emotional. The first bird attack is a quick swoop of a small gull that pecks Melanie in the head and draws blood, bringing Mitch to her aid. As the attacks persist, Melanie and the Brenners are forced to barricade themselves in the house, now prisoners of the birds and a reversal of the situation in the pet shop. Radio reports tell of attacks spreading to nearby communities, and in the film's final ambiguous shot, Mitch leads the women slowly to his car through a landscape filled with perched birds of different species apparently massing for the next attack, and they drive away to an uncertain future as the sun rises on a new world.

As with the killer plants in M. Night Shyamalan's later *The Happening* (2008), *The Birds* offers no explanation for the avian attacks. In the key scene in the local restaurant, an ornithologist who happens to be there explains that normally birds of different feathers do not flock together, making the situation seem even more ominous. While the conversation about the birds' mysterious behaviour occurs, we hear a server place orders for fried chicken, hinting that the threat may be nature's deliberate revenge on humanity. (Rachel Carson's profoundly influential *The Silent Spring* was published in 1962, just a year before the film's release.) Alternatively, we might read the monstrous birds as metaphoric of the characters' repressed tensions: the attacks begin in Bodega Bay when Melanie comes to town (as a hysterical woman in the restaurant points out), her arrival also triggering the jealousy of Mitch's former girlfriend, local schoolteacher Annie Hayworth (Pleshette), who is still in love with Mitch, and the possessiveness of Mitch's mother, a widow whose wish to hold onto her son recalls the domineering Mrs. Bates of *Psycho*.

Whatever the reason for the avian aggression, *The Birds* emphasises, like so many apocalyptic films to follow, how tenuous civilization is and how quickly it can collapse. When the birds attack the town, before Hitchcock cuts to the famous high-angle ('bird's-eye point-of-view') shot looking down at the destruction,

DIRECTOR Alfred Hitchcock
PRODUCER Alfred Hitchcock
SCREENPLAY Evan Hunter
CINEMATOGRAPHY
Robert Burks
EDITOR George Tomasini
PRODUCTION COMPANY
Alfred Hitchcock Productions, Universal
MAIN CAST Rod Taylor, Tippi Hedren, Jessica Tandy, Suzanne Pleshette, Veronica Cartwright

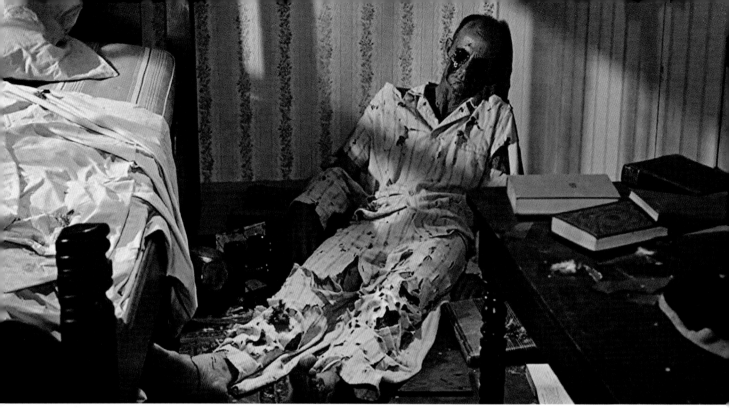

chaos erupts in mere moments: a customer in a gas station, strafed by birds, drops the pump hose while filling his car's gas tank; gas spills on the ground; another customer unknowingly lights a cigarette and drops a match; the place explodes in a hellish ball of flame and then people flee in all directions, helpless. Hitchcock subtly emphasises the precarious nature of our social order, beginning with Melanie out in the open bay, a city fish out of water, exposed and lacking solid grounding underfoot, her pale glove stained bright red by blood at the fingertips from the bird's attack. In the sobering opinion of the town drunk, also in the restaurant, 'It's the end of the world.'

Further Reading:

Horwitz, Margaret M. '*The Birds*: A Mother's Love'. In *A Hitchcock Reader*, ed. Marshall Deutelbaum and Leland Poague, pp. 279–287. Ames: Iowa State University Press, 1986.

Paglia, Camille. *The Birds*. London: British Film Institute, 1998.

Sharrett, Christopher. 'The Myth of Apocalypse and the Horror Film: The Primacy of *Psycho* and *The Birds*'. In *Framing Hitchcock*, pp. 355–372. Detroit: Wayne State University Press, 2002.

Wood, Robin. *Hitchcock's Films Revisited*, revised ed. New York: Columbia University Press, 2002.

Blade
1998 – 120 mins
Stephen Norrington

Although Black Panther first appeared in comics in the 1960s, a decade before Blade (Eric Brooks), the latter was the first Black comic book superhero to be adapted as a feature film. (Robert Townsend's *Meteorman* [1993] worked in reverse, becoming a Marvel comic after the film.) *Blade* followed the infamously awful *Howard the Duck* (1986), which was the first Marvel property to be released as a feature in the US, and its success initiated Marvel's long run of comic book adaptations and the development of the Marvel Comic Universe. It was followed by two sequels, *Blade II* (2002) and *Blade: Trinity* (2004), both also starring Wesley Snipes as the superhuman vampire-slayer and both written by David S. Goyer, who also directed the latter, as well as inspiring two videogames and a television series (2006). Director Stephen Norrington (he subsequently directed the film version of *The League of Extraordinary Gentlemen* comic books [2003]) began his career doing

DIRECTOR Stephen Norrington
PRODUCER Peter Frankfurt, Wesley Snipes, Robert Engelman
SCREENPLAY David S. Goyer
CINEMATOGRAPHY Theo van de Sande
EDITOR Paul Rubell
MUSIC Mark Isham
PRODUCTION COMPANY Marvel Enterprises, Amen Ra Films, Imaginary Forces
MAIN CAST Wesley Snipes, Stephen Dorff, Kris Kristofferson, N'Bushe Wright, Donal Logue, Udo Kier, Arly Jover

makeup and effects for such films as *Gremlins** (1984), *Aliens* (1986), and *The Witches* (1990), and he brings to *Blade* a combination of comic book style and choreographed action with the bloodletting of vampire mythology.

In the world of *Blade*, vampires and humans have existed together from time immemorial. The vampires run a corporate empire and meet in a boardroom, capitalist bloodsuckers as well as literal ones. Blade, part-human and part-vampire – 'something else', as his helper Whistler (Kristofferson) describes him – wages a private war against them, but the renegade vampire Deacon Frost (Dorff) is threatening to upset tradition by obtaining the big whatsit, the resurrection of the vampire god and the complete takeover of the human race ('tonight the age of men comes to an end'). Created in 1973 by writer Marv Wolfman and artist Gene Colan as one of several supporting characters in Marvel's *The Tomb of Dracula* comic book, Blade is portrayed in the film as less conflicted, more of a killing machine. In his fight against the vampire horde Blade mainly relies, like a samurai, on a sword strapped on his back, but he also carries all sorts of other weapons including a handgun that looks like the oversized model wielded by *Judge Dredd* (first film version, 1995), and he drives a sleek black car that evokes the Batmobile, while Whistler functions as his Alfred. There is even a Joker of sorts in Frost's henchperson, Mercury (Jover), who continually sports a psychotic smile.

In addition to its comic book sensibility, *Blade*'s visual design in some ways anticipates that of *The Matrix* (1999), released the following year. Neo's black overcoat seems to have been inspired by Blade's costume, and when Blade fires on Frost, the latter's heightened perception is depicted as a 'bullet time' dodging of the shells.

Blade tells Dr. Jenson (Wright) that the world she lives in is in reality merely 'sugar-coated topping', which also evokes the illusory world of the Matrix. Yet in *Blade* even this surface world seems bleak, filled with people on the streets who hardly seem to notice Blade striding among them with his weapons visible or while fighting Frost. In Blade's cruel world, as he says, you have to learn to pull the trigger if you want to survive – which Dr. Jenson learns to do, beginning with Pearl, the giant Jabba-like mound of festering flesh that provides tech support for the vampires. Frost evokes the spectre of slavery and race relations when referring to Blade's 'Uncle Tom routine', but the film is more interested in the action sequences than in exploring the nation's fraught history of race relations.

Further Reading

Carrington, André M. *Speculative Blackness: The Future of Race in Science Fiction*. Minneapolis: University of Minnesota Press 2016.

Coleman, Robin R. Means. *Horror Noire: Blacks in American Horror Films from 1890s to Present*. New York and Abingdon, UK: Routledge, 2011.

Nama, Adilifu. *Super Black: American Pop Culture and Black Superheroes*. Austin: University of Texas Press 2011.

Ní Fhlainn, Sorcha. *Postmodern Vampires: Film, Fiction, and Popular Culture*. London and New York: Palgrave Macmillan, 2019.

Wilson, Natalie. *Willful Monstrosity: Gender and Race in 21st Century Horror*. Jefferson, NC: McFarland, 2020.

The Blair Witch Project
1999 – 81 mins
Daniel Myrick and Eduard Sánchez

Co-directed by Daniel Myrick and Eduardo Sánchez, two film students at the University of Central Florida, *The Blair Witch Project* was a surprising hit, earning millions at the box office on a miniscule budget of $60,000 and making it one of the most successful independent movies in film history. Its success fuelled a franchise that includes novels, comic books, video games, a documentary about the making of the film (*The Woods Movie* [2015]), a mockumentary expanding on the supposed backstory (*Curse of the Blair Witch* [1999]), and two sequels: *Book of Shadows: Blair Witch 2* (2000), directed by Joel Berlinger (*Paradise Lost: The Child Murders at Robin Hood Hills* [1997]), more conventional in style; and *Blair Witch* (2016), directed by Adam Wingard (*Pop Skull* [2007], *You're Next* [2011]). Its success spurred the cycle of 'found footage' horror films that

DIRECTOR Daniel Myrick, Eduard Sánchez
PRODUCER Robin Cowie, Gregg Hale
SCREENPLAY Daniel Myrick, Eduardo Sánchez
CINEMATOGRAPHY Neal Fredericks
EDITOR Daniel Myrick, Eduardo Sánchez
MUSIC Antonio Cora
PRODUCTION COMPANY Haxan Films, Artisan Entertainment
MAIN CAST Heather Donahue, Michael C. Williams, Joshua Leonard

followed (see, for example, *Paranormal Activity** [2007]) which feature scenes that unfold in real time, without editing, as in the style of videogames and observational documentary, shot by a camera that is acknowledged by the characters as being present within the narrative world (as opposed to the conventional manner, in which the camera is an invisible observer of events), wielded by one of the characters.

Evoking the earlier *Cannibal Holocaust* (1980), the opening titles of *Blair Witch* tell us, 'In October of 1994, three student filmmakers disappeared in the woods near Burkittsville, Maryland, while shooting a documentary. A year later, their footage was found.' The film we see is supposedly the footage shot by the three students, Heather, Mike, and Josh, chronicling their search for the legendary Blair Witch and their chaotic trip into the woods, where they become lost and terrified over several days and eventually disappear.

With camcorder footage shot from two cameras, the film makes deft use of suggestion and mood in the manner of Val Lewton (*Cat People** [1942], *I Walked with a Zombie** [1943]) rather than relying on graphic horror, tapping into fears of the wilderness that date back to the Puritans (see also *The Witch** [2015]). Offscreen space and sound frequently suggest an unseen presence, with twigs snapping around them in the woods, muffled voices, and screams in the far distance. In place of elaborate special effects and monsters, the frightened student filmmakers find bundles of sticks, some in the shape of human effigies, piles of rocks, and blood-soaked scraps of clothing – some of them sprung upon the actors, so their surprise and disorientation are to some degree unstaged. The film begins with some conventional documentary footage of interviews with local residents, but then chronicles the trio's deteriorating mental states and mounting panic in the woods, culminating in the famous scene when Heather talks tearfully into the camera, nostrils aquiver, before the climax in the crumbling house, where the abandonment of traditional documentary certainty parallels her fear and loss of control.

According to the faux legend invented for the film, the Blair Witch is the ghost of Elly Kedward, a woman who had been banished from Blair Township (now Burkittsville, Maryland) for witchcraft in 1785 and subsequently died. The canny promotional campaign for *The Blair Witch Project* was the first to involve the creation of a convincing website with an extremely detailed backstory offering a timeline of events relating to the Blair Witch and the founding of Burkitttsville and numerous clickable options for finding out more about her and other related faux historical figures and events. Many people were persuaded that the film was based on historical truth, and at the height of its popularity and for some time thereafter there was a spike in tourism in Burkittsville that provided a boost to the local economy.

Further Reading:

Heller-Nicholas, Alexandre. *Found Footage Horror Films: Fear and the Appearance of Reality*. Jefferson, NC: McFarland, 2014.

Highley, Sarah L., and Jeffrey Andrew Weinstock, eds. *Nothing That Is: Millennial Cinema and the Blair Witch Controversies*. Detroit: Wayne State University Press, 2004.

Roscoe, Jane, and Craig Hight. *Faking It: Mock-Documentary and the Subversion of Factuality*. Manchester: Manchester University Press, 2001.

Stern, D. A. *The Blair Witch Project: A Dossier*. New York: Onyx, 1999.

Turner, Peter. *The Blair Witch Project*. Leighton Buzzard: Auteur, 2015.

Brain Damage
1988 – 86 mins
Frank Henenlotter

Writer-director Frank Henenlotter (*Basket Case* [1982], *Frankenhooker* [1990]) has described *Brain Damage* as a combination of *The Tingler** [1959] meets *The Trip* (1967), but the film's creature, Aylmer, 'the awe-inspiring famous one', is also reminiscent of a Cronenbergian parasite and something that has plopped in from *Eraserhead** (1977). Henenlotter considers himself an exploitation filmmaker, like Herschell Gordon Lewis (*Two Thousand Maniacs!** [1964]) – about whom Henenlotter made a documentary, *Herschell Gordon Lewis: The Godfather of Gore* (2010) – but with decidedly better production values and greater wit. *Brain Damage* complicates the gore of Lewis by mixing disturbing images of body horror with humour, making the resultant blend more disturbing.

Aylmer is given a history more elaborate than that of the Maltese Falcon, and like that bejewelled 'dingus' it literally provides 'the stuff that dreams are made of'. Lacking limbs, Aylmer forms a symbiotic relationship with his human host, attaching itself somewhere on the body so it can be carried around to hunt for brains, which it eats on a regular basis, and in return providing a beguiling blue, very addictive drug that gives an intense hallucinogenic high. Evoking such Bs as *The Brain Eaters* (1958) and *Zontar: The Thing from Venus* (1966), this pitiless puppet master attaches itself to the neck of its host by irregular rows of twitching teeth and hypodermic hooks in a mouth that looks simultaneously silly and sardonic.

The plot begins when Aylmer escapes from Morris (Barnes) and Martha (Saint Peter), who have been his hosts, and enters a new victim, a young man named Brian (Hearst), who lives in a neighbouring apartment. Like Brian, we are unaware of what is going on until Aylmer reveals itself, popping up from behind Brian's shoulder and casually saying 'Hi!' like an old friend. Aylmer is brilliantly voiced, appropriately, by John Zacherle, the iconic television horror host of the 1950s who was known for inserting comic cutaways into the classic horror movies he showed. (Zacherle also appears in *Frankenhooker*.)

Certainly, Aylmer embodies Brian's libido, with several jokes connecting the creature with the phallus, most explicitly when the woman Brian picks up at the night club begins to fellate him in the alley ('Feels like you've got a real monster in there', she observes). Isolating himself, Brian plays in the bathtub with an erect Alymer, who requires periodic immersion in water, and he moans orgasmicly whenever Aylmer injects its juice into his brain. But the film isn't much interested in this theme, or in the potential for commenting on urban alienation and violent crime when Brian, riding in the subway with his girlfriend Barbara (Lowry), kisses her and so allows Aylmer to suck out her brains through his mouth, and no one notices (even though one passenger is reading a newspaper with the headline 'Killers Loose in City'). Yet even more sobering is the scene in the cheap hotel room where Brian nobly but vainly tries to kick his 'juice' habit, shaking in agony on the floor, while Aylmer natters away at him, taunting Brian as he wades patiently in the sink. It

DIRECTOR Frank Henenlotter
PRODUCER Edgar Ievins
SCREENPLAY Frank Henenlotter
CINEMATOGRAPHY
Bruce Torbet
EDITOR Frank Henenlotter,
James Y. Kewi
MUSIC Matthias Donnelly,
Clutch Reiser, Gus Russo
PRODUCTION COMPANY
The Brain Damage Company
MAIN CAST Rick Hearst,
Jennifer Lowry, Theo Barnes,
Lucille Saint Peter, John
Zacherle (voice of Aylmer,
uncredited)

is a harrowing vision of addiction, the inner dialogue of the addict fighting a losing battle with himself – until Aylmer breaks out in song, reciting the lyrics to the big band hit 'Elmer's Tune' (made famous by Glenn Miller) in their entirety, and the scene's existential profundity sinks into the enjoyably preposterous.

Further Reading:

Hallenbeck, Bruce G. *Comedy-Horror Films: A Chronological History, 1914–2008*. Jefferson, NC: McFarland, 2009.

Juno, Andrea, and V. Vale. *Incredibly Strange Films*, ed. V. Vale and Andrea Juno, pp. 8–17. San Francisco: RE/search #10, 1986.

McDonagh, Maitland. *Filmmaking on the Fringe: The Good, the Bad, and the Deviant Directors*. New York: Citadel, 1995.

Bram Stoker's Dracula
1992 – 128 mins
Francis Ford Coppola

Early in his career Francis Ford Coppola worked for Roger Corman on *The Terror* (1963), allowing him the opportunity to make his first feature based on his own screenplay, the psychological horror film *Dementia 13* (1963). Decades later he returned to the horror genre with *Twixt* (2011), an uneven work inspired in part by the writings of Edgar Allan Poe. Betwixt these films he directed *Bram Stoker's Dracula*, a big-budget movie with high production values and high-concept casting that won three Oscars (for Costume Design, Sound Editing, and Makeup), the only *Dracula* adaptation to win Academy Awards. It remains, as the title suggests, the most faithful adaptation of Bram Stoker's novel to date, although it does introduce some changes to the book's ungainly narrative, particularly in the ending when Mina (Ryder) decapitates Dracula (Oldman) and releases him from his vampire curse.

DIRECTOR Francis Ford Coppola
PRODUCER Francis Ford Coppola, Fred Fuchs, Charles Mulvehill
SCREENPLAY James V. Hart
CINEMATOGRAPHY Michael Ballhaus
EDITOR Nicholas C. Smith, Glen Scantlebury, Anne Goursaud
MUSIC Wojciech Kilar
PRODUCTION COMPANY American Zoetrope, Osiris Films
MAIN CAST Gary Oldman, Winona Ryder, Anthony Hopkins, Keanu Reeves, Richard E. Grant, Cary Elwes, Billy Campbell, Sadie Frost, Tom Waits

The film acknowledges the awkward epistolary structure of the novel, in which the narration consists of a collection of letters, diary entries, and recording transcriptions, by having scenes begin with the characters providing voiceover narration and with text identifying the letter or diary entry. More importantly, the film is especially faithful to the spirit of repression that informs the novel and its historical Victorian context. Even the silent trick film Dracula (Oldman) and Mina (Ryder) attend is about repressed sexuality, showing a man who imagines himself with two nude women who then, to his disappointment, 'turn' into his wife. Like Stoker's novel, the plot plods forward but throbs with energy during the vampire sequences, which are rife with erotic overtones. As he is being seduced by Dracula's three wives in his Transylvanian castle, the first one appears, tellingly, to the dreamily moaning Jonathan Harker (Reeves) by rising up from between his legs in bed. It is clear why Lucy (Frost) is Dracula's first victim in London: where Mina represses her sexual desire, Lucy is looser, flirting with the American Quincy Morris ('It's so big, let me touch it', she says of his Bowie knife) even before she is bitten.

Similar to John Badham's Dracula (1979) with Frank Langella, Coppola combines the Count's erotic appeal with a sense of sweeping romanticism. Five hundred years earlier, we learn, Vlad Dracula's wife Elisabeta committed suicide erroneously thinking he had died in battle; his undying love survives centuries as he seeks to regain her through a contemporary woman who reincarnates her spirit, just as Kharis does in The Mummy* (1932), which itself borrowed from Tod Browning's Dracula* (1931) with Bela Lugosi. When Dracula is about to turn Mina into a vampire and his mate forever, at the last moment his love proves so true that he nobly refuses to seal her fate. Mina mercifully ends his torment by impaling and decapitating him in a narrative change that suggests the depth of her unleashed passion and perhaps a kind of feminist empowerment (in the novel, by contrast, Dracula is dispatched by Harker and Morris). The intercutting of Harker and Mina's marriage with the defilement and death of Lucy by Dracula recalls the famous montage in Coppola's The Godfather (1972) as it seeks to transform Vlad from blasphemous demon to transcendent lover.

In keeping with the period in which the film is set, Coppola chose to use traditional optical effects rather than CGI. Especially noteworthy are the beautifully eerie moments when Nosferatu-like shadows creep along the walls moving independently of Dracula himself. Gary Oldman, known as an actor capable of remarkable physical transformations, is well cast as the shape-shifting vampire who in the film looks different in almost every scene, whether aging forward or backward or in another form altogether, and manages to create a distinctive Dracula even as his performance nods to Lugosi's. Of the other actors, Keanu Reeves does capture a sense of Harker's bourgeois blandness although he seems to be in Jonathan Harker's Excellent Adventure, while Anthony Hopkins's Van Helsing interestingly conveys a hint of Hannibal Lecter, and Tom Waits tops Dwight Frye as the mad Renfield.

Further Reading:

Deaville, James. 'The Beauty of Horror: Kilar, Coppola, and Dracula'. In Music in the Horror Film: Listening to Fear, ed. Neil Lerner, pp. 187–205. London and New York: Routledge, 2009.

Dika, Vera. 'From Dracula – with Love'. In The Dread of Difference: Gender and the Horror Film, ed. Barry Keith Grant, pp. 388–400. Austin: University of Texas Press, 1996.

Elsaesser, Thomas. 'Specularity and Engulfment: Francis Ford Coppola and Bram Stoker's Dracula'. In Contemporary Hollywood Cinema, ed. Steve Neale and Murray Smith, pp. 191–208. London and New York: Routledge,1998.

Generani, Gustavo. 'Bram Stoker's Dracula: Breaking the Imperial-Anthropological Time'. Horror Studies 9, no. 1 (2018): 119–139.

Worland, Rick. The Horror Film: An Introduction. Malden, MA and Oxford: Blackwell, 2007.

The Bride of Frankenstein
1935 – 80 mins
James Whale

Universal's follow-up to *Frankenstein* (1931) was the first of the studio's numerous monster sequels of the 1930s. (*Dracula's Daughter* was released the following year and then the unhallowed race was on.) After *The Old Dark House* (1932) and *The Invisible Man* (1933), *Frankenstein* director James Whale revisited his monster with *The Bride of Frankenstein* and extended his remarkably sympathetic treatment of him. The inspiration for the much less accomplished *The Bride* (1985) (Sting as Dr. Frankenstein and Jennifer Beales as the mate?!), the plot of *Bride of Frankenstein* picks up immediately where the earlier film leaves off, bracketed by a frame tale involving Mary Shelley, Percy Shelley, and Lord Byron in which Mary (Lanchester, who also plays the eponymous bride) reveals that there is more to the Frankenstein story than has thus far been told.

DIRECTOR James Whale
PRODUCER Carl Laemmle Jr.
SCREENPLAY John Balderston, William Hurlbut
CINEMATOGRAPHY John J. Mescall
EDITOR Ted J. Kent
MUSIC Franz Waxman
PRODUCTION COMPANY Universal Pictures
MAIN CAST Boris Karloff, Colin Clive, Elsa Lanchester, Ernest Thesiger, Valerie Hobson, Dwight Frye, O. P. Heggie

Henry Frankenstein (Clive) now rejects his earlier work to create life but is finally cajoled into creating a mate for the monster (Karloff) by his old mentor, Dr. Pretorius (Thesiger), who uses the creature as a threat to convince Frankenstein. The film begins with a horrifying opening scene in which the parents of the little girl drowned in *Frankenstein* are killed by the creature, who has survived the fire at the windmill that concluded the earlier movie, the father strangled in the pit under the burned mill and the mother unceremoniously tossed into it. Una O'Connor's shrill screams follow, punctuating the grisly scene. After Pretorius shows Henry his collection of miniature homunculi, the former proclaims that together they will create 'a new world of gods and monsters' – the phrase providing the title for the 1998 film about the final period of Whale's life.

Aided in part by Karloff's brilliant performance, *Bride of Frankenstein* pushes identification with the creature further than the first film. This time he saves a drowning girl rather than causing a girl to drown, but the misunderstood monster is hunted down by the angry mob of villagers, captured, and imprisoned in chains. The scene in which he is transported to the town jail, lashed to a pole, has distinct overtones of the crucifixion, while Christian imagery is also invoked, for example, in the touching scenes of the monster with his friend, the blind man (Heggie), in his cottage (he is attracted to the cottage by the blind man's playing of 'Ave Maria' on the violin), which suggests the Last Supper as they share bread and wine before being interrupted by two hunters. Some have argued that Whale's homosexuality may explain his extraordinary empathy with the creature, shunned as he is by society. Certainly, the mincing Pretorius is coded as gay, and Ernest Thesiger, the actor who portrayed him, was, like Whale, homosexual. The scene where the two hunters interrupt the creature's idyll with the blind man ('friend') may be read as the imposition of normative masculinity on and disruption of a homosexual relationship.

After a reprise of the first film's famous creation scene with its wild expressionism (this time, 'She's alive! Alive!'), production designer Kenneth Strickfaden's laboratory equipment from *Frankenstein* was reused in *Bride of Frankenstein* (as it would be later in Mel Brooks' *Young Frankenstein** [1974]). When the poor creature is rejected by his new mate (Lanchester), he flies into a rampage that also conveniently provides apparent narrative closure and poetic justice: now able to speak, he tells Henry and Elizabeth to leave the lab ('Yes! Go! You live!') while to Pretorius and his intended bride he says, 'You stay. We belong dead.' Shedding a tear, he destroys the tower laboratory, killing them and himself (although, as we subsequently find out four years later in *Son of Frankenstein* [1939], he had only lapsed into a coma).

Further Reading:

Curtis, James. *James Whale: A New World of Gods and Monsters*. Minneapolis: University of Minnesota Press, 2003.

Manguel, Alberto. *Bride of Frankenstein*. London: British Film Institute, 1997.

Weaver, Tom, Michael Brunas, and John Brunas. *Universal Horrors: The Studios Classic Films, 1931–1946*, 2nd edn. Jefferson, NC and London: McFarland, 2007.

Young, Elizabeth. 'Here Comes the Bride: Wedding Gender and Race in *Bride of Frankenstein*'. In *The Dread of Difference: Gender in the Horror Film*, 2nd edn, ed. Barry Keith Grant, pp. 359–387. Austin: University of Texas Press, 2015.

Bubba Ho-Tep
2002 – 92 mins
Don Coscarelli

One might suspect that even John Carpenter (*Halloween** [1978], *In the Mouth of Madness** [1994]), who early in his career made a biopic about Elvis Presley – *Elvis* (1979) – could never have imagined a film like *Bubba Ho-Tep*. Written and directed by Don Coscarelli (writer and director of all four films in the *Phantasm* franchise), the plot of *Bubba* finds an elderly Elvis Presley (Campbell) – or a delusional Elvis impersonator named Sebastian Haff – and John Fitzgerald Kennedy (Davis) – or, again, a delusional senior who thinks he is JFK – as two residents of a Texas retirement home battling a 3,000-year old Egyptian soul-sucking mummy in cowboy boots feeding off the easy prey of old folks in the retirement home. According to Kennedy's research in *The Everyday Man and Woman's Book of Souls*, a being like Bubba that consumes souls can ingest them through any major bodily orifice, although Elvis assumes its preferred point of entry is through the rectum because the mummy apparently wrote graffiti on one of the toilet stall walls while defecating.

Tana leaves also figure in somehow.

The film is quite funny, with Campbell and Davis performing this ludicrous scenario with deadpan serious-ness. There are memorable discussions about chocolate dingdongs and other topics of urgent significance. Even the mummy has his comic banter, hurling insults at Elvis in their climactic fight ('Eat the dog dick of Anubis, you ass wipe'). The two men from the funeral parlor who load the corpses into their hearse in the morning are like the gravediggers in *Hamlet*, with comic repartee that nudges at deeper philosophical ques-tions ('Makes you wonder, doesn't it?'). Once the dynamic duo discovers the existence of the malevolent mummy, Bubba and Elvis ponder what they should do, and Jack reasonably responds: 'Changing rest homes might be a good idea.' But the President and the King instead decide to take a stand (more accurately, a seat in a motorised wheelchair) against the supernatural soul-sucker.

At the same time as *Bubba Ho-Tep* succeeds as an offbeat horror comedy movie, tucked within it is a poignant statement about society's treatment of the elderly and of aging. Elvis and Jack were living a dreary existence, alone with their memories and fantasies, humoured and forgotten and condescended to by caregivers and younger folk. But battling Bubba gives them a purpose. Campbell is outstanding as an aged and dispirited Presley who regains himself when confronted with an actual spirit, pretending to be Elvis pretending to be Sebastian Haff pretending to be Elvis. His physical movements are constrained yet controlled, including the sultry sneer of the lip. On another level, the film, like *Phantom of the Paradise** (1974), is about the tyranny of the culture industry and its destruction of individual authenticity. Thinking in voiceover, Elvis remarks that he wanted to escape his life as a cultural icon because 'It wasn't even me anymore. Just this thing they made up' – a walking automaton going through the motions, not unlike Bubba. In the end, Elvis defeats his darker self and dies in the process, but with his soul intact – a glorious wish-fulfilling fantasy given the string of more than twenty formula musical comedies he was forced to

DIRECTOR Don Coscarelli
PRODUCER Don Coscarelli, Jason R. Savage
SCREENPLAY Don Coscarelli
CINEMATOGRAPHY Adam Janeiro
EDITOR Scott J. Gill, Donald Milne
MUSIC Brian Tyler
PRODUCTION COMPANY Silver Sphere Corporation
MAIN CAST Bruce Campbell, Ossie Davis, Ella Joyce, Heidi Marnhout, Bob Ivy, Larry Pennell

churn out in the 1960s after an auspicious beginning with *Loving You* (1957), *Jailhouse Rock* (1957), and *King Creole* (1958).

Further Reading

Berns, Fernando Gabriel Pagnoni, and Diego Foronda. 'Elegiac Masculinity in *Bubba Ho-Tep* and *Late Phases*'. In *Gender and Contemporary Horror in Film*, ed. Samantha Holland, Robert Shail, and Steven Gerrard, pp. 23–38. Bingley, UK: Emerald Publishing, 2019.

Coscarelli, Don. *True Indie: Life and Death in Filmmaking*. New York: St. Martin's Press, 2018.

Simpson, Philip L. "Ask Not What Your Rest Home Can Do for You": Self-Agency and Public Service in *Bubba Ho-Tep*'. In *Elder Horror: Essays on Film's Frightening Images of Aging*, ed. Cynthia J. Miller and A. Bowdoin Van Riper, pp. 12–21. Jefferson, NC: McFarland, 2019.

Thompson, Hannah. '"You Nasty Thing from Beyond the Dead": Elvis and JFK versus The Mummy in *Bubba Ho-Tep*'. In *Undead in the West: Vampires, Zombies, Mummies, and Ghosts on the Cinematic Frontier*, ed. Cynthia J. Miller and A. Bowdoin Van Riper, pp. 237–52. Lanham, MD: Scarecrow Press, 2012.

Wilkinson, Simon A. *Hollywood Horror from the Director's Chair: Six Filmmakers in the Franchise of Fear*. Jefferson, NC: McFarland, 2008.

Bud Abbott and Lou Costello Meet Frankenstein
1948 – 83 mins
Charles Barton

The horror comedy, dating back at least to *The Cat and the Canary** (1927), was a favourite for Hollywood comedy teams, but none did it better than Abbott and Costello. In this, their first pairing with Universal's classic horror monsters, the comic duo play Chick Young (Abbott) and Wilbur Grey (Costello), two railway freight handlers who become involved with the terrible trio of Dracula (Lugosi), the Wolfman (Chaney), and the Frankenstein monster (Strange). The two funnymen flirted with the fantastic in the haunted house comedy *Hold that Ghost* (1941) and in *The Time of Their Lives* (1946), where they played ghosts themselves, before embarking on their series of monster meetings. The film's commercial success paved the way for their

DIRECTOR Charles Barton

PRODUCER Robert Arthur

SCREENPLAY John Grant, Frederic I. Rinaldo, Robert Lees

CINEMATOGRAPHY Charles Van Enger

EDITOR Frank Gross

MUSIC Frank Skinner

PRODUCTION COMPANY Universal

MAIN CAST Bud Abbott, Lou Costello, Bela Lugosi, Lon Chaney Jr., Glenn Strange, Lenore Aubert, Jane Randolph, Frank Ferguson

subsequent appointments with the studio's other monsters: *Abbott and Costello Meet the Killer, Boris Karloff* (1949), *Abbott and Costello Meet the Invisible Man* (1951), *Abbott and Costello Meet Dr. Jekyll and Mr. Hyde* (1953), and *Abbott and Costello Meet the Mummy* (1955).

For the monsters, though, who hadn't appeared since *House of Dracula* (1945), it would be their last appearance in a Universal horror film. As the series ran its course, the films declined in both humour and horror, the comic duo meeting *Captain Kidd* (1952) and the *Keystone Kops* (1955) and joining the *Foreign Legion* (1950) and even going to *Mars* (1953). The comedians met the last of the Universal Studios monsters, the Creature from the Black Lagoon, on television's *Colgate Comedy Hour* in 1954.

At the railway station Wilbur takes an urgent overseas telephone call from Lawrence Talbot (Chaney), who urges them not to deliver two arriving crates for McDougal's House of Horrors, the local wax museum. The crates contain the remains of Count Dracula and the Frankenstein monster, but before he can convey his warning, the rising of the full moon transforms Talbot into a werewolf. After the hapless pair deliver and unpack the crates, Dracula emerges from his coffin and, amidst some comic business involving Wilbur, whose hysterical warnings no one will believe ('I saw what I saw when I saw it', he insists), animates the Frankenstein monster with a portable power charger he inexplicably has. As we find out, Dracula is in cahoots with a renegade surgeon with a Frankenstein complex, Dr. Sandra Mornay (Aubert), who promises to fulfill the vampire's wish to have the monster fitted with a new brain, one with 'no will of his own. No fiendish intellect to oppose his master.' As she boasts, she has found a brain that will exceed his expectations – Wilbur's ('so simple, so pliable'). In the climax, the Wolfman grabs Dracula as the vampire morphs into bat form and jumps with him off a steep cliff, presumably killing them both, while the monster, after throwing Dr. Mornay through a window to her death, is then consumed by fire – all the action interspersed with farce as the boys run about attempting to escape the mayhem.

Apart from Abbott and Costello, the rest of the cast plays it straight. Indeed, this was the only time on film Lugosi repeated the role he had created in *Dracula** (1931), although he would portray vampires in several other movies including *Mark of the Vampire* (1935), *Spooks Run Wild* (1941) with the Bowery Boys, and *The Return of the Vampire* (1943). The appositely named Glenn Strange had starred in many Westerns before replacing Karloff as Frankenstein's monster in *House of Frankenstein* (1944) and *House of Dracula* (1945); and although Lugosi's Dracula seems oddly corporeal, Chaney brings the same gravitas to the role of tortured soul Lawrence Talbot that he did to *The Wolf Man** (1941). While Dracula's transformations into a bat are poorly animated, detracting from their frightful potential, Talbot's transformations are excellently done. The film's best moment, though, occurs when Dracula steers the newly awakened but groggy Frankenstein monster away from the hypnotised and immobile Wilbur, reassuringly telling the creature, 'Don't be afraid, he won't hurt you.'

Further Reading:

Carmichael, Deborah. 'Abbott and Costello Meet Frankenstein: Laughing in the Face of an Uncertain Future.' In *The Laughing Dead: The Horror-Comedy Film from Bride of Frankenstein to Zombieland*, ed. Cynthia J. Miller and Bowdoin Van Riper, pp. 127–37. Lanham, MD: Rowman & Littlefield, 2016.

Miller, Jeffrey S. *The Horror Spoofs of Abbott and Costello*. Jefferson, NC and London: McFarland, 2000.

Hallenbeck, Bruce G. *Comedy-Horror Films: A Chronological History, 1914–2008*. Jefferson, NC: McFarland, 2009.

Weaver, Tom, Michael Brunas, and John Brunas. *Universal Horrors: The Studios Classic Films, 1931–1946*, 2nd edn. Jefferson, NC and London: McFarland, 2007.

The Burrowers
2008 – 96 mins.
J. T. Petty

The woods may be lovely – and, indeed, the cinematography of *The Burrowers* presents them so, in glorious shots that would grace any classic Western – but they are also dark and deep. The fearful associations of the 'untamed' wilderness have carried over into the horror genre, as expressed in horror movies from *Creature from the Black Lagoon* (1954)* to *The Witch* (2015)*. The Puritan mind associated Native Americans with demonic evil, a psychic projection that *The Burrowers* reverses. Written and directed by J. T. Petty (*Hellbenders* [2012], *Mimic 3: Sentinel* [2003]), this is no mere exercise in genre hybridity, like *Curse of the Undead* (1959), with its vampire gunslinger, or *Billy the Kid vs. Dracula* (1966). Rather, the film uses the Western, with its traditionally racist view of indigenous cultures, to offer a devastating critique of the racism upon which westward expansion and the genocide of Native Americans were founded.

The film begins like John Ford's classic Western *The Searchers* (1956), in which rabid Indian-hater Ethan Edwards (John Wayne) searches for years for his niece, kidnapped by renegade Comanche, not to rescue her but to kill her because she has been defiled. In *The Burrowers*, set in 1879 (eleven years after *The Searchers*

DIRECTOR J. T. Petty
PRODUCER William Sherak, Jason Shuman
SCREENPLAY J. T. Petty
CINEMATOGRAPHY Phil Parmet
EDITOR Andy Grieve, Rob Sullivan
MUSIC Joseph LoDuca
PRODUCTION COMPANY Blue Star Pictures
MAIN CAST William Mapother, Sean Patrick Thomas, Doug Hutchison, Karl Geary, Clancy Brown, David Busse

begins), the women and children of a pioneer family are taken away by someone or something, and the neighbouring men, assuming it was Indians, organise a search party to find and rescue them. The film offers several other references to *The Searchers*, such as when the pursuers find a child's doll and, most astonishingly, when one of them, Parcher (Mapother), shoots out the eyes of a dead Indian, an act of religious defilement, as Ethan explains when he does the same in *The Searchers*.

It turns out, though, that the women have not been taken by Indians but have been snatched by creatures the Indians, who already know about them, call burrowers. The burrowers paralyze their prey with a natural toxin, bury their victims alive, and return to eat them later after rot has begin to soften them. We learn that the burrowers used to feed on buffalo, but now that the buffalo are gone the burrowers have had to find another source of food – namely, humans. It is whites who have upset the delicate balance of nature, unable to live in harmony with the land. Despite learning this, the band of pursuers persists in holding onto their racist perspective as they agree to kill the monsters while still planning to rescue the missing settlers from the Indians. In their pursuit, they meet a cavalry platoon under the command of Henry Victor (Hutchison), a vain and rabid racist clearly modelled on Gen. George Armstrong Custer (at one point he is shown trimming his handlebar moustache with scissors as the vain Custer does in another subversive Western, *Little Big Man* [1970]).

In the brutally ironic ending of *The Burrowers*, Victor misconstrues the danger because of his own racist perspective ('All we can do is make sure these Indians never do nothing like this again') and so fails to learn about the native drug used to combat the creatures. Here, the cavalry does not come to the rescue; instead, we see two Ute braves, who know the secret of the drug, lynched and swinging from ropes. One cowboy advises another 'Find your girl, kill the burrowers, build a house on the prairie, and play American.' The country is built on bloodshed, but the subterranean nature of the burrowers suggests repression, while their abject maws are a horrific representation of the idea that the nation will never exorcise its racist demons without unearthing and confronting its violently racist past.

Further Reading

Fine, Kerry, Michael K. Johnson, Rebecca M. Lush, and Sarah L. Spurgeon, eds. *Weird Westerns: Race, Gender, Genre*. Lincoln: University of Nebraska Press, 2020.

Green, Paul. *Encyclopedia of Weird Westerns*, 2nd edn. Jefferson, NC: McFarland, 2016.

Miller, Cynthia J., and Bowdoin Van Riper, eds. *Undead in the West: Vampires, Zombies, Mummies, and Ghosts on the Cinematic Frontier*. Lanham, MD: Scarecrow Press, 2012.

Miller, Cynthia J., and Bowdoin Van Riper, eds. *Undead in the West II: They Just Keep Coming*. Lanham, MD: Scarecrow Press, 2013.

Candyman
1992 – 99 mins
Bernard Rose

King Kong* (1933) evoked the fear of racial miscegenation in the figure of the dark ape, the beast in love with the (white) beauty, but explicit questions of race in horror only emerged with the casting of a black actor as the protagonist of *Night of the Living Dead** in 1968. *Candyman* translates American culture's racial fears and anxieties into the terms of horror and locates it within urban America. Director Bernard Rose (*Paperhouse* [1988]) took Clive Barker's source story 'The Forbidden' (contained in Book 5 of Barker's *Books of Blood* [1985]) and relocated it from Great Britain to the Cabrini-Green public housing development in Chicago, infamous at the time as a case study for the failures of inner city public housing, and changed the emphasis from class to race – although the two are, of course, inextricable, as *Candyman* shows. The film was followed by two sequels, *Candyman: Farewell to the Flesh* (1995) and *Candyman: Day of the Dead* (1999), all three featuring Tony Todd as the title monster.

Helen Lyle (Madsen), a graduate student in sociology at the University of Chicago, is researching urban legends (the ones we hear of involve babysitters and evoke *Halloween** [1978]), when she comes upon a local one involving the Candyman, about which she decides to write her thesis. From one of her professors we learn Candyman's backstory: he was the son of a prosperous former slave (he became wealthy, significantly, during the Civil War, when the nation was ripped asunder, like Candyman's victims) who sired a child by a white woman whom he loved; in retribution, her father had Candyman's hand cut off and replaced with his killing hook, stripped naked and smeared with honey from a local apiary, and then stung to death by the bees. According to the legend, Candyman can be summoned by saying his name five times while looking in a mirror.

Investigating the unsolved murder of a woman in Cabrini-Green that residents attribute to Candyman, Helen goes with her friend and fellow graduate student Bernadette (Lemmons) on a field trip to the projects to learn about how the people who live there use the 'mythical figure' of Candyman to cope with what she describes as 'the unconscious fears of modern urban society'. Helen summons him according to the legend, and he explains to her that he needs the belief of people in order to survive and that because Helen's research threatens to demythify him, innocent blood – hers – must be shed to perpetuate that belief ('Believe in me, be my victim'). He arranges circumstances so that she seems to have killed several people actually dispatched by Candyman, placing her within the nightmare existence of the people she was at first regarding with a tourist gaze.

The first trip to Cabrini-Green by the two women seems like they are entering an alien world – although it is only eight blocks away! Helen climbs through the hole behind the bathroom wall cabinet in the murdered woman's apartment like Alice going through the rabbit hole. Unlike Helen's academic distance from her subjects, the film emphasises people's connectedness rather than difference, as in the opening high-angle shots

DIRECTOR Bernard Rose
PRODUCER Steve Golin,
Sigurion Sighvatsson, Alan Poul
SCREENPLAY Clive Barker,
Bernard Rose
CINEMATOGRAPHY
Anthony B. Richmond -
EDITOR Dan Rae
MUSIC Philip Glass
PRODUCTION COMPANY
Propaganda Films, PolyGram
Filmed Entertainment
MAIN CAST Virginia Madsen,
Tony Todd, Xander Berkeley,
Kasi Lemmons, Vanessa A.
Williams, DeJuan Guy

behind the credits of the city that show roadways bustling with cars, a hive of activity, like the bees that burst from Candyman's chest. In the course of fighting Candyman, Helen gets too close to her topic, like Kathleen in *The Addiction** (1995), and changes from aloof academic to active participant. In the final shot, recalling the end of *The Shining** (1980), the camera tracks in to a close-up of a wall mural depicting her along with Candyman, now absorbed into and part of the folklore she had been investigating.

Further Reading:

Briefel, Aviva, and Sianne Ngai. '*Candyman*: Urban Space, Fear, and Entitlement'. In *Horror Film Reader*, ed. Alain Silver and James Ursini, pp. 281–303. New York: Limelight, 2000.

Coleman, Robin R. Means. *Horror Noire: Blacks in American Horror Films from 1890s to Present*. New York and Abingdon, UK: Routledge, 2011.

Thompson, Kirsten Moana. *Apocalyptic Dread: American Film at the Turn of the Millennium*. Albany: State University of New York Press, 2007.

Towlson, Jon. *Candyman*. Leighton Buzzard: Auteur, 2018.

Carnival of Souls
1962 – 80 mins
Herk Harvey

The only feature film directed by Herk Harvey, who made dozens of educational and industrial shorts for the Centron Corporation, an independent production company based in Lawrence, Kansas, *Carnival of Souls*, despite of – or, perhaps, because of – its small budget, is particularly effective at creating an eerie, dreamlike atmosphere that perfectly expresses the plight of its main character, Mary Henry (Hilligoss), whose soul is in a purgatorial limbo. Harvey shot the film on an extremely small budget in Lawrence and Salt Lake City, where the abandoned Saltair Pavilion, once an important national vacation venue, was located. Much of the crew were Centron employees, as was the screenwriter, John Clifford, who was given carte blanche with the only stipulation from Harvey being that the final scene had to feature a crowd of ghouls in the dilapidated ballroom of Saltair. Amusement parks have featured in numerous horror films, and *Carnival of Souls*, now a cult favourite widely seen over the years on late-night television, inspired a direct-to-video remake (1998) and a loose remake, *Yella* (2008), directed by Christian Petzold, as well as the look of George Romero's zombies in *Night of the Living Dead** (1968).

In Kansas, Mary is a passenger in a car with two other young women when they become involved in a drag race with some young men and end up plunging into a river as both vehicles are jockeying for position on a narrow wooden bridge. While the police try unsuccessfully to locate the car in the river, Mary somehow surfaces, the only survivor, although she is unable to remember what happened. Moving to Salt Lake City to take up a job as a church organist, she is definitely not in Kansas anymore as periodically she sees a stranger, 'The Man' (Harvey), lurking near, and she finds herself drawn to the abandoned pavilion, which seems to beckon like Hill House or the Overlook Hotel.

The film suggests that Mary's soul is in turmoil and that she needs to come to terms with her own death. The minister in Kansas tells her that she should put more 'soul' into her playing, and the one in Salt Lake City says he feels sorry for her 'lack of soul'. For Mary, the church is merely a business transaction, as she tells John (Berger), the other roomer in the house, who replies, correctly, that her spiritually deficient attitude likely induces nightmares. Mary seems antisocial, although from a psychoanalytic perspective the film suggests she may have a fear of intimacy with men. On one level, The Man is a projection of her fear of all men, whether the smug Dr. Samuels (Levitt) or the sleazy John. But it is also the men, the doctor and ministers, who seek to prevent Mary from achieving spiritual peace by exploring the pavilion. When she finally does so, she sees The Man (Death?) at the undead ball dancing with herself, after which the undead pursue and overtake her. This death dance is the one social event no one, not even Mary, can avoid.

The plot, including the twist ending where the car is finally dredged up from the river back in Kansas with the bodies of three women in it, recalls the famous ending of the *Twilight Zone* episode 'The Hitch-Hiker' with Inger Stevens, and the scene in the department store when Mary becomes briefly disconnected from the world is reminiscent of another episode of the show, 'The After-Hours', with Anne Francis,

DIRECTOR Herk Harvey

PRODUCER Herk Harvey

SCREENPLAY John Clifford, Herk Harvey

CINEMATOGRAPHY Maurice Prather

EDITOR Bill de Jamett, Dan Palmquist

MUSIC Gene Moore

PRODUCTION COMPANY Herts-Lion International Corp.

MAIN CAST Candace Hilligoss, Francis Feist, Sidney Berger, Art Ellison, Herk Harvey, Stan Levitt

who discovers while shopping that she is in fact a mannequin in the store. Both episodes were written by Rod Serling (the former based in turn on an earlier radio play) and broadcast during the show's first season in 1960, and both may have been an influence on Clifford and Harvey.

Further Reading

Brown, Julie. 'Carnival of Souls and The Organs of Horror'. In Music in the Horror Film: Listening to Fear, ed. Neil Lerner, pp. 1–20. New York and London: Routledge, 2010.

Kawin, Bruce F. 'Carnival of Souls'. In Selected Film Essays and Interviews. London and New York: Anthem Press, 2013.

Riley, James. "Have You No Respect? Do You Feel No Reverence?': Narrative and Critical Subversion in Herk Harvey's Carnival of Souls'. In Crash Cinema: Representation in Film, ed. Mark Goodall, Jill Good, and Will Godfrey, pp. 14–24. Newcastle: Cambridge Scholars Publishing, 2007.

Price, Michael H., and Todd Camp. Herk Harvey's Carnival of Souls and Other Futile Inquiries. Parkville, MD: Midnight Marquee Press, 2009.

Carrie
1976 – 98 mins
Brian De Palma

Based on Stephen King's 1974 book of the same name, his first published novel, *Carrie* was also the first of the many screen adaptations based on his fiction (a representative share of them are included in this book). It garnered two Oscar nominations – Sissy Spacek for Best Actress as the telekinetic teenager of the title and Piper Laurie for Best Supporting Actress for her maniacal mother, Margaret White – and was the first significant box-office success for director Brian De Palma (*Sisters** [1972], *Phantom of the Paradise** [1974]). Its popularity generated a sequel, *The Rage: Carrie 2* (1999), with Amy Irving reprising her role as classmate Sue Snell; a 2002 made-for-television film; a 2013 remake; and an unsuccessful 1988 Broadway musical. The film's depiction of high school life and teenage female empowerment – 'It has nothing to do with Satan, it's me', as Carrie tells her mother – has guaranteed its iconic status in horror as well as popular culture more generally.

Introverted teenager Carrie White has her first period in the high school gym shower at the same time as she becomes aware of her dawning power of telekinesis. (De Palma's 1978 *The Fury* also features a similar premise involving telekinesis, but with a teenage boy.) Kept ignorant of menstruation by her fanatically religious mother, Carrie experiences a new sensual awareness of her own body – enticingly filmed by De Palma in slow motion and soft focus – but it quickly turns frightening for her with the sight of blood, associating feminine agency with horror. Perceiving Carrie's turn to womanhood and driven mad by her own lustful indulgence in the past, her mother attempts to repress the girl's growth by locking her in a closet to pray, as she has done so many times before. But this time Carrie is determined to come out of the closet, which she does by asserting her own wishes over her mother's and defiantly going to the prom with school heartthrob Tommy Ross (Katt).

The film builds inevitably toward the extraordinary prom scene, the extended set piece that provides the powerful climax and a cathartic explosion of violence in which no one is spared. (Of course, the fact that the school is named Bates High School already promises that the event will not go well.) After the bucket of pig's blood is dumped on her by cruel classmate Chris Hargensen (Allen) while being crowned prom queen, Carrie's unleashed rage is indiscriminate as she imagines that everyone has been in on the prank and laughing at her, just as her mother predicted. She is all the more enraged for having had a moment of happiness, as she seemed finally to have been accepted by her peers, even Tommy, who seemed truly to like her. The two of them dance, spinning in a *pas de deux* with the rotating camera in one lengthy shot, the speed gradually increasing once they kiss, an expression of her giddy joy. But then, drenched in blood, her blue eyes glaring through the red, she takes her vengeance as the film abruptly shifts to a red tint and a split screen, a technique De Palma has often employed, the change in visual register a sudden shock that mirrors the shock of the event itself.

DIRECTOR Brian De Palma
PRODUCER Paul Monash
SCREENPLAY
Lawrence D. Gordon
CINEMATOGRAPHY Mario Tosi
EDITOR Paul Hirsch
MUSIC Pino Donaggio
PRODUCTION COMPANY
Red Bank Films
MAIN CAST Sissy Spacek, Piper Laurie, Amy Irving,
Betty Buckley, Nancy Allen,
William Katt, John Travolta,
P. J. Soles, Sydney Lassick

De Palma's treatment ultimately stands as a rebuke to Hitchcock's famous assertion that in *Sabotage* (1936) it was a mistake to allow the bomb to go off on the bus and kill the boy unaware he is carrying it, as well as all the other passengers, because it alienated the audience. Just as in *Sabotage* Hitchcock builds suspense by cutting between the boy with the deadly package and clocks ticking away the time until noon, when the bomb is set to detonate, so in the prom scene in *Carrie* De Palma cuts multiple times from the dance floor to the bucket of pig's blood, rubbing our noses in it, as it were. More than once the camera tracks along the path of the rope, taking us to its inevitable end, the bucket. Even though Carrie kills them all, reserving particularly awful deaths for her sarcastic English teacher (Lassick) and kindly gym teacher Miss Collins (Buckley), surely the apocalyptic mayhem that turns the prom scene into a blazing inferno taps into the secret fantasies of every adolescent who has ever been bullied at school.

Further Reading

Bliss, Michael. *Brian De Palma*. Metuchen, NJ and London: Scarecrow Press, 1983.

Creed, Barbara. *The Monstrous-Feminine: Film, Feminism, Psychoanalysis*. London and New York: Routledge, 1993.

Mitchell, Neil. *Carrie*. Leighton Buzzard: Auteur, 2014.

Stamp, Shelley. 'Horror, Femininity, and Carrie's Monstrous Puberty'. In *The Dread of Difference: Gender in the Horror Film*, 2nd edn, ed. Barry Keith Grant, pp. 329–345. Austin: University of Texas Press, 2015.

The Cat and the Canary
1927 – 86 mins
Paul Leni

John Willard's 1922 Broadway play *The Cat and the Canary*, part of a cycle of spooky mystery thrillers, has proven sufficiently sturdy to have inspired several film versions, among them Rupert Julian's lost *The Cat Creeps* (1930), unrelated to the 1946 film also titled *The Cat Creeps*), Elliott Nugent's more comedic version of 1939 starring Bob Hope and Paulette Goddard, and a 1979 British version directed by Radley Metzger. The very popular first silent version, directed by German émigré filmmaker Paul Leni (*Waxworks*, 1924), was significant in introducing German expressionism to American cinema and for helping to establish Universal's expressionist approach to horror. (Leni made only four films in Hollywood. The final one, *The Last Warning*

DIRECTOR Paul Leni
PRODUCER Carl Laemmle
SCREENPLAY Robert F. Hill, Alfred A. Cohen
CINEMATOGRAPHY Gilbert Warrenton
EDITOR Martin G. Cohen
PRODUCTION COMPANY Universal
MAIN CAST Laura LaPlante, Creighton Hale, Lucien Littlefield, Flora Finch, Arthur Edmund Carewe, Tully Marshall, Martha Mattox

[1928], was generically similar to *The Cat and the Canary* and also starred Laura La Plante. Leni died less than a year after the film's release as a result of blood poisoning.) Leni's film version set the template for the 'old dark house' genre, so named for another important early example, *The Old Dark House* (1932), directed by James Whale (*Frankenstein* [1931], *The Bride of Frankenstein** [1935]), on which Leni's film was a clear influence. *The Cat and the Canary*'s blend of the funny and the frightening also influenced later horror comedies such as the monster films of Abbott and Costello (see *Bud Abbott and Lou Costello Meet Frankenstein** [1948]).

The plot revolves around the death of the wealthy Cyrus West and the reading of his will twenty years later to determine who inherits his fortune. Hopeful family members gather for the midnight reading at West's mansion on the Hudson, which in the periodic exterior shots looks more like Nosferatu's *schloss* than the manor of a privileged patroon. The place even has cobwebs on the outside. At the same time, a violent madman has apparently escaped from the local asylum and is hiding in the mansion, which has been maintained all these years by the joyless Mammy Pleasant (Mattox). The romantic subplot is provided by ingénue Annabelle West (La Plante) and bumbling Paul Jones (Hale). The will stipulates that if Annabelle is judged insane, then the estate would be inherited by another family member named in a second sealed envelope which someone has apparently already opened. This stipulation launches the unknown killer's plot to drive Annabelle mad. The lawyer, Mr. Crosby (Marshall), observes to her that the greedy relatives are like cats around a canary, which is also how the asylum guard describes the escaped maniac and his victims.

Before coming to Hollywood at the invitation of Universal boss Carl Laemmle, Leni had worked as a director and a set designer, and the German expressionist influence is clear in the sets of *The Cat and the Canary*, designed by Leni and built by Charles D. Hall, who later designed the sets of *Dracula** (1931), *Frankenstein* (1931), and *The Invisible Man* (1933), among other films. There are shots filmed with distorting lenses, and shadows move along walls as if cast by Nosferatu. When Mr. Crosby tells Annabelle that she is 'in a cage, surrounded by rats', she is photographed through the slates of a wooden chair as if they are the bars of a prison cell. Leni's camera is frequently mobile, adding visually to the tension, perhaps at once most wittily and disturbingly positioned from the point of view of the falling portrait of Cyrus West, as if his ghost is there presiding over events. Overall, while the characters' fears are often played for laughs, the film maintains a sinister atmosphere brought to fruition in the shots of the hairy hand that slowly and threateningly moves into the frame, and the bulging eye and upwardly thrusting fangs of The Cat when we finally see him in the climax.

Further Reading:

Fowkes, Katherine A. *Giving Up the Ghost: Spirits Ghosts, and Angels in Mainstream Comedy Films*. Detroit: Wayne State University Press, 1999.

Jones, David Annwn. *Re-envisaging the First Age of Cinematic Horror, 1896–1934*. Cardiff: University of Wales Press, 2018.

Natale, Simone. 'Specters of the Mind: Ghosts, Illusion, and Exposure in Paul Leni's *The Cat and the Canary*'. In *Cinematic Ghosts: Haunting and Spectrality from Silent Cinema to the Digital Era*, ed. Murray Leeder, pp. 59–76. New York and London: Bloomsbury, 2015.

Rigby, Jonathan. *American Gothic: Six Decades of Classic Horror Cinema*. Cambridge: Signum, 2017.

Spadoni, Robert. *Uncanny Bodies: The Coming of Sound Film and the Origins of the Horror Genre*. University of California Press, 2007.

Cat People
1942 – 74 mins
Jacques Tourneur

Val Lewton, a fiction writer and previously a story editor for David O. Selznick, was appointed head of the unit set up by RKO for the purpose of making low-budget horror films that might rival Universal's dominance of the genre. In addition to the budgetary constraints (under $150,000) and short running times allowed, the studio provided sensational titles on which the films would be based. Working with these constraints, Lewton and his team managed to produce several excellent B films that, turning their limitations into virtues, moved horror in a more psychological direction than the earlier Universal movies with their reliance on monsters. Lewton's films reveal a transition from the earlier German expressionist style, which had been absorbed so successfully at Universal (see, for example, The Bride of Frankenstein* [1935]) to film noir, a genre that RKO would later embrace. Jacques Tourneur, the director of Cat People, the first of the nine horror films Lewton produced for the studio, also directed two of the other films, I Walked with a Zombie* and The Leopard Man (1943). Written, like the sequel, The Curse of the Cat People (1943), by DeWitt Bodeen (as was another film in the series, The Seventh Victim [1943]), Cat People was the first film on which Tourneur would work with the great cinematographer Nicholas Musuraca (the two later teamed up again for one of the classic film noirs, Out of the Past [1947]).

In the plot, Serbian-born fashion illustrator Irena Dubrovna (Simone Simon) begins a relationship with ship designer Oliver Reed (Smith). Coming to her apartment building for the first time, Oliver remarks upon entering, 'I never cease to marvel at what is behind a Brownstone front' – a justification for the reuse of the grandiose interior mansion set from The Magnificent Ambersons [1942]), as well as a comment that applies to the idea of intense passions lurking within apparent ordinariness. (Oliver, played blandly by the appropriately named Smith, describes himself as 'a good plain Americano'.) Irena tells Oliver about her heritage, that she comes from a village where the people had been enslaved and consequently resorted to witchcraft, becoming cat people – a story that the modern and boringly sensible Oliver brushes off merely as a fairy tale heard in childhood. They marry, but Irena believes that she, too, will transform into a panther if aroused erotically or emotionally, so their marriage remains unconsummated. Enter the local psychiatrist, Dr. Louis Judd (Conway), who provides the Freudian explanation for Irena's fear of sex as childhood trauma and repression.

Unlike Paul Schrader's more graphic and explicit 1982 remake, here Irena's transformations are mostly hinted at rather than made graphically explicit. Shadows and darkness are everywhere in the film, often look-ing like bars of a cage, emphasising Irena's repression. One justly famous scene involves Alice (Randolph), her perceived rival for Oliver's affections, going for a late-night swim in a public pool alone. The shadow by the exit stairway may be just that of a house cat, while the play of the water's reflections on the shadowy tiled walls seems somehow ominous – after which Alice, jittery, leaves the pool and retrieves her robe, which is now shredded as if by claws.

DIRECTOR Jacques Tourneur
PRODUCER Val Lewton
SCREENPLAY DeWitt Bodeen
CINEMATOGRAPHY
Nicholas Musuraca
EDITOR Mark Robson
MUSIC Roy Webb
PRODUCTION COMPANY
RKO Radio Pictures
MAIN CAST Simone Simon,
Tom Conway, Kent Smith,
Jane Randolph, Jack Holt

In another famous scene, Irena follows Alice through a deserted Central Park at night, crosscutting between the legs of Alice and of the following Irena, both in their high heels punctuating the silence of the night, until we no longer hear or see Irena's; after a brief silence, there is the startling sound of what might be a hissing cat but then becomes recognisable as the airbrakes of a city bus that suddenly comes into frame and stops. Even the deadly attack by a presumably transformed Irena on Dr. Judd is treated circumspectly. Only at the end, when we see a dead panther on the ground near the zoo cages to where a mortally wounded Irena staggered just before, is Irena's supernatural curse presented as actual.

Further Reading

Gunning, Tom, "'Like unto a Leopard': Figurative Discourse in *Cat People* and Todorov's *The Fantastic*'. *Wide Angle* 10:3 (1988): 30–39

Newman, Kim. *Cat People*. London: British Film Institute, 1999.

Siegel, Joel. *Val Lewton: The Reality of Terror*. New York: Viking Press, 1973.

Telotte, J. P. *Dreams of Darkness: Fantasy and the Films of Val Lewton*. Urbana: University of Illinois Press, 1985.

Worland, Rick. *The Horror Film: An Introduction*. Malden, MA and Oxford: Blackwell, 2007.

Child's Play
1998 – 87 mins
Tom Holland

Devilish dolls have figured in numerous horror movies, whether as the projection of a psychologically disturbed ventriloquist ('The Ventriloquist's Dummy' in the portmanteau film *Dead of Night* [1945] is perhaps the most well-known example) or the embodiment of the supernatural (*Annabelle* [2014]). Often, the narratives play on the uncanny ambiguity of whether the doll is actually sentient or not, but *Child's Play* makes it clear from the start that Chucky is truly the embodiment of evil: in the very first scene a serial killer, Charles Lee Ray (Dourif), uses voodoo ('gris-gris') to transfer his soul into a large high-tech child's doll as he is dying from a policeman's bullet in the aisle of a toy store. Tom Holland, writer of the first *Psycho* sequel, *Psycho II* (1983), and of the cult horror movie *Fright Night* (1985), and director of two Stephen King adaptations – 'The Langoliers' (published in *Four Past Midnight*, 1990), a two-part television miniseries in 1995, and King's 1984 novel *Thinner* as a feature film the following year – walks that fine line in *Child's Play* between humour and horror. The six sequels that followed – *Child's Play 2* (1990), *Child's Play 3* (1991), *Bride of Chucky* (1998), *Seed of Chucky* (2004), *Curse of Chucky* (2004), and *Cult of Chucky* (2017) (there was also a remake in 2019, as well as comics and a video game) – moved the franchise more toward the comic, but Holland's foundational film balances its killings with comedy just as Chucky's face combines childish innocence and chilling evil.

As Chucky, Ray seeks vengeance on his enemies, including detective Mike Norris (Sarandon), who had fatally shot him in the toy store. Chucky wields his knife without compunction as he seeks revenge and then to transfer his soul into the boy Andy (Vincent), whose mother Catherine (Hicks) had bought the doll as a gift for her six-year-old son's birthday. As bodies begin to mount ('friends 'til the end', Chucky's pre-recorded greeting promises), the authorities at first think that Andy is acting out his youthful aggression, but we, like Andy, know better, and soon enough Chucky reveals himself.

Then Chucky seems unstoppable, his diminutive size making him more elusive as he darts in and out from under furniture and slashes at legs. Indeed, even when battered, burnt, and dismembered, Chucky somehow manages to escape, disappearing like the supposedly dead Michael Myers in *Halloween** (1978). In the climactic confrontation, Chucky is trapped in the fireplace and burned beyond recognition ('This is the end, friend', says Andy as he strikes the match), but charred Chucky keeps coming, like a tiny Terminator, even as his little body flies brutally and ludicrously backwards when shot.

Child's Play pays playful homage to several of its horror influences. The low-to-the-ground tracking shots might be from Chucky's point of view, recalling a similar use of the moving camera in *Halloween*, the prototypical slasher film that informs *Child's Play*. The death of Catherine's best friend Maggie (Manoff) echoes that of Damien's mother in *The Omen** (1973), just as the film's final freeze-frame shot of Andy glancing back at smoked Chucky before the door closes nods to the famous last shot of that film. The

DIRECTOR Tom Holland
PRODUCER David Kirschner
SCREENPLAY Don Mancini, John Lafia, Tom Holland
CINEMATOGRAPHY Bill Butler
EDITOR Edward Warschilka, Roy E. Peterson
MUSIC Joe Renzetti
PRODUCTION COMPANY United Artists
MAIN CAST Chris Sarandon, Brad Dourif, Catherine Hicks, Alex Vincent, Dinah Manoff, Neil Giantoli

fact that Chucky is a 'Good Guys' doll might seem to suggest the thin line between good and evil that characterises human nature (nicely embodied in the ambiguous face of Chucky), or a critique of capitalism, as in the progressive horror film. The Good Guys seems thoroughly corporatised, with its own television cartoon show and a wide line of accessories that includes Good Guys guns and a Good Guys tool chest, which provides Chucky with his first murder weapon, a miniature hammer.

Further Reading

Kane, Paul, and Marie O'Regan, eds. *Voices in the Dark: Interviews with Horror Writers, Directors, and Actors*. Jefferson, NC: McFarland, 2011.

Lennard, Dominic. *Bad Seeds and Holy Terrors: The Child Villains of Horror Film*. Albany: SUNY Press, 2014.

Paul, William. *Laughing Screaming: Modern Hollywood Horror and Comedy*. New York: Columbia University Press, 1994.

Colour out of Space
2019 – 111 mins
Richard Stanley

Perhaps the best adaptation of H. P. Lovecraft to date in its fidelity to the author's vision, *Colour out of Space*, based on Lovecraft's 1927 story, marks an impressive return to the fantastic for director Richard Stanley. After beginning his feature film career with *Hardware* (1990) and *Dust Devil* (1992) and then, after being fired from the third version of H. G. Wells's *The Island of Dr. Moreau* (finished by John Frankenheimer) shortly after shooting began, Stanley had concentrated on documentaries for several years before returning with this updating of Lovecraft that remains true to the author's sensibility from the opening shots of a fog-enshrouded forest accompanied by a voiceover quotation from the beginning of the story about the 'deep woods that no axe has ever cut'. The fifth adaptation of Lovecraft's story, Stanley's version succeeds best at visualising the author's abstract notion of alien lifeforms beyond human comprehension and his abiding sense of cosmic horror. (See also John Carpenter's *In the Mouth of Madness** [1994]).

Stanley overlays the story of the unspeakable horrors that befall a New England farm family, the Gardners, after a meteorite containing an alien life form lands in their front yard, with the themes of repression and tensions within the nuclear family that inform many of the great horror films (see, for example, *The Birds** [1963], *The Hills Have Eyes** [1977], and *The Shining** [1980]). The life form lives in the well water and, as in the Lovecraftian *Annihilation* (2018), infects all living organisms nearby – the surrounding plant life, the crops, the farm animals, and people. As the crops mutate and the animals grow weird (echoes of Carpenter's *The Thing* [1982] here, especially with the flock of alpaca eventually fusing into one mass), the film treads the *Dark Waters* (2019) of ecological horror.

But the lifeform also brings about psychological changes in the Gardners, especially Nathan, the father (Cage), that only release the repressed tensions already present in the family, former city dwellers who have escaped (retreated?) to the country. Nathan's failures and repressed anger, which have clearly affected his two teenage children, Lavinia (Arthur) and Benny (Meyer), gradually emerges as his mind slips away. Tommy Chong is amusingly cast as the pothead neighbour who really spaces out, but the alien's genetic jumble of Theresa (Richardson) and her youngest child, Jack (Hilliard), is certainly no laughing matter. As their constant moans reveal, this is a mother's smothering, protective impulses literally and horribly realised.

The film drops the definite article from Lovecraft's title, which is an improvement because, being beyond our comprehension, it is entirely possible that there are other colours out there in the vast reaches of the cosmos as well. Less effective are the alien entity point-of-view shots that recall those of *It Came from Outer Space* (1953) and the attempt to visualise what the Gardners see once they drink the infected water, the sense of cosmic beings beyond human understanding – 'some place where things ain't as they is here', as Lovecraft's farmer explains with his dying words in the story. Although the alien entity has been buried in the waters of the new dam at the end of the film, as in the story, the mutated praying mantis that still hovers about suggests

DIRECTOR Richard Stanley
PRODUCER Daniel Noah, Josh C. Waller, Elijah Wood, Lisa Whalen
SCREENPLAY Richard Stanley, Scarlett Amaris
CINEMATOGRAPHY Steve Annis
EDITOR Brett W. Bachman
MUSIC Colin Stetson
PRODUCTION COMPANY SprectreVision
MAIN CAST Nicolas Cage, Joely Richardson, Madeleine Arthur, Q'orianka Kilcher, Tommy Chong, Elliot Knight, Brendan Meyer, Julian Hilliard

that, like repression, it will eventually return with a monstrous future fate for the entire town of Arkham and beyond.

Further Reading:

Joshi, S. T., and David Schultz. *An H. P. Lovecraft Encyclopedia*. Westport, CT: Greenwood Press, 2001.

Migliore, Andrew, and John Strysik. *Lurker in the Lobby: A Guide to the Cinema of H. P. Lovecraft*. San Francisco: Night Shade Books, 2006.

Mitchell, Charles. *The Complete H. P. Lovecraft Filmography*. Westport, CT: Greenwood Press, 2001.

Oakes, David A. *Science and Destabilization in the Modern American Gothic: Lovecraft, Matheson, and King*. Westport, CT: Greenwood Press, 2000.

Smith, Don G. *H. P. Lovecraft in Popular Culture: The Works and Their Adaptations in Film, Television, Comics, Music and Games*. Jefferson, NC: McFarland, 2006.

Contagion
2011 – 106 mins
Steven Soderbergh

A gripping depiction of a pandemic caused by a new viral mutation that within months kills one-twelfth of the world's population, *Contagion* expresses expected anxieties in the age of such diseases as Legionnaire's Disease, Norwalk Virus, N1H1 (bird flu), swine flu, SARS, Ebola, West Nile Virus, AIDS, and, of course, Covid-19. Well researched and entirely plausible, *Contagion* downplays the more reassuring narratives of earlier films about deadly microbes such as *The Satan Bug* (1965) and *Outbreak* (1995) for a mosaic structure more suitable to a global threat that spreads rapidly. 'Nothing spreads like fear', the film's publicity warned, as it shows what might happen when a new contagious disease that begins with a cough and flu-like aches and advances within days to convulsions, coma, and death sweeps the world. Although director Steven Soderbergh had made no other horror movies previously (*Unsane* was released in 2018), the crime and corruption that informs American life as portrayed in many of his films works its way into *Contagion* as well.

DIRECTOR Steven Soderbergh
PRODUCER Michael Shamberg, Stacey Sher, Gregory Jacobs
SCREENPLAY Scott Z. Burns
CINEMATOGRAPHY Peter Andrews
EDITOR Stephen Mirrione
MUSIC Cliff Martinez
PRODUCTION COMPANY Participant Media, Imagenation Abu Dhabi, Double Feature Films
MAIN CAST Gwyneth Paltrow, Kate Winslet, Matt Damon, Jude Law, Laurence Fishburne, Marion Coutillard, Bryan Cranston, Jennifer Ehle, Sanaa Lathan

Soderbergh often employs avant-garde stylistic techniques, and *Contagion*'s style perfectly captures the inevitable and uncontainable community spread of the outbreak. The narrative is at times interrupted with montages in which the quick editing, accompanied by Cliff Martinez's insistently rhythmical electronic score, emphasises the interconnecting mobility of society today. People are seen touching shared public surfaces everywhere as they go about their daily business. The film begins immediately with one of these montages, initiated by a cough on the soundtrack but without dialogue for its duration. We see Beth Emhoff (Paltrow), who turns out to be Patient Zero, using touchscreens and exchanging documents at the restaurant and airport, and others unwittingly following and thereby spreading the virus to other cities internationally.

The fact that Beth contracts the new disease while cheating on her husband seems an unfortunate lapse into conventional morality. Otherwise, like the disaster films of the late 1970s, *Contagion* shows a calamitous event in which some characters live and others die irrespective of their morality or the star status of the actors portraying them. The first person we see in the film is Gwyneth Paltrow, a likeable star, but she soon dies. The later close-up of her face followed by the sudden shock of seeing it being peeled back from her skull makes us realise after a moment that Beth is dead and that her cadaver is undergoing an autopsy. Like the brutal murder of Marion Crane in *Psycho** (1960), this scene violates viewers' tacit contract with the star system, amplifying the horror. As we come to understand the scale of the threat, we are hampered from identifying with many of the film's numerous stars, for any of them could fall victim to the virus and a horrible death – as, indeed, happens to Kate Winslet's Dr. Mears.

Contagion also emphasises how easily social order may crumble. Once the epidemic takes hold, an effective montage shows a variety of public and urban spaces now eerily empty of people and populated instead by posters for the missing and impromptu memorials for victims. In this sense the film also taps into widespread doubt about the effectiveness of governmental intervention in disaster scenarios, a doubt that has only grown with each passing year and new emergency. The film depicts conflicting and uncoordinated responses at the federal and state levels – a scenario subsequently played out early in the 2020 Covid-19 pandemic (when *Contagion* became one of the most popular films on Netflix). Its view of the inability of government to act decisively and quickly in times of crisis undoubtedly has resonated with audiences disaffected with gridlock in contemporary Washington.

Further Reading:

Baker, Aaron. 'Global Cinema and *Contagion*'. *Film Quarterly* 66, no. 3 (Spring 2013): 5–14.

Ostherr, Kirsten. *Cinematic Prophylaxis: Globalization and Contagion in the Discourse of World Health*. Durham and London: Duke University Press, 2005.

Schweitzer, Dahlia. *Going Viral: Zombies, Viruses, and the End of the World*. New Brunswick: Rutgers University Press, 2018.

Sutton, Victoria. *The Things that Keep Us Up at Night: Reel Bio-Horror*. Lubbock, TX: Vargas Publishing, 2014.

The Crazies
1973 – 103 mins
George A. Romero

Like George Romero's earlier *Night of the Living Dead** (1968), *The Crazies* confounds the easy distinction between 'us' and 'them' that characterises the classic studio era horror and science fiction film. Set in Evans City, Pennsylvania (an independent filmmaker, Romero shot his early horror films around his home base of Pittsburgh), the plot involves an accidentally released and highly infectious biochemical weapon that causes death or insanity and the deadly chaos that ensues as the military struggle to contain it. As with Romero's other early horror films *Night of the Living Dead* (1968), *Jack's Wife* (aka *Hungry Wives*, *Season of the Witch*, 1972), and *Martin** (1977), *The Crazies* systematically blurs all distinction between the normal and the 'crazies', consequently undermining the relative moral values conventionally assigned to each. In doing so, *The Crazies* offers a scathing critique of the American military and government during the Vietnam War era. (A 2010 remake, with Romero involved as one of the executive producers, relocates the action to rural Iowa, situating the murderous madness explicitly within the American heartland.)

The biochemical weapon 'Trixie' seeps into the town's water system after the plane transporting it crashed in the area days earlier. The military move in with eventual orders to shoot to kill as martial law is declared. Firefighter David (McMillan) and his pregnant girlfriend Judy (Carroll), a nurse, along with fellow firefighter and Vietnam veteran Clank (Jones), try to survive and make it out of the town. The effect of the virus is vividly shown in the shocking opening in which a man sets fire to his house with his children still in it after killing his wife and then, in a moment of clarity, is horrified to discover what he has done. The soldiers herd the townspeople into the local high school, which becomes a burgeoning bedlam of the infected as the town erupts into a site of deadly confrontations between the military, the mad, and uninfected civilians trying to resist the imposition of governmental will or defend themselves.

David had been a Green Beret in Vietnam, which provides a plausible backstory for his ability to survive, but more importantly, provides a context for the film's political critique. The military is shown to be inept, a victim of its own bureaucracy, its mission compromised from the start, with Major Ryder (Spillman) and Col. Peckem (Hollar) continuously barking orders and tossing their radio phones aside in frustration. As the military becomes violently oppressive, the local priest, who presumably is infected, protests the army's treatment of the townspeople by dousing himself with gasoline and setting himself on fire in a shot that inevitably recalls the shocking video of Buddhist monk Thích Quang Đuc's self-immolation on a Saigon street in 1963. The soldiers, dressed in their NBC suits and gas masks, seem threateningly anonymous as they round up confused and frightened families, even pillaging their belongings as they do so, and shooting those who resist. The scene is unavoidably reminiscent of the infamous My Lai massacre, in which a village of unarmed civilians were killed by a platoon of American soldiers in March 1968. The film even associates the soldiers with Nazis rounding up Jews in a shot showing a pile of watches and other belongings of victims being collected by

DIRECTOR George A. Romero
PRODUCER A. C. Croft
SCREENPLAY George A. Romero
CINEMATOGRAPHY S. William Hinzman
EDITOR George A. Romero
MUSIC Bruce Roberts
PRODUCTION COMPANY Pittsburgh Films
MAIN CAST Will McMillan, Lane Carroll, Harold Wayne Jones, Harry Spillman, Richard Liberty, Lloyd Hollar, Lynn Lowry, Richard France

soldiers. The military has little hesitation in preparing a backup plan in which the town would be nuked, as we see in stock footage of a scrambling B-52 (a plane employed for carpet bombing runs in Vietnam), undisturbed about potential collateral damage.

In *The Crazies*, then, the army is hardly the cavalry coming to the rescue, as it is in so many Cold War monster movies. Indeed, quite the opposite, as it manages to thwart any possibility of rescue when soldiers mistake Dr. Watts (France), who may have developed an antidote, for an infected local. Throughout, viewers are left to wonder whether specific individuals have succumbed or not as soldiers ask, 'How can you tell who's infected and who isn't?'

Further Reading

Gagne, Paul R. *The Zombies that Ate Pittsburgh: The Films of George A. Romero*. New York: Dodd, Mead, 1987.

Phillips, Kendall R. *Dark Directions: Romero, Craven, Carpenter, and the Modern Horror Film*. Carbondale: Southern Illinois University Press, 2012.

Towlson, John. *Subversive Horror Cinema: Countercultural Messages of Films from Frankenstein to the Present*. Jefferson, NC: McFarland, 2014.

Williams, Tony. *The Cinema of George A. Romero: Knight of the Living Dead,* 2nd edn. London: Wallflower, 2015.

Wood, Robin. *Robin Wood on the Horror Film: Collected Essays and Reviews*, ed. Barry Keith Grant. Detroit: Wayne State University Press, 2018.

Creature from the Black Lagoon
1954 – 79 mins
Jack Arnold

The last of the classic Universal monsters, the Gill Man appeared first in *Creature from the Black Lagoon* and then spawned two sequels – *Revenge of the Creature* (1955) and *The Creature Walks Among Us* (1956). The first two films were directed by Jack Arnold, Universal's director of choice for its monster movies during the period (*Tarantula* [1955], *The Incredible Shrinking Man* [1957]), the latter by veteran assistant director John Sherwood (*The Monolith Monsters* [1957]). All three films were produced by William Alland, producer of several science fiction films in the 1950s including *This Island Earth* (1955). (He also played Jerry Thompson, the reporter whose face is hidden in shadows in *Citizen Kane* [1941].) Originally filmed and released in 3D (as seen by the superfluous shots of Carlson and Denning swimming toward and firing their spearguns at the camera), *Creature* taps into worldwide folklore of sea-dwelling creatures to evoke a foreboding mood of repression and mystery.

DIRECTOR Jack Arnold
PRODUCER William Alland
SCREENPLAY Harry Essex, Arthur A. Ross
CINEMATOGRAPHY William E. Snyder
EDITOR Ted J. Kent
MUSIC Henry Mancini, Hans J. Salter, Herman Stein
PRODUCTION COMPANY Universal
MAIN CAST Richard Carlson, Julie Adams (as Julia Adams), Richard Denning, Antonio Moreno, Nestor Paiva, Whit Bissell

The Black Lagoon itself, located in 'the upper reaches of the Amazon' is, as we are told twice, cut off from civilization like 'another world'. (The film was actually shot in Wakulla Springs, south of Tallahassee in Florida, which also stood in for an African Jungle in two Johnny Weissmuller Tarzan movies and is now a state park.) The Universal studio logo, with its spinning globe showing the Western hemisphere, allows American viewers, notoriously ignorant of geography, to have a vague sense of where the Amazon might be. Dark and deep, entering it is like crossing a watery Borgo Pass. *Creature* was the first underwater 3D film, and so it includes several lengthy underwater scenes that were themselves a novelty at the time, but these scenes also 'immerse' us in this other world of the Gill Man. This is crucial to the film's thematic thrust for, as with all of Universal's classic monsters, a sense of sympathy for the Creature is evoked, an attitude that is increasingly emphasised in the trajectory of the trilogy until the extraordinarily poignant ending of the final film, *The Creature Walks Among Us*, in which the captured Gill Man, whose gills have been surgically removed, staggers to the sea to which he knows he can never return, but moves toward it anyway, out of frame, as the image fades.

The opening narration combines an acknowledgment of Creation as God's work (so as not to offend Evangelical audiences, one presumes) with the scientific principles of evolution as we are shown animal tracks coming out of the water onto land. The Creature's existence is first suspected because of the discovery of a fossilised claw, and his presence is initially shown metonymically by his webbed hand reaching out of the water. Later we see a close-up of the clutching hand of the Creature's first victim, killed in his tent, and then a claw is caught by the expedition's net, which extends the motif to underscore the evolutionary connection between the Gill Man and modern human man.

This connection is explored in the tension between the two male protagonists, David Reed (Carlson) and Mark Williams (Denning), and their relationship to Kay Lawrence (Adams). The two actors represent heroic masculinity in the horror and science fiction genres – Carlson starred in *The Magnetic Monster* (1953) and *It Came from Outer Space*, Denning in *Target Earth* (1954), *Creature with the Atom Brain*, and *Day the World Ended* (both 1955) – and both men appear here running around bare-chested in bathing suits, holding their diaphragms in and thrusting their chests out, knives at the waist, looking very macho. The scene in which Kay swims (in her specially designed bathing suit), unaware that the Creature is swimming along with her below the surface, is a lyrical *pas de deux* that parallels the men's courting dance around her, David chivalrous and Mark aggressive. For Mark, too, the Creature is merely an asset, like the amphibian man for the government in Guillermo del Toro's *The Shape of Water* (2017), and the film jettisons him as it does the Creature in favour of David.

Further Reading

Baxter, John. *Science Fiction in the Cinema*. New York: Paperback Library, 1970.

Jancovich, Mark. *Rational Fears: American Horror in the 1950s*. Manchester, UK and New York: Manchester University Press, 1996.

McConnell, Frank. *The Spoken Seen: Film & the Romantic Imagination*. Baltimore and London: Johns Hopkins University Press, 1975.

Reemes, Dana M. *Directed by Jack Arnold*. Jefferson, NC and London: McFarland, 1988.

Weaver, Tom. *The Creature Chronicles: Exploring the Black Lagoon Trilogy*. Jefferson, NC and London: McFarland, 2018.

The Dead Zone
1983 – 103 mins
David Cronenberg

After a string of distinctive and personal made-in-Canada horror films beginning with *Rabid* (1977) and culminating with the brilliantly audacious *Videodrome* (1983), Canadian director David Cronenberg teamed with Stephen King and producer Debra Hill (*Halloween** [1978] and other John Carpenter films) in what seemed to be a decided move into more mainstream filmmaking with *The Dead* Zone. Yet, even while the film is faithful in spirit to King's novel, *The Dead Zone* is also consistent with Cronenberg's concern with desire, repression, and trauma. (Cronenberg's next film, his 1986 remake of *The Fly** [1958], showed his continued ability to balance auteurist impulses with genre constraints.) In his earlier films (*Rabid*, *The Brood* [1979], *Scanners* [1981], but also *The Fly*), conflict is played out on the characters' bodies; while in later films such as *Naked Lunch* (1991), *M Butterfly* (1993), and *Spider* (2002) the horror is psychological and explored as such by Cronenberg's subjective camerawork, which conflates fantasy and reality. In this sense, *The Dead Zone*, like *Videodrome*, is a transitional film, albeit more accessible on a narrative level.

Johnny Smith (Walken), a teacher, suffers a terrible automobile accident when his little Volkswagen beetle smashes into an overturned 18-wheeler – another of King's monster trucks (see also *Pet Sematary* [1983] and *Maximum Overdrive* [1986, King's only directorial effort to date]) – putting him into a coma for five years. When he finally awakens, he discovers that he has lost his job, his girlfriend Sarah (Adams), and his physical health, but he has gained the power of second sight, able to glimpse a traumatic event in a person's past, present, or future when he touches them. The ability weighs heavily on Johnny, and he begins to withdraw from human contact, identifying with fellow schoolteacher Ichabod Crane in 'The Legend of Sleepy Hollow' (1820), about whom Washington Irving writes: 'As he was a bachelor, and in nobody's debt, nobody troubled his head any more about him.' Metaphorically and literally, Johnny's visions are sapping him of his vitality, pushing him toward death. Floundering in self-pitying loneliness, he rails against God for his fate, his despair expressed in the film's washed out, wintry landscape and pale visual palette.

However, gradually Johnny comes to regard his curse as a gift, as it allows him to save lives and to capture a local serial killer. He finds a purpose when he attends a political rally and shakes the hand of Greg Stillson (Sheen), a right-wing populist demagogue running for office (his story is more detailed in the novel), and has a vision of him in the future as a crazed president launching a first-strike nuclear attack that starts World War III. Johnny's determination to take action to prevent the tragedy from happening crystallises like the billboard with the giant image of Stillson's face that comes together as workmen erect it outside his window before the rally.

In the novel Johnny also has a brain tumor, so one might question whether his visions are truly prophetic or a symptom of madness; but it is never mentioned in the film, although he likewise suffers from headaches, and because Johnny's visions have all been true there is no reason to question their veraci-

DIRECTOR David Cronenberg
PRODUCER Debra Hill
SCREENPLAY Jeffrey Boam
CINEMATOGRAPHY Mark Irwin
EDITOR Ronald Sanders
MUSIC Michael Kamen
PRODUCTION COMPANY Dino De Laurentiis Company
MAIN CAST Christopher Walken, Brooke Adams, Tom Skerritt, Herbert Lom, Anthony Zerbe, Colleen Dewhurst, Martin Sheen

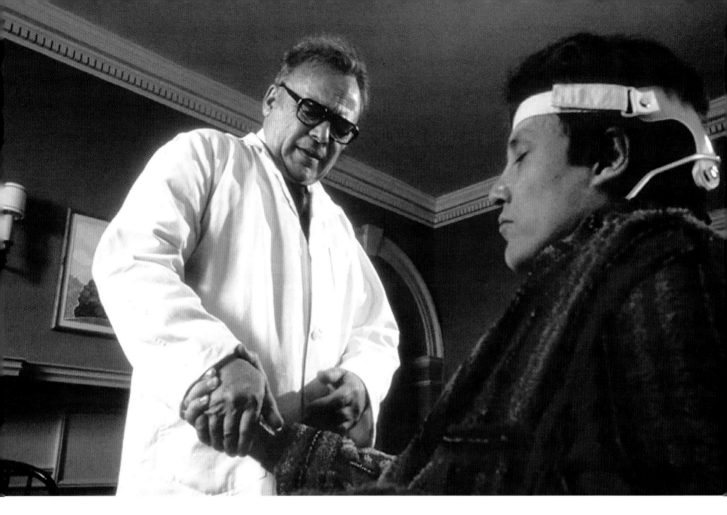

ty (unlike in *Videodrome*, where the viewer, like protagonist Max Renn, is unsure at times whether he is hallucinating). Thus, we must take seriously the question that Johnny's doctor (Lom) does not, and some variation of which we all have considered at some point: if you were able to go back in time knowing what you know now, would you kill Adolph Hitler? True horror, the film suggests, is not the existence of paranormal foresight, but finding the courage to act on what it might reveal.

Further Reading:

Beard, William. *The Artist as Monster: The Cinema of David Cronenberg*. Toronto: University of Toronto Press, 2006.

Handling, Piers, ed. *The Shape of Rage: The Films of David Cronenberg*. Toronto: General Publishing/ New York: Zoetrope, 1983.

Rodley, Chris, ed. *Cronenberg on Cronenberg*, revised ed. London: Faber and Faber, 1997.

Magistrale, Tony. *Hollywood's Stephen King*. New York: Palgrave Macmillan, 2003.

The Devil's Rejects
2005 – 109 mins
Rob Zombie

The middle installment in Rob Zombie's Firelfy trilogy, between *House of 1000 Corpses* (2003) and *3 from Hell* (2019), *The Devil's Rejects* is a postmodern pastiche of American hillbilly horror that offers its indebtedness to the genre's history even as it demonstrates audacious ambition on the part of its maker. Writer-director Zombie (he directed the remake of *Halloween** [1978] in 2007), also a musician whose music is saturated with horror themes, here dives deeper into the crazed clan he created for the earlier film. *The Devil's Rejects* focuses on three members of the psychotic Firefly clan, Otis (Moseley), Baby (Moon Zombie, the filmmaker's wife), and its patriarchal head, Captain Spaulding (Haig), all three reprising their roles from *House of 1000 Corpses* (2003).

The film begins with a bang – or, more precisely, many bangs. Several months after the events of *House of 1000 Corpses*, Sheriff John Quincey Wydell (Forsythe) and a detachment of Texas state troopers surround and engage in a bloody shootout with the Fireflies at their rundown farm, 'the most horrific crime scene

DIRECTOR Rob Zombie
PRODUCER Mike Elliott, Andy Gould, Marco Mehitz, Michel Ohoven, Rob Zombie
SCREENPLAY Rob Zombie
CINEMATOGRAPHY Phil Parmet
EDITOR Glenn W. Garland
MUSIC Tyler Bates
PRODUCTION COMPANY Cinelamda
MAIN CAST Sid Haig, Bill Moseley, Sheri Moon Zombie, Ken Foree, Matthew McGrory, Lew Temple, William Forsythe, Leslie Easterbrook, David Sheridan

since Jack the Ripper stalked the streets of London' according to the news reporter. Cinematographer Phil Parmet, who also shot *The Burrowers** (2008), provides the film with a harsh, saturated look that recalls *The Texas Chainsaw Massacre** (1974), while the hand-held shots add a sense of documentary immediacy (Parmet had been one of the cameramen for Barbara Kopple's influential 1976 documentary *Harlan County, USA*).

As the story unfolds, *The Devil's Rejects* (the term the terrible trio invoke to describe themselves) proudly invokes its numerous influences in the inserted film clips and from hillbilly horror movies such as *Two Thousand Maniacs!** (1964) to the classic Western, particularly toward the end in the scenes at Charlie's roadhouse. The Fireflys' torture, sexual humiliation, and murder of their victims recalls such earlier horror films as *The Last House on the Left** (1972), *Henry: Portrait of a Serial Killer** (1986), and, most obviously, *The Texas Chainsaw Massacre*, while the casting of Michael Berryman is a nod to *The Hills Have Eyes** (1977). The climactic shootout with police at the highway roadblock – beautifully choreographed to Lynyrd Skynyrd's 'Free Bird' – evokes simultaneously the famous endings of *Bonnie and Clyde* (1967), *The Wild Bunch* (1969), *Butch Cassidy and the Sundance Kid* (1969), and *Thelma & Louise* (1991).

The film's boldest allusion is its attempt to duplicate Hitchcock's startling strategy in *Psycho** (1960) of getting the audience to identify with the monstrous rather than with normality. The first half of *The Devil's Rejects* focuses on the torture and killing of five members of a traveling country band, Banjo and Sullivan, whom the Fireflys take hostage in a rundown motel room; the second half shows the mental collapse of Sheriff Wydell, who personally captures the three Fireflies and in turn tortures them before they escape once again, only to meet their end in the final showdown (although somehow they survive for *3 from Hell*). In the second half of the film the monsters come the victims, while the now insane Wydell becomes the monster, torturing the Fireflys as they had tortured others, a clear demonstration of Nietzsche's warning that he who fights monsters should be aware he doesn't become one in the process. Zombie's point is articulated by the crazed Wydell: 'I tried to walk the line, but I know now there is no line' – although, unlike in *Psycho*, Zombie fails to realign the viewer's perspective in a way that resonates as complexly as does Hitchcock.

We never discover why the Fireflys have names of Groucho's characters in the classic Marx Brothers' comedies. It may be merely a part of Zombie's patchwork pastiche, but when Wydell and his deputy realise the connection and summon local film critic Marty Walker ('a self-proclaimed Marx Brothers expert, if I say so myself'), it is surely the only scene in any horror film in which a film critic is asked to help crack a case (even if he is ridiculed by Wydell as a 'Hollywood-lovin' pussy').

Further Reading:

Blake, Linnie. '"I Am the Devil and I'm Here to Do the Devil's Work"': Rob Zombie, George W. Bush, and the Limits of American Freedom'. In *Horror after 9/11: World of Fear, Cinema of Terror*, ed. Aviva Briefel and Sam J. Miller, pp. 186–199. Austin: University of Texas Press, 2011.

McCollum Victoria. *Post 9-11 Heartland Horror: Rural Horror Films in an Era of Urban Terrorism*. Abingdon, Oxon and New York: Routledge, 2017.

Morris, Jeremy. 'The Justification of Torture-Horror: Retribution and Sadism in *Saw*, *Hostel*, and *The Devil's Rejects*'. In *The Philosophy of Horror*, ed. Thomas Richard Fahey, pp. 42–56. Lexington: University Press of Kentucky, 2010.

Taylor, Laura Wiebe. 'Popular Songs and Ordinary Violence: Exposing Basic Human Brutality in the Films of Rob Zombie'. In *Terror Tracks: Music, Sound and Horror Cinema*, ed. Philip Hayward, pp. 229–237. London: Equinox Publishing, 2009.

Dr. Jekyll and Mr. Hyde
1931 – 96 mins
Rouben Mamoulian

Along with Mary Shelley's *Frankenstein* (1918) and Bram Stoker's *Dracula* (1897), Robert Louis Stevenson's novella *The Strange Case of Dr. Jekyll and Mr. Hyde* (1886) is the most often filmed of horror tales. Among the several silent versions, the most well-known is the 1920 film with John Barrymore, while Rouben Mamoulian's 1931 version is perhaps the most celebrated of sound versions, earning Fredric March his first Academy Award for Best Actor in 1932 (shared with Wallace Beery for *The Champ*). The paradigmatic doppelganger story of the beast within, Stevenson's story has also inspired numerous variations such as *Dr. Jekyll and Sister Hyde* (1991), *Dr. Jekyll and Mrs. Hyde* (1995), *Mary Reilly* (1996), *The Nutty Professor* (1963), and, of course, *Abbott and Costello Meet Dr. Jekyll and Mr. Hyde* [1953]). Mamoulian's film, released before the implementation of the Production Code, emphasises the tale's erotic and libidinous aspects, particularly as it relates to sadism (unlike MGM's bowdlerised version a decade later with Spencer Tracy). 'I hurt you because I love you', Hyde tells Ivy (Hopkins), the object of his lust and cruelty. (For this reason, several minutes were cut for the film's re-release in 1936, but later restored.)

More so than in Stevenson's story, Mamoulian's version depicts Jekyll as the victim of Victorian repression – even to the point of the camera showing a pot boiling over, an image repeated in the film's final shot. Whenever Jekyll's desires are impeded, the explanation is merely that 'It isn't done'. His biggest frustration is that he wants to marry his fiancée Muriel Carew (Hobart) immediately, but her father, General Sir Danvers Carew (Hobbes), orders them to wait for the sake of propriety, proudly admitting that he had to wait years for his own marriage. 'Can a man dying of thirst forget water?' Jekyll asks his colleague Lanyon (Herbert). His sappy love scene early on with Muriel ('we shall live on love and moonlight') sounds like the trite romantic clichés that mask desire, as in *Murders in the Rue Morgue** (1932).

Beside himself with such desire, Jekyll is shown in the bravura shot from his perspective with which the film begins that anticipates such extended uses of the subjective camera as in the noirs *Lady in the Lake* (1946) and *Dark Passage* (1947), so that we do not see Jekyll (or Hyde) until he comes before a mirror – suggesting at once both the indeterminacy and the doubling of his personality. Society seems excessively oppressive, Jekyll a justified rebel against it. His darting movements express the energy unleashed through Hyde ('What I want, I get'), and rather than walk with a crooked or stooped mien like other Hydes, March straightens up as Hyde, emboldened by his denial of denial. From this perspective, Jekyll's exceptional commitment to his clinic for the poor is explicable as obsessive sublimation rather than simply noble good works, like the guilty payoff he gives to music hall singer Ivy on behalf of Jekyll.

But in the film desire seems inextricable from aggression and domination, and although his goal is a noble one, to free humanity of repression and remorse by living through it, in the end a dejected Jekyll, defeated by his own inner nature, reverts not just to Hyde but to conventional morality by insisting to Lanyon that

DIRECTOR Rouben Mamoulian
PRODUCER Rouben Mamoulian
SCREENPLAY Samuel Hoffenstein, Percy Heath
CINEMATOGRAPHY Karl Struss
EDITOR William Shea
MUSIC Johann Sebastian Bach, adapted by Herman Hand
PRODUCTION COMPANY Paramount
MAIN CAST Fredric March, Miriam Hopkins, Rose Hobart, Holmes Herbert, Halliwell Hobbes, Edgar Norton, Temp Pigott

he has explored an area of knowledge that was reserved as 'God's domain'. Wally Westmore's makeup emphasises the simian aspect of Hyde's character, associating him with primitive instincts ('some dim animal relation to the earth', is how Jekyll describes it in his university lecture), suggesting the baser nature of desire. March's makeup was applied in different colours, and photographing him with a series of colour filters revealed the different layers of makeup, enabling the actor's transition to Hyde to be shown in one continuous shot (a technical tour-de-force that underscores the continuity of desire and domination in the human psyche), although unfortunately his later transformations are presented with an uninspired series of lap-dissolves as in *The Wolf Man** (1941).

Further Reading

Luhr, William, and Peter Lehman. *Authorship and Narrative in the Cinema*. New York: Capricorn, 1977.

Prawer, S. S. *Caligari's Children: The Film as Tale of Terror*. New York: Da Capo, 1980.

Sevastakis, Michael. *Songs of Love and Death: The Classic American Horror Film of the 1930s*. Westport, CT: Greenwood, 1993.

Veeder, William, and Gordon Hirsch, eds. *Dr. Jekyll and Mr. Hyde: After One Hundred Years*. Chicago: University of Chicago Press, 1988.

Welsch, Janice R. 'The Horrific and the Tragic'. In *The English Novel and the Movies*, ed. Michael Klein and Gillian Parker, pp 165–179. New York: Frederick Ungar, 1981.

Dracula
1931 – 85 mins
Tod Browning

There have been many adaptations of Bram Stoker's 1897 source novel, including F. W. Murnau's *Nosferatu – Eine Symphonie Des Grauens* (1922), Terence Fisher's *Dracula* (1958), Werner Herzog's *Nosferatu – Phantom der Nacht* (1979), John Badham's *Dracula* (1979), and Francis Ford Coppola's *Bram Stoker's Dracula** (1992). But it was Bela Lugosi's incarnation of the undead Count, first on stage and then in the 1931 movie directed by Tod Browning (*The Unknown** [1927], *Freaks** [1932]), that engraved the physiognomy of Dracula forever in the collective imagination. The 1927 production of the play featured the then-unknown Hungarian actor as the eponymous vampire, and, with the death of the originally cast Lon Chaney, Lugosi recreated his stage role for the film. Billed as 'the strangest love story ever told', the film was released, with intended irony, on Valentine's Day.

DIRECTOR Tod Browning
PRODUCER Carl Laemmle Jr.
SCREENPLAY Garrett Fort, Dudley Murphy
CINEMATOGRAPHY Karl Freund
EDITOR Milton Carruth, Maurice Pivar
PRODUCTION COMPANY Universal Pictures
MAIN CAST Bela Lugosi, Edward Van Sloan, Dwight Frye, Helen Chandler, David Manners, Herbert Bunston

The film was adapted from the 1924 play based on Stoker's novel by Irish actor Hamilton Deane and American writer John L. Balderston (he also worked on the scripts of *The Bride of Frankenstein** [1935] and *Mad Love** [1935]), which explains its rather stage-bound quality. Much of the action, including the anti-climactic death of the vampire, takes place offscreen, and Dracula in his bat form never seems more than a rubber toy dangling on a wire. Nevertheless, it is one of those perfect instances of casting, with Lugosi's vampire becoming a central icon of western culture, so familiar that children can learn math from a juvenilised version of him on public television's *Sesame Street* while eating Count Chocula breakfast cereal. The atmospheric cinematography, featuring the pin spots on Lugosi's face, was provided by Karl Freund (responsible for the camerawork for several of the most important German expressionist films, including *Metropolis* [1926], and in Hollywood a cinematographer (*Murders in the Rue Morgue** [1932]) and director (*The Mummy** [1932], *Mad Love** [1935]) of some important horror movies of the 1930s.

While Freund's work was crucial to the look of Dracula, one doesn't need Freud to understand the vampire's obviously sexual connotation. In the film, as in Stoker's novel, the vampiric Count clearly represents an unleashed and frightening sexual energy that was strongly repressed during the Victorian era, when the novel was published. (See also *Bram Stoker's Dracula*.) There is little in Dracula of the existential angst that haunts more contemporary vampires such as those of *The Addiction** (1995) or *Interview with the Vampire** (1994), although Lugosi's cold-blooded vampire does muse wistfully to Mina at one point that: 'To die, to be really dead, that must be glorious… There are far worse things awaiting man than death.'

Dwight Frye is unforgettable as Renfield, especially in the moment when the camera looks down the hold of the abandoned ship, the light penetrating just enough to see his crazed face while he laughs maniacally, all rationality gone. Van Helsing (Van Sloan), far from the action-hero makeover he received for the 2004 film *Van Helsing*, is, as in the novel, an avuncular figure of benevolent patriarchy. When he and the young hero, Jonathan Harker (Manners), destroy the vampire by tracking him to his lair and impaling him while he sleeps, it is more than an individual heroic act and nothing less than staking the claim of monogamous heterosexuality. In the film's final shot, with Dracula now 'really dead', the young couple, Jonathan and Mina (Chandler), the latter thankfully freed from Dracula's spell, ascend a long staircase to the heavenly light of day, accompanied by the promise of wedding bells on the soundtrack as the final fadeout suggests they will live happily ever after.

Further Reading:

McNally, Raymond T., and Radu Florescu. *In Search of Dracula: A True History of Dracula and the Vampire Legends*. New York: Warner Paperback Library, 1973.

Rhodes, Gary D. *Tod Browning's Dracula*. Sheffield: Tomahawk Press, 2015.

Skal, David J. *Hollywood Gothic: The Tangled Web of Dracula from Novel to Stage to Screen*. New York: Faber and Faber, 2004.

Waller, Gregory A. *The Living and the Undead: From Stoker's Dracula to Romero's Dawn of the Dead*. Urbana: University of Chicago Press, 1986.

Wolf, Leonard. *A Dream of Dracula: In Search of the Living Dead*. New York: Popular Library, 1972.

Eraserhead
1977 – 89 mins
David Lynch

The opening shot of David Lynch's remarkable first feature film, of the hapless Henry Spencer (Nance) seeming to float headless in space, not only anticipates the ending, but also encapsulates the experience of the entire film: a surreal, unanchored vision of contemporary alienation and anomie to rival that of Kafka and filled with a sense of physical anxiety, revulsion, and horror of the body to match David Cronenberg. Five years in the making while Lynch (*Blue Velvet* [1986]) was studying filmmaking at the American Film Institute, *Eraserhead* was first exhibited as a midnight movie, quickly attaining cult status and playing in some theatres for years.

On one level, *Eraserhead* is about environmental devastation. Its brutal, blighted landscapes make the industrial wastelands of such other horror movies as *The Texas Chainsaw Massacre** (1974) seem almost bucolic

DIRECTOR David Lynch
PRODUCER David Lynch
SCREENPLAY David Lynch
CINEMATOGRAPHY
Frederick Elmes,
Herbert Cardwell
EDITOR David Lynch
MUSIC David Lynch,
Fats Waller, Peter Ivers
PRODUCTION COMPANY
American Film Institute
MAIN CAST Jack Nance,
Charlotte Stewart, Allen Joseph,
Jeanne Bates, Laurel Near,
Judith Roberts

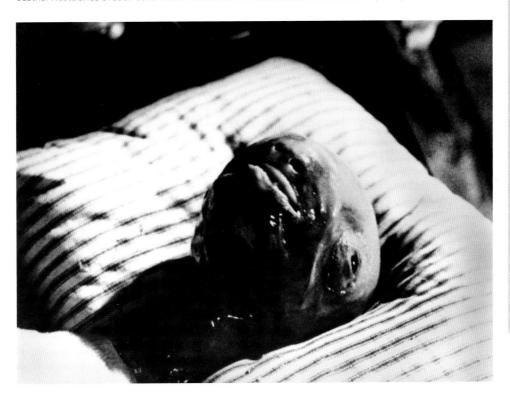

by comparison. Mr X (Joseph) tells Henry that the place has gone from pastures to hell hole in thirty years. Shot entirely at night, every scene is dark and gloomy, although beautifully lit. Industrial piping extrudes into living spaces, as does the incessant industrial noise. Lynch created the carefully constructed soundtrack, which features electronic tones; mechanical hisses, cranking and stamping; rain; fog horns; a howling, hollow, Fellini-esque wind; and, of course, the awful and incessant cries of the baby creature. Henry and Mary's baby might be deformed because of industrial pollution: like the monstrous baby in Larry Cohen's *It's Alive** (1974), it is indeed alive – but what, exactly, is it? The creature lacks limbs, is skinless, resembling nothing so much as a newborn bird fallen from its nest. Swathed in dirty bandages, the baby's persistent wails sound like the bleating of a mutant sheep, a nightmarish version of a baby suffering from colic.

From a psychoanalytic perspective, the film envisions an overwhelming sense of male horror at the prospect of marriage, sex, and the responsibilities of parenting. Desire and guilt, dread and fear haunt Henry, perhaps as a result of a previous sexual encounter with Mary X (Stewart). Now he is pressured into marrying her because she is pregnant, and so the torturous dinner with Mary's parents, who are as bizarre as the monstrous family in *Texas Chainsaw Massacre*. At the same time Henry feels guilty regarding Mary, he desires the Beautiful Girl across the Hall (Roberts), his conflicted imagination conjuring a succession of scenarios involving bodily revulsion, particularly of the female body. There are numerous shots in which the camera seems to penetrate unidentified orifices, threatening engulfment and erasure, and of slimy viscera, frequently associated with women. The tiny chicken-like creatures ('They're new!') served at the X family's dinner, the legs of which begin twitching and oozing liquid onto the plate as Henry is about to carve, sum up these fears. Eventually Henry cuts away the baby's swathing to reveal that it has no body at all, just pulsating innards which exude a nightmarish volume of blood, pus, and other abject fluids when Henry stabs it.

Eraserhead follows dream logic rather than conventional dramaturgy: when the Beautiful Girl asks Henry where his wife is, he replies that 'She must have gone back to her parents again. I'm not sure' – and she simply, inexplicably, drops out of the narrative. Henry ultimately imagines his identity taken over by the wailing baby, his head literally popping off and the baby creature replacing him in his clothes. His brain matter is fed into some steampunk machine (compare the visual design of Lynch's *Dune* [1984]) that produces pencils with erasers – a fitting end for this most self-effacing of antiheroes. The film offers no sense of normality from which its monstrousness deviates. Its main character undergoes no psychological deterioration with mad visions clearly marked. Wherever we are – whether in a surreal alternate universe, Henry's mind, or Lynch's, we are in this dream within a dream from the outset, with no exterior perspective – like the view of a brick wall offered by Henry's window.

Further Reading:

Hoberman, Jim, and Jonathan Rosenbaum. *Midnight Movies*. New York: Da Capo, 1986.

McGowan, Todd. *The Impossible David Lynch*. New York: Columbia University Press, 2007.

Sheen, Erica, and Annette Davidson, eds. *The Cinema of David Lynch: American Dreams and Nightmare Visions*. London and New York: Wallflower Press, 2004.

Wilson, Eric G. *The Strange World of David Lynch: Transcendental Irony from Eraserhead to Mulholland Drive*. New York and London: Continuum, 2007.

Wood, Paul A. *Weirdsville USA: The Obsessive Universe of David Lynch*. London: Plexus, 1997.

The Evil Dead
1981 – 85 mins
Sam Raimi

The second film by Sam Raimi (*Darkman* [1990], *Spider-Man* [2002] and its two sequels [2004, 2007], *Drag Me to Hell* [2009]), *The Evil Dead*, about five college students vacationing in an isolated cabin in a remote wooded area who accidentally release a group of slumbering demons, provided the template for *The Cabin in the Woods* [2012], among others, and launched a media franchise consisting of two sequels written and directed by Raimi, *Evil Dead II* (1987) and *Army of Darkness* (1992); a 2013 reboot, *Evil Dead*; as well as comic books, several survival horror video games, a stage musical, *Evil Dead: The Musical*, and a television series, *Ash vs Evil Dead* (2015–18). *The Evil Dead* screened out of competition at the 1992 Cannes Film Festival and, championed by Stephen King, quickly built a cult reputation. Ash Williams, the film's protagonist (Campbell,

DIRECTOR Sam Raimi
PRODUCER Bruce Campbell, Sam Raimi, Rob Tapert
SCREENPLAY Sam Raimi
CINEMATOGRAPHY Tim Philo
EDITOR Edna Ruth Paul
MUSIC Joseph LoDuca
PRODUCTION COMPANY Renaissance Pictures
MAIN CAST Bruce Campbell, Ellen Sandweiss, Hal Delrich, Betsy Baker, Theresa Tilly

who also plays Elvis in *Bubba Ho-Tep** [2002], has himself become a cult icon), is the lone survivor of a long horrific night. Inspired by *Night of the Living Dead** (1968), *The Texas Chainsaw Massacre** (1974), and *The Hills Have Eyes** (1977) – a poster for the latter is visible among the bric-a-brac in the cabin – *The Evil Dead* offers a non-stop gore-fest laced with humour that rivals that of Peter Jackson (*The Frighteners** [1996]), the other master of splatstick).

The five students – Ash Williams, his girlfriend Linda (Baker); Ash's sister, Cheryl (Sandweiss); their friend Scott (Delrich); and his girlfriend Shelly (Tilly) – arrive at a remote 'cabin in the woods' in rural Tennessee. There they find in the basement some artifacts and a tape recorder left by an archaeologist, who explains on the tape that he had been researching the 'Naturan Demanto' (in the sequels, the 'Necronomicon'), a 'Sumerian Book of the Dead', and includes some incantations which release several demons that proceed to possess the woods and, in turn, all of the characters with the exception of Ash. Things go from bad to worse as the night unfolds, the demons turning increasingly viscous as the possessed bodies of Ash's friends are burned, pummelled, stabbed, dismembered, and disintegrated with the help of Claymation and other special effects.

When Scott asks Cheryl what had attacked her in the woods (her prolonged screaming surely an homage to Sally's in *Texas Chainsaw Massacre*), she replies that it was the 'woods themselves', but the real aggressor is Raimi's bold, energetic camerawork – literally in the final shot – but throughout, right from the opening scene that crosscuts between the group's car driving to the cabin and the camera gliding ominously along stream and through woods, as if it were a demonic entity, one of those 'forces that roam the forest and dark bowers of man's domain', as the archaeologist describes them on his tape recording. Raimi's penchant for such peripatetic photography, perhaps fully realised in the gunfights in his Western *The Quick and the Dead* (1995), here includes sweeping tracking shots, one of them crashing through a cabin window, and point-of-view shots from the demons' perspective and from inside a grave, as well as odd or unmotivated camera placement, with upside-down shots, canted angles, and shots from floor level.

Although the possessed Cheryl is chained in the cellar, the film is hardly interested in the themes of repression or oppression, or even in the implications of Ash's decapitation of his girlfriend. Indeed, the characters are barely fleshed out before their flesh begins to rot off. Toward the end of the film the archaeologist's projector throws a blood-soaked image on the cabin wall as blood drips down the lens – an image that perfectly summarises *The Evil Dead* itself.

Further Reading:

Egan, Kate. *The Evil Dead*. London and New York: Wallflower Press, 2011.

Muir, John Kenneth. *The Unseen Force: The Films of Sam Raimi*. New York: Applause Theatre and Cinema Books, 2004.

Riekke, Ron, and Jeffrey A. Sartain, eds. *The Many Lives of the Evil Dead*: *Essays on the Cult Film Franchise*. Jefferson, NC and London: McFarland, 2019.

Warren, Bill. *The Evil Dead Companion*. New York: St. Martin's Griffin, 2000.

Wiater, Stanley. *Dark Visions: Conversations with the Masters of the Horror Film*. New York: Avon, 1992.

The Exorcist
1973 – 122 mins
William Friedkin

In the early 1970s, with the unpopular war in Vietnam at its height, generating massive and sometimes violent protests across the country, and the Watergate scandal growing (President Richard Nixon resigned before he could be impeached in 1974), civil and political institutional order seemed to many to be crumbling, leading to a cycle of disaster movies and horror films, both attesting to national trauma. *The Exorcist*, based on the bestselling 1971 novel by William Peter Blatty and adapted and produced by him, was pivotal in this regard. A massive hit at the box office and one of MGM's most successful films ever, audiences lined up the see it, with some viewers, according to press reports, having extreme physical reactions ranging from fainting and vomiting to heart attacks. It conjured two sequels, *Exorcist II: The Heretic* (1977) and *The Exorcist III* (1990), the latter written and directed by Blatty; two prequels, *Exorcist: The Beginning* (2004, directed by Paul Schrader), and *Dominion* (2005); and a television series (2016–18). In 2000 a director's-cut version was released, restoring several minutes of material deleted for the original release, including an alternate take of Regan's spider walk down the townhouse stairway with her mouth dripping blood.

A suddenly unruly adolescent girl, Regan MacNeil (Blair), is possessed by a demon (identified in *Exorcist II* as Pazuzu), causing her to commit taboo acts such as stealing, urinating in public, and, perhaps most shocking of all, abusing herself with a crucifix as her body grows putrescent. To many conservative parents at the time, their rebellious and blasphemous children seemed beyond their understanding, as if they were possessed. Regan lives with her actress mother Chris (Burstyn) in Georgetown, an upscale neighbourhood of Washington, DC, the center of national political power, and Chris has just completed working on a movie about political activism that seems to be empty of any real politics (she describes it as a 'Walt Disney version of the Ho Chi Minh story') when Regan's problematic behaviour begins. The horror of an innocent child uttering vile blasphemies and profanities ('Your mother sucks cocks in Hell') informs other horror movies like *The Prodigy* (2019), but *The Exorcist*'s Regan set the bar for such devilish delinquents.

When the demon asks Father Karras (Miller) to loosen the straps that bind Regan to her bed, the priest responds by saying that if it is indeed the devil, he could make them disappear himself. The demon counters that that would be 'much too vulgar a display of power' – yet this is what the film itself does and what it is most remembered for. Director Friedkin (*The French Connection* [1971]) pushed his two female stars physically to create some of the film's effects, while such memorable moments as Regan's projectile regurgitation of green bile and her rotating head have become iconic moments often referred to and parodied in popular culture.

Max Von Sydow brings an existential gravitas to his role as the presiding priest of the exorcism, Father Merrin, because of his roles in several of Ingmar Bergman's films such as the spiritually questing Knight in

DIRECTOR William Friedkin
PRODUCER William Peter Blatty
SCREENPLAY
William Peter Blatty
CINEMATOGRAPHY
Owen Roizman, Billy Williams
EDITOR Bud Smith,
Evan A. Lottman, Norman Gay
MUSIC Jack Nitzsche
PRODUCTION COMPANY
Hoya Productions
MAIN CAST Ellen Burstyn, Max Von Sydow, Lee J. Cobb, Jack MacGowran, Jason Miller, Kitty Winn, Linda Blair

The Seventh Seal (1957). But *The Exorcist* also invites a reading involving repression and the family. Regan's changing behaviour is initially viewed as repressed anger regarding her absent father, from whom Chris is separated and who we never see although his presence is weighty, nonetheless. After the first visit from Lt. Kinderman (Cobb), Chris puts the safety lock on her front door, although of course the danger comes from within rather than out there. By film's end, with the exorcism successful, the unruly daughter is returned to her mother and God the Father is acknowledged, the threat of counter-cultural protest stifled.

Further Reading

Blatty, William Peter. *William Peter Blatty on The Exorcist from Novel to Film*. New York: Bantam, 1974.

Britton, Andrew. 'The Exorcist'. In *Britton on Film: The Complete Film Criticism of Andrew Britton*, ed. Barry Keith Grant, pp. 232–236. Detroit: Wayne State University Press, 2009.

Creed, Barbara. *The Monstrous-Feminine: Film, Feminism, Psychoanalysis*. London and New York: Routledge, 1993.

Kermode, Mark. *The Exorcist*, 2nd edn. London: British Film Institute, 1998.

Travers, Peter, and Stephanie Reiff. *The Story behind The Exorcist*. New York: New American Library, 1974.

The Fall of the House of Usher
1928 – 13 mins
James Sibley Watson and Melville Webber

There have been several adaptations of Poe's 1939 short story 'The Fall of the House of Usher', a gothic tale of disease, madness, paranoia, and perhaps incest, including, coincidentally, another one made in France by Jean Epstein (*La Chute de la maison Usher*) the same year as Watson and Webber's more deliriously experimental short film. (Also in 1928, another experimental filmmaker, Charles Klein, adapted another of Poe's stories, 'The Tell-Tale Heart'.) Watson had previously served as an editor of the important literary magazine *The Dial*, championing the works of modernists such as the poets William Carlos Williams and Marianne Moore, so he was quite familiar with contemporary movements in art, including, as is clear in *The Fall of the*

DIRECTOR James Sibley Watson and Melville Webber
CINEMATOGRAPHY James Sibley Watson and Melville Webber
EDITOR James Sibley Watson and Melville Webber
MUSIC Alec Wilder
PRODUCTION COMPANY Film Guild
MAIN CAST Herbert Stern, Hildegarde Watson, Melville Webber

House of Usher, German expressionist cinema. Together, Watson and Webber, working in Rochester, New York, made one of the first truly avant-garde American experimental films with their 'film version', as the credits put it, of Poe's story. (Later, they would make one of the first American experimental sound films, *Lot in Sodom* [1933], emphasising the sexual element in the story of the sinful cities of Sodom and Gomorrah from the Book of Genesis.) Unlike most Poe adaptations, Watson and Webber's film is less concerned with plot than with mood, seeking to create through the plastic means of the cinematic medium the 'insufferable gloom' of the eponymous House.

Poe's story is told by an unidentified narrator who had been a friend of Roderick Usher in the past and who comes to visit his old friend at Usher's urgent behest. Upon his arrival at the Usher mansion, the narrator is shocked by his old friend's sickly and agitated condition. Trying to cheer his friend, the narrator learns of a family curse, and after Usher's twin sister Madeline dies, he helps Usher temporarily entomb her in a vault below the house. Days later, Usher confesses that they buried her prematurely, after which she appears in the doorway, frightening Usher to death. The narrator escapes just as the House itself cracks open, implodes, and sinks into the fetid tarn. The film begins with an image of the text of Poe's story but shown as a kaleidoscopic jumble, as if to say that something is awry in Usher house, and that the film is going to be more faithful to the spirit of the story than to its letter.

In the story Poe refers to the black tarn and the occasional preternatural light around the Usher mansion, and Watson and Webber make excellent use of black-and-white contrasts and shadows to create a sense of menacing darkness. In one shot of Madeline Usher walking up a staircase, she casts a giant shadow on the wall reminiscent of the famous similar shot in *Nosferatu* (1922). Impressively, they also use white to expressive effect. For example, Madeline Usher's surprise appearance in the doorway after being prematurely entombed is visualised as a pair of feet climbing two superimposed flights of white stairs, the whiteness underscoring her soulless state. Poe connects the metaphorical associations of the house with its disturbed master, and so the film's distorted sets and props, the stylised facial makeup, and the canted angles that tilt during the shot, all suggest Usher's madness in the manner of *The Cabinet of Dr. Caligari* (1920). The filmmakers employ a wide range of optical effects to visualise the story's sense of the unwholesome relationship between the Usher siblings and the mental and moral decay that envelops the family home like the 'pestilent and mystic vapour' that hangs over the place, including superimpositions, reverse motion, prism lenses, and even a bold, jagged wipe down the middle of the screen intended to signify the crack in the house's masonry the narrator discerns at the beginning of the story and which rips the house asunder at its inevitable end.

Further Reading

Huckvale, David. *Poe Evermore: The Legacy in Film, Music, and Television*. Jefferson, NC: McFarland, 2014.

Jones, David Annwn. *Re-envisaging the First Age of Cinematic Horror, 1896–1934*. Cardiff: University of Wales Press, 2018.

Smith, Don G. *The Poe Cinema: A Critical Filmography of Theatrical Releases Based on the Works of Edgar Allan Poe*. Jefferson, NC: McFarland, 2003.

Perry, Dennis R., and Carl H. Sederholm. *Poe, 'The House of Usher', and the American Gothic*. New York: Palgrave Macmillan, 2009.

Woodson, Thomas, ed. *Twentieth Century Interpretations of The Fall of the House of Usher: A Collection of Critical Essays*. Englewood Cliffs, NJ: Prentice-Hall, 1969.

Fallen
1998 – 124 mins
Gregory Hoblit

Directed by Gregory Hoblit, who has worked primarily on television as a producer and director of cop shows (*Hill Street Blues*, *NYPD Blue*, *L.A. Law*), *Fallen* is a fascinating hybrid of film noir procedural and supernatural horror film. What seems at first a relatively routine investigation into copycat murders after the execution of a serial killer (Koteas) brought to justice by Philadelphia police detective John Hobbes (Washington) turns into an apocalyptic revelation regarding one of the fallen Host. Aided by the performances of John Goodman and pre-*Sopranos* James Gandolfini as Hobbes's fellow officers and Donald Sutherland as his superior, the film's narrative is especially noteworthy as a rare instance of misdirection in which we discover at the end that it is not the narrator who is unreliable, but the viewer, adding to the climactic frisson.

The film begins with Hobbes stumbling through the woods as Denzel Washington in voiceover declares, 'I want to tell you about the time I almost died'. Everything that follows until the end is a flashback from the narrator's perspective, beginning with the execution of the serial killer Edgar Reese, who before dying taunts the assembled witnesses, especially his captor Hobbes, whom he mocks by singing the Rolling Stones' 'Time Is on My Side'. When several murders in the manner of Reese follow, and after Hobbes witnesses a string of people taunting him with the same song, he meets Gretta Milano (Davidtz), an angelologist from whom he learns the truth: the fallen angel Azazel, a vindictive, now disembodied demon that enjoys meting out death for its own sake and with the ultimate goal of toppling civilization ('Babylon'), had possessed Reese and can possess any human host, moving from one to another by the slightest touch, and is now mocking Hobbes.

Azazel causes a number of deaths, including Hobbes' brother, the circumstances making it seem as if Hobbes is responsible and forcing him to flee the city to a remote cabin in the woods. There he prepares for the final confrontation with Azazel, bringing us back to where the film began and to the climax and narrative twist. The revelation forces viewers to reconsider everything that has come before in the film, analogous to the way that Hobbes has to radically change his previously uncomplicated worldview once he learns about the existence of the fallen angel. Analogously, the film at first seems like a detective noir, but as the mystery unfolds, the conventional noir elements – shadows, rain, dark palette – comes to represent heavenly as well as human corruption.

Azazel's choice of The Stones' 'Time Is on My Side' effectively suggests the near immortality of Azazel compared to the brief candle of a human lifespan, and also builds on the dark connotations of the famous rock group's music, already used in other movies of the supernatural such as *Interview with the Vampire** (1994) and *The Devil's Advocate* (1997) and so well chronicled in the Maysles Brothers' documentary *Gimme Shelter* (1970), in which the audience at the infamous Altamont concert is whipped into a frenzy that resulted in the fatal stabbing death of a fan in the crowd. *Fallen* ends with a shot of a crowded city street in broad daylight, seeming even more crowded by the use of a telephoto lens that flattens the depth of field

DIRECTOR Gregory Hoblit
PRODUCER Charles Roven, Dawn Steel
SCREENPLAY Nicholas Kazan
CINEMATOGRAPHY Newton Thomas Sigel
EDITOR Lawrence Jordan
MUSIC Tan Dun
PRODUCTION COMPANY Turner Pictures
MAIN CAST Denzel Washington, John Goodman, Donald Sutherland, Embeth Davidtz, James Gandolfini, Elias Koteas

and makes the horde of people seem to jostle in close proximity – an easy environment for Azazel to move in and also suggestive of the pervasive presence of evil in the world today. The shot is accompanied by the Stones' 'Sympathy for the Devil' ('Been around for a long, long year/ Stole many a man's soul to waste'), which they also performed at Altamont. Although God presumably exists, we are left to wonder to what extent we have been abandoned and world history has been influenced by the intervention of the fallen.

Further Reading:

Krzywinska, Tanya. 'Demon Daddies: Gender Ecstasy and Terror in the Possession Film'. In *Horror Film Reader*, ed. Alain Silver and James Ursini, pp. 247–267. New York: Limelight, 2000.

Stanford, Peter. *Angels: A Visible and Invisible History*. London: Hodder & Stoughton, 2019.

Fatal Attraction
1987 – 119 mins
Adrian Lyne

Following such precursors as and *Play Misty for Me* (1971) and *Looking for Mr. Goodbar* (1977), the erotic thriller emerged generically in the 1980s as a result of rapidly changing concepts of sex and gender and evolving attitudes in culture generally and the workplace specifically that challenged previously prevailing patriarchal norms. In the erotic thriller, sex and suspense are inextricable; sexual transgression, even between consenting adults, inevitably turns deadly. The cycle, which includes such movies as *Jagged Edge* (1985) and *Basic Instinct* (1992), was established with the surprising box-office success of *Fatal Attraction*. Director Adrian Lyne explored similar territory in *9½ weeks* (1986), *Indecent Proposal* (1993), and his remake of *Lolita* (1997), and while *Jacob's Ladder* (1997) is more ambitious in narrative structure, it, too, explores the dark corridors of the male mind. Adapted by James Dearden from his short film *Diversion* (1980), *Fatal Attraction* involves a one-night stand between a married family man, Dan Gallagher (Douglas, the icon of yuppie angst), and a professional woman, Alex Forrest (Close), which brings nightmarish repercussions as Alex becomes increasingly psychotic and possessive, ultimately trying to kill Dan and his family.

At the time of its release, *Fatal Attraction* was widely condemned for its scapegoating of the professional female, but it may be read as a projection of Dan's fear and guilt, wherein the result of his affair with Alex is, on one level, the return of his repressed dissatisfaction with his marriage. Dan feels trapped by domesticity, his discontent imaged forth in the family's cramped apartment, so he fantasises a relationship with no distracting responsibilities in the form of Alex. But then, to assuage his guilt, Dan projects responsibility onto her – at one point he calls her 'sick' – making her a monstrous Other because she does not recognise what he calls 'the rules' for such affairs. Her golden, curled tresses are no doubt part of his initial attraction, but then she comes to seem a Medusa-like figure of feminine rage. Alex will not be 'reasonable', will not be treated like the sides of beef that hang outside her apartment building. She refuses to be silenced, telephoning Dan insistently and leaving an audio cassette in his car that questions his masculinity – both instances of an assertive female voice that seems beyond his masculine control. Indeed, it is not Alex but Dan who is silenced, as her adamant refusal to have an abortion leaves him, as he admits, 'no say'.

Like the serial slashers, Alex is coded as a monster in the climax. She invades the family home on a murderous rampage and seems almost supernaturally unstoppable, like Jason Vorhees and Michael Myers. When Alex is apparently drowned in the bathtub by Dan, after an improbably lengthy period she pops up from beneath the water and then must be killed again, this time shot by Dan's wife, Beth (Archer). The Archers' marriage is thus renewed through violence, and she and Dan embrace, reunited.

The final shot is almost Sirkian in its irony, as the camera pans to the fireplace mantle, the hearth of the family home, showing a photograph of the married couple – a still image – and a pair of bronzed baby shoes. Both objects connote immobility and stasis, undercutting the notion that anything has changed in Dan

DIRECTOR Adrian Lyne
PRODUCER Stanley R. Jaffe, Sherry Lansing
SCREENPLAY James Dearden
CINEMATOGRAPHY Howard Atherton
EDITOR Michael Kahn, Peter E. Berger
MUSIC Maurice Jarre
PRODUCTION COMPANY Jaffe/Lansing Productions, Paramount Pictures
MAIN CAST Michael Douglas, Glenn Close, Anne Archer

and Beth's marriage. Rather, the objects are a comment on their re-affirmed embrace of traditional values – a very reassuring resolution, especially for male viewers after witnessing the most nightmarish consequences of indulging in the fantasy of marital infidelity.

Further Reading:

Conlon, James. 'The Place of Passion: Reflections on *Fatal Attraction*'. In *The Dread of Difference: Gender in the Horror Film*, 2nd edn. ed. Barry Keith Grant, pp. 459–467. Austin: University of Texas Press, 2015.

Grant, Barry Keith. 'Rich and Strange: The Yuppie Horror Film'. *Film International* 14, nos. 3–4 (2016): 6–19.

Pearce, Lynne, and Gina Wisker, eds. *Fatal Attractions: Rescripting Romance in Contemporary Literature and Film*. London: Pluto Press, 1998.

Williams, Linda Ruth. *The Erotic Thriller in Contemporary Cinema*. Bloomington and Indianapolis: Indiana University Press, 2005.

Willis, Sharon. *High Contrast: Race and Gender in Contemporary Hollywood Film*. Durham and London: Duke University Press, 1997.

The Fly
1958 – 94 mins
Kurt Neumann

The first film adaptation of George Langelaan's 1957 short story 'The Fly' is more horror than science fiction, for while its premise of matter teleportation is the stuff of the latter, it is treated with the tropes of the former. Although shot in colour by noted cinematographer Karl Struss (his many credits include *Sunrise: A Song of Two Humans* [1927], *Island of Lost Souls* [1932], and the 1931 version of *Dr. Jekyll and Mr. Hyde**), it hatched two black-and-white sequels, *Return of the Fly* (1959) and *Curse of the Fly* (1965), a distinctively different

DIRECTOR Kurt Neumann
PRODUCER Kurt Neumann
SCREENPLAY James Clavell
CINEMATOGRAPHY
Karl Struss
EDITOR Merrill G. White
MUSIC Paul Sawtell
PRODUCTION COMPANY 20th
Century Fox
MAIN CAST Al (David)
Hedison, Patricia Owens,
Vincent Price, Herbert Marshall,
Charles Herbert

remake by David Cronenberg in 1986, and an opera composed by Howard Shore, who also composed the music for Cronenberg's film, first performed in 2008. Directed by Kurt Neumann (*Rocketship X-M* [1950], *Kronos* [1957], *She-Devil* [1957]), who died only weeks after the film's release, *The Fly*'s plot about a scientist's experiment in teleportation that goes horribly wrong exploits the fear of insects (entomophobia, one of the most common of phobias), not unlike the later mockumentary *The Hellstrom Chronicle** (1971), but ups the ante with a literal fly in the ointment.

Hélène Delambre (Owens) tells the horrifying story in flashback after she is arrested for the grisly murder of her husband André (Hedison), a Montreal scientist whose head and arm were crushed beyond recognition in a hydraulic press. She explains that André had been working on a matter transporter machine and that in attempting to teleport himself his atoms combined with those of a common housefly that had accidentally entered the machine with him. In Cronenberg's version, the scientist's atomic structure more plausibly fuses with the atoms of the fly, creating a new hybrid creature ('Brundlefly'), whereas here in the original Delambre somehow has a large insect head and arm and the fly a tiny human head and arm, yet both creatures seem to have a human brain (although Delambre says his is slipping away). Hélène is horrified when she sees her transformed husband – as shown in the memorable point-of-view shot from André/the fly's perspective as a mosaic of images of images of Hélène screaming that mimics the compound eye of a fly.

The detective investigating the case, Inspector Charas (Marshall), thinks Hélène is insane, but as she is about to be taken away, he and André's brother Francois (Price) see the fly with the white head for which Hélène had been frantically searching, trapped in a spider's web in the garden. In close-up we see the fly with André's head and arm trapped in the web screaming 'Help me! Help me!' in a high-pitched whine as a large spider is about to consume it, and at the last moment Charas crushes them both with a rock. 'I shall never forget that scream as long as I live', he says, shaken – an experience that would seem to be equally true for so many baby boomer children who saw *The Fly* in Saturday matinees when it was first released.

In the final scene the nuclear family appears reconstituted, Francois seeming to take André's place with the now free Hélène and her son, Philippe (Herbert). Such an ending might signify a return to the status quo after the mad scientist's fate offers the conventional wisdom that there are some things man is not meant to know. But *The Fly*, surprisingly, offers a different, less conservative moral. Philippe says he also wants to be an explorer like his father, and Francois explains that his brother died searching for truth and that: 'The search for the truth is the most important work in the whole world and the most dangerous' – justifying André's work as more than mere hubris. This ending, more upbeat than that of Langelaan's story, provides a note of caution rather than a prescriptive taboo, although its motive may be merely commercial, to prepare for the sequel (in which Phillipe pursues his father's experiments and in the process acquires a fly leg as well as arm and head).

Further Reading:

Knee, Adam. 'The Metamorphosis of *The Fly*'. *Wide Angle* 14, no. 1 (1992): 20–34.

Hendershot, Cyndy. *I Was a Cold War Monster: Horror Films, Eroticism and the Cold War Imagination*. Bowling Green, OH: Popular Press, 2001.

Lennard, Dominic. *Brute Force: Animal Horror Movies*. Albany: SUNY Press, 2019.

Sobchack, Vivian. *Screening Space: The American Science Fiction Film*, 2nd edn. New Brunswick, NJ and London: Rutgers University Press, 2004.

Tudor, Andrew. *Monsters and Mad Scientists: A Cultural History of the Horror Movie*. Oxford: Blackwell, 1989.

Frankenstein
1910 – 14 mins
J. Searle Dawley

The first of dozens of film adaptations of Mary Shelley's classic novel, the Edison Company's production was, as the opening intertitle tells us, 'a liberal adaptation'. With the exception of the creation scene in which there are several cutaways to point-of-view shots of Frankenstein watching the monster be created in a boiling chemical stew, the film is relatively unsophisticated narratively, with each scene equalling one shot and the film space like a theatrical proscenium. Of greater interest is the film's approach to the tone and theme of Shelley's tale, and how it anticipates much of classic Hollywood cinema in its endorsement of dominant ideology. It retains the essential idea of the protagonist creating life, but radically alters the plot and the theme to suggest that an embrace of heterosexual 'love' will conquer any monstrous evil that may lurk within. (In this sense it is exactly opposite the more open and inclusive vision of Mel Brooks's *Young Frankenstein** [1974]).

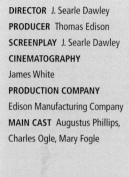

DIRECTOR J. Searle Dawley
PRODUCER Thomas Edison
SCREENPLAY J. Searle Dawley
CINEMATOGRAPHY
James White
PRODUCTION COMPANY
Edison Manufacturing Company
MAIN CAST Augustus Phillips,
Charles Ogle, Mary Fogle

As the film begins, Frankenstein (Phillips) is heading off for college. A mere two years later, he has discovered the 'mystery of life', and we see him contemplating a skull like Hamlet. Frankenstein then performs his experiment, but for some inexplicable reason he fails to achieve his goal of creating the perfect human being because the 'evil in his mind' – presumably, the presumption of meddling in God's territory, although we are never told this explicitly – causes him to produce a hideously distorted monster. As portrayed by Charles Ogle, a prolific character actor during the silent period, the creature has a macrocephalic head, hunched back, and extended claw-like hands and feet. The creation scene is shown backwards, the skeleton body of the creature seeming to form rather than burn in the fire, and then anticipating what would become a standard convention of the genre with the close-up of the creature's hand slowly appearing through the doorway before being shown in full.

As in the novel, Frankenstein is 'appalled' at the sight of his creation and rejects him. In an extraordinary scene that may be actually happening or a representation of a feverish dream, Frankenstein collapses in bed as the creature appears to him through the curtains above the headboard, then disappears before the servant enters. Frankenstein returns to his family home where the creature follows, haunting him. He appears on Frankenstein's wedding night, but instead of carrying Elizabeth (Fogle) off, she faints at the sight of the creature, who seems, oddly, more pitiable and concerned for her welfare than threatening.

We are told that Frankenstein's 'better nature asserts itself' – meaning that he is now commendably channelling his energy into heterosexual monogamy – and so 'the creation of an evil mind is overcome by love and disappears' – that is, the creature looks into a mirror, sees himself, and like one of Georges Méliès's film faeries, suddenly vanishes into thin air thanks to stop-motion photography. According to the description of the film in the Edison Kinetogram, the company's bi-weekly bulletin: 'Here comes the point which we have endeavored to bring out, namely: That when Frankenstein's love for his bride shall have attained full strength and freedom from impurity it will have such an effect upon his mind that the monster cannot exist.' Interestingly, though, his reflection remains in the mirror momentarily, and is then replaced by that of Frankenstein, suggesting that while the doctor has successfully integrated into the dominant social order – he and Elizabeth now embrace – the monster still lurks within.

Further Reading

Buenzo, Daniele Pio. 'The Theme of the Doppelganger in James Searle Dawley's *Frankenstein*'. In *Transmedia Creatures: Frankenstein's Afterlives*, ed. Francesca Saggini and Anna Enrichetti Soccio, pp. 173–186. Lewisburg, PA: Bucknell University Press, 2019.

Frayling, Christopher. *Frankenstein: The First Two Hundred Years*. London: Reel Art Press, 2017.

Phillips, Kendall R. *A Place of Darkness: The Rhetoric of Horror in Early American Cinema*. Austin: University of Texas Press, 2018.

Forrey, Steven Earle. *Hideous Progenies: Dramatisations of Frankenstein from the Nineteenth Century to the Present*. Philadelphia: University of Pennsylvania Press, 1990.

Freaks
1932 – 64 mins
Tod Browning

Directed by Tod Browning (*The Unknown** [1927]) the year after he directed *Dracula** (1931), *Freaks* is noto-rious for casting actual 'freaks' (many of whom, such as Koo Koo, the Bird Girl; the limbless Prince Randian, 'The Human Torso'; and conjoined twins Daisy and Violet Hilton, were in fact real sideshow performers). After early screenings the original version of the film was cut by almost half an hour, including the castration of Hercules, to mollify outraged audiences (it was banned in the U.K. for thirty years) already put off by having to look at them and their vengeance, and a new prologue with the carnival barker was added.

While little of Tod Robbins's original story, 'Spurs' (1923), remains other than the marriage of a dwarf and an average-sized woman, the film does make two crucial changes: In the story the 'freaks' have no

DIRECTOR Tod Browning
PRODUCER Tod Browning
SCREENPLAY Willis Goldbeck,
Leon Gordon, Edgar Allan
Woolf, Al Boasberg
CINEMATOGRAPHY
Merritt B. Gerstad
EDITOR Basil Wrangell
PRODUCTION COMPANY
MGM
MAIN CAST Wallace Ford,
Leila Hyams, Olga Baclanova,
Harry Earles, Daisy Earles,
Henry Victor, Roscoe Ates

communal code which binds them together and, in fact, are quite the opposite, 'children' who engage in egotistical bickering; and the dwarf who marries the bareback rider is as much a vindictive monster in the story as a victim. The film's plot is set in a traveling circus, where the so-called freaks share a moral protocol, 'the code of the freaks' – according to the carney, 'a law unto themselves for mutual protection in a hostile world'. When the trapeze artist Cleopatra (Baclanova) overhears one of the midgets, Hans (Earles), mention a cache of money he has saved, she devises a plan with her lover, the strong man Hercules (Victor), to marry Hans and then poison him to inherit the money. The easily deluded and smitten Hans marries Cleo and is immediately treated brutally by her as she begins to poison him. In the climax, the 'freaks' discover her plot and unite to seek vengeance by killing Hercules and mutilating Cleopatra.

Early on the film emphasises that the so-called freaks are not really very different from us, as we see them doing mundane domestic chores like hanging laundry. Two of the physically normal people, Cleopatra and Hercules, seem morally monstrous, willing to exploit and even kill for material gain, while the 'freaks' seem admirably loyal by contrast. Browning thus boldly reverses the relationship between the monstrous and the normal, yet in presenting the strangely bodied circus people as objects of our voyeuristic gaze, the film falls into the same trap it preaches against. Just as the film's sensational advertising copy emphatically positions the 'freaks' as horrible monsters at which we may gawk, the climax, succumbing to generic convention, presents them as frightening monsters. In an intense rainstorm, they slither and crawl through the mud, associating them with muck, with that which is unclean, to exact their revenge on Cleopatra (Browning had already made Lon Chaney move similarly in *West of Zanzibar* [1928], in which

his character's legs are paralyzed). Lightning flashes alternate with disturbing darkness, allowing us only to glimpse them momentarily in vignettes as they move forward close to the ground. The camera looks straight on as they threateningly approach it, and, by extension, us.

In short, the swarming vengeance of the 'freaks' seems to endorse the very view of them as monsters rather than as people. As they approach Cleopatra in the unknown darkness of the forest, the film cuts away, as if what is to follow is too horrible to witness, to the final scene. Back at the circus, the carney reveals to his audience, and to us, 'the most astounding living monstrosity of all time' – Cleopatra, now a chicken with a human head nestled in a bed of hay, clucking away.

Further Reading:

Fiedler, Leslie. *Freaks: Myths and Images of the Secret Self*. New York: Simon and Schuster, 1978.

Hawkins, Joan. '"One of Us": Tod Browning's *Freaks*'. In *Freakery: Cultural Spectacles of the Extraordinary Body*, ed. Rosemarie Garland Thomson, 265–276. New York and London: New York University Press, 1996.

Skal, David J., and Elias Sadava. *Dark Carnival: The Secret World of Tod Browning, Hollywood's Master of the Macabre*. New York: Doubleday, 1995.

Norden, Martin F., and Madeleine Cahill. 'Violence, Women, and Disability in Tod Browning's *Freaks* and *The Devil Doll*'. In *Horror Film Reader*, ed. Alain Silver and James Ursini, pp. 151–165. New York: Limelight, 2000.

Smith, Angela M. *Hideous Progeny: Disability, Eugenics, and Classic Horror Cinema*. New York: Columbia University Press, 2011.

The Frighteners
NZ/US, 1996 – 110 min
Peter Jackson

Financed by a major American studio, as was the case with Peter Jackson's subsequent *The Lord of the Rings* trilogy (2001–3) and K*ing Kong* (2005), *The Frighteners* was made for Universal, with Robert Zemeckis (*Back to the Future* [1985], *Forrest Gump* [1994]) as executive producer. Zemeckis initially hired Jackson and his personal and professional partner Fran Walsh to write the script for him to direct, but later decided that Jackson should direct it. Jackson shot the film with a cast of American stars in his home country of New Zealand, far away from Universal executives, on a budget of US$30 million. The film's multitude of special effects, including spectral ghosts, animated portraits, breathing houses, and a trip up the tunnel to the light of the afterlife, were created by Weta Digital, the company Jackson co-founded to create the effects for his previous feature, *Heavenly Creatures* (1994), and which has provided the FX for many major Hollywood science fiction and fantasy films since.

Jackson granted Zemeckis the right to final cut instead of Universal, an arrangement which seemed to have worked harmoniously, although the film was not a box-office success at the time of its release – in part because *The Frighteners* features the same distinctive but uneasy blend of comedy and horror that Jackson brought to his early features *Bad Taste* (1988), *Meet the Feebles* (1989), and *Braindead* (1992), movies that made him the preeminent figure of splatstick. (See also Sam Raimi's *The Evil Dead** [1981] and Frank Henenlotter's *Brain Damage** [1988].) While *The Frighteners* frequently references American serial killer culture, its kiwi quirkiness is pervasive.

The complex plot centres on Frank Bannister (Fox), a con man who cheats homeowners by pretending to exorcise poltergeists and other spirits. Ironically, he does have the ability to see dead people, and he works with a trio of co-conspiritors who create ghostly manifestations in people's homes in order to convince them to hire Bannister to drive the spirits out. Like Jackson himself, Bannister rehearses his spectral cast and choreographs their 'special effects', checking for ghostly presences through a souped-up radio and a special 'viewfinder'. As a horror filmmaker Jackson is himself a 'frightener', and one who might be said to be possessed by his visions, haunted by them just as Bannister is haunted by his ghosts. Bannister learns to triumph over the ghosts of his past, his guilt over the death of his first wife, and embrace love again while at the same time defeating the spirit of a dead serial killer (Busey) posing as the Grim Reaper, the living woman haunted by him (Wallace in full madwoman mode with a shotgun, like the crazed hippo Heidi in *Meet the Feebles*), and a maniacal FBI agent (Combs) who makes Special Agent Dale Cooper of *Twin Peaks* (1990–1991) look perfectly normal by comparison.

Gore gags appear even at the most suspenseful moments, as when a Raggedy Ann doll attacks Lucy Lynskey (Alvarado) as if it were the Bride of Chucky, or when a ghostly Judge (Astin) pauses during a chase in a museum to fornicate with a mummy (as he boasts, he isn't known as 'the hanging judge' for nothing).

DIRECTOR Peter Jackson
PRODUCER Peter Jackson, Jamie Selkirk
SCREENPLAY Fran Walsh, Peter Jackson
CINEMATOGRAPHY John Blick, Alun Bollinger
EDITOR Jamie Selkirk
MUSIC Danny Elfman
PRODUCTION COMPANY WingNut Films, Universal Pictures
MAIN CAST Michael J. Fox, Trini Alvarado, Peter Dobson, John Astin, Dee Wallace Stone, Jeffrey Combs, Jake Busey

Yet *The Frighteners* is not simply a ghost comedy in the tradition of *Topper* (1937) or *Ghost* (1990), for the supernatural forces in the film can be gruesomely malevolent, literally ripping the hearts out of the living. Just as *Meet the Feebles* imagines muppets with genitalia, one might say that *The Frighteners* imagines *Harvey* (1950) in the world of *Hellraiser* (1987). If, in the end, the terrible house of the climax seems disappointingly like videogame space and heaven merely a haven of excellent libraries, premium cigars, and beautiful women, the film's mixed success vividly reveals the textual tensions that frequently arise when filmmakers from elsewhere work within American cinema's genre system.

Further Reading

Conrich, Ian. 'Kiwi Gothic: New Zealand's Cinema of a Perilous Paradise'. In *Horror International*, ed. Steven Jay Schneider and Tony Williams, pp. 114–127. Detroit: Wayne State University Press, 2005.

Grant, Barry Keith. *A Cultural Assault: The New Zealand Films of Peter Jackson*. Nottingham, UK: Kakapo Books, 1999.

Leotta, Alfio. *Peter Jackson*. London and New York: Bloomsbury, 2016.

Sibley, Brian. *Peter Jackson: A Film-maker's Journey*. New York: Harper Collins, 2016.

Funny Games
US/FR/UK/GER/ITAL, 2007 – 111 mins
Michael Haneke

While Gus Van Sant's near shot-for-shot 1998 remake of Alfred Hitchcock's *Psycho** (1960) seems pointless, Michael Haneke's remake of his own *Funny Games* (1997) in English a decade after the original is more than merely repetitive, gaining extra force for American viewers by engaging with Hollywood cinema. The attack on bourgeois western culture and its alienating effects in Haneke's films, beginning with his first, *The Seventh Continent* (1989), and often involving media (*Benny's Video* [1992], *Caché* [*Hidden*, 2005]), works powerfully within the context of the home invasion cycle which, unsurprisingly, has only become more prevalent in the new millennium with such films as *Panic Room* (2002), *You're Next* (2011), and *The Purge** (2013) and its sequels. These films express the fear of vulnerability regarding the integrity of the familial home, a theme consistent with Haneke's examination of cultural collapse, as in *Time of the Wolf* (2003). For an American remake, *Funny Games US* is as surprisingly bleak as the first version, unlike George Sluiser's 1993 American remake of his own *The Vanishing* (*Spoorloos* [1988]), which changed the downbeat ending of the original to provide satisfying narrative closure. *Funny Games US* is filled with games – funny peculiar rather than funny ha-ha – characters playing them with each other and the director with the viewer. Haneke, like Hitchcock in *Psycho*, plays the audience masterfully, implicating them in their own questionable desires.

The insular world of the film's doomed bourgeois family is emphasised immediately in the opening credit sequence, in which George (Roth) and Ann Faber (Watts) – Haneke often uses variations of these first names to indicate his characters' representativeness – play a game taking turns identifying pieces of classical music as they drive along a country road, trees a brilliant summer green, sailboat in tow, on their way to their isolated lakeside country vacation home. The images, aided by the music, suggest a flowing harmony and privileged peacefulness – but their bubble is about to burst, as the ensuing title credit is accompanied by the harsh, uptempo sounds of John Zorn's saxophone, announcing the film's intention to subject them, and us, to a shattering experience. We quickly discover its form in the two young psychopaths, Paul (Pitt) and Peter/Tom (Corbet). The Fabers' world is shattered as easily as the eggs that serve as the trivial pretext for the young men's murderous violence. Haneke knows that to make an omelette you have to crack some eggs.

Unlike the original *Funny Games*, the Hollywood version necessarily taps into the American myth of the individual male hero only to completely deny it. Paul refers to George as the 'captain' of his ship, but he is neither the captain of his soul nor the master of his fate. Rather, he is metaphorically castrated almost from the start, when Peter smashes George's kneecap with one of his own expensive golf clubs. Further, although the differences from Haneke's original are minimal, the star status of Watts and Roth, playing the victimised couple who cannot save themselves or their child (Gearhart), heightens the expectation that they will survive and makes the situation tougher for American audiences than it would if they had seen the original German art film instead.

DIRECTOR Michael Haneke
PRODUCER Hamish McAlpine, Christian Baute, Chris Coen, Andro Steinborn, Naomi Watts
SCREENPLAY Michael Haneke
CINEMATOGRAPHY Darius Khondji
EDITOR Monika Willi
PRODUCTION COMPANY Celluloid Dreams, Tartan Films, Film4 Productions
MAIN CAST Naomi Watts, Tim Roth, Michael Pitt, Brady Corbet, Devon Gearhart

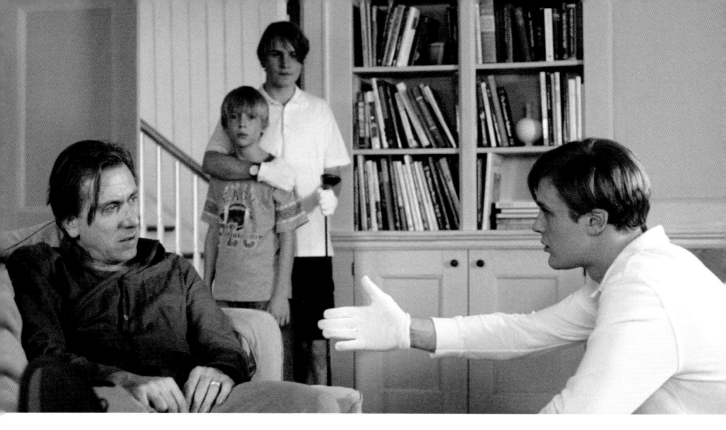

Paul periodically looks at the camera, breaking the fourth wall, and his dialogue often speaks to viewers as much as it is addressed to the other characters. In this way Haneke positions us not just as spectators, but as virtual co-conspirators in their torture and humiliation, and then makes us regret it by rubbing our faces in it. Paul tells us that we want a real ending with 'plausible plot development', but we are given no explanation for the young men's murder spree – or rather, they give numerous reasons, any of which would serve in a more conventional home invasion movie. But these aren't merely gestures of Brechtian distanciation, because the film invariably engages us even as it distances us. Through a controlled deployment of editing, framing, and tempo, most of the violence is left to our own imagination, taking place offscreen. As Peter explains when George asks why they don't just kill them now: 'You shouldn't forget the importance of entertainment.'

Further Reading

Price, Brian, and John David Rhodes, eds. *On Michael Haneke*. Detroit: Wayne State University Press, 2010.

McGettigan, Andrew. 'A Bleak Burlesque: Michael Haneke's *Funny Games* as a Study in Violence'. In *New Takes in Film-Philosophy*, ed. Havi Carel and Greg Tuck, pp. 223–239. Basingstoke, UK and New York: Palgrave Macmillan, 2011.

Rowe, Christopher. *Michael Haneke: The Intermedial Void*. Evanston, IL: Northwestern University Press, 2017.

Wheatley, Catherine. *Michael Haneke's Cinema: The Ethics of the Image*. New York and Oxford: Berghahn, 2009.

Ganja & Hess
1973 – 113 mins
Bill Gunn

Blaxploitation filmmaking was at its height in the early 1970s, spurred by the success of such movies as *Shaft* (1971) and *Superfly* (1972), among others. After the commercial success of *Blacula* (1972), independent production company Kelly-Jordan Enterprises approached writer and actor Bill Gunn, who had already written several produced screenplays including Hal Ashby's *The Landlord* (1970), with the idea of making a black vampire film. And while Gunn certainly delivered a lot of blood and nudity, it is contextualised within an opaque narrative that seems to resist the coherence of classic narrative style. In this way it is akin to the foundational blaxploitation film *Sweet Sweetback's Baadasssss Song* (1971), but with a theme of cultural appropriation generally replacing the racial animus of Melvin Van Peebles's film. Equal parts vampire movie, blaxploitation film, and art cinema, *Ganja & Hess* is utterly unique in the blaxploitation cycle.

Dr. Hess Green (Jones, whose only other lead role in a feature film was as Ben in *Night of the Living Dead** [1968]) is a wealthy black anthropologist who, in the course of researching the imaginary culture of Mythria, an ancient African society of blood drinkers, becomes a vampire himself after his assistant, George Meda (Gunn),

DIRECTOR Bill Gunn
PRODUCER Chiz Schultz
SCREENPLAY Bill Gunn
CINEMATOGRAPHY
James E. Hinton
EDITOR Victor Kanefsky
MUSIC Sam Waymon
PRODUCTION COMPANY
Kelly-Jordan Enterprises
MAIN CAST Marlene Clark,
Duane Jones, Bill Gunn, Sam
Waymon, Leonard Jackson

suffers a breakdown and stabs him with an ancient cursed dagger before committing suicide. Green calmly laps up Meda's blood from the tiled bathroom floor, now, it seems, an immortal vampire. Later he falls in love with and marries Meda's estranged wife, Ganja (Clark), who eventually discovers the truth but is turned into a vampire by him. Soon Green becomes spiritually uneasy, and after attending a gospel service at a church in the city returns home to his stately suburban mansion where he commits suicide by standing in the shadow of a giant crucifix. The film ends with Ganja and the unresolved question of whether she will continue her vampiric ways or follow Green to death.

This is the broad outlines of the film's plot, but it is presented elliptically, omitting much conventional exposition. As well, its tone shifts radically, most noticeably alternating lengthy, lyrical passages, such as those of Hess and Ganja as their relationship develops, with the scenes of vampiric violence. When Hess attends the church service, the film seems to shift abruptly in style to that of a direct cinema documentary, giving the extended sequence a strong sense of authenticity. Another contrast involves Green's luxurious mansion, filled with artifacts of African cultures and nestled in the quiet woods, which contrasts starkly with the noisy and crowded city, suggesting the class privilege that allows for the study of one culture by another, a theme the film shares with the later *Candyman** (1992). And like *The Addiction** (1995), *Ganja & Hess* interprets the vampire as a metaphor for addiction generally. But more radically, it also suggests that vampirism may be understood not only as the exploitation of others,

of draining their lifeblood whether literally or metaphorically, but also that vampirism is itself a form of slavery, dooming the victimiser as much as the victim.

The film's producers, unhappy with its box-office performance, sold it to Heritage Enterprises, which cut it by more than half an hour and re-released it as *Blood Couple* later the same year, although it failed to do any better. In retrospective acknowledgement of its importance, Spike Lee remade *Ganja & Hess* as *Da Sweet Blood of Jesus* (2014).

Further Reading:

Benshoff, Harry. 'Blaxploitation Horror Films: Generic Reappropriation or Reinscription?' *Cinema Journal* 39, no. 2 (Winter 2000): 31–50.

Coleman, Robin R. Means. *Horror Noire: Blacks in American Horror Films from 1890s to Present*. New York and Abingdon, UK: Routledge, 2011.

Diawara, Manthia, and Phyllis Klotman. '*Ganja & Hess*: Vampires, Sex, and Addictions'. *Jump Cut* 35 (1990): 30–36.

Sherrod, Harrison M. 'The Blood of the Thing (Is the Truth of the Thing): Viral Pathogens and Uncanny Ontologies in *Ganja & Hess*'. In *Beyond Blaxploitation*, ed. Novotny Lawrence and Gerald R. Butters, Jr., pp. 102–113. Detroit: Wayne State University Press, 2016.

Get Out
2017 – 104 mins
Jordan Peele

Get Out was a major box-office phenomenon of 2017, breaking several box-office records for first-time director Jordan Peele, who also wrote the screenplay. Peele had previously worked with Keegan-Michael Key on the hit television comedy sketch show *Key and Peele* (2012–2015), which, like *Get Out*, demonstrates a darkly comic understanding of pop culture conventions. But while *Get Out* does contain some comic moments, it is no laughing matter. Right from the opening scene, in which a black man wanders the mean streets of white suburbia and falls prey to violence, the film addresses the complexities of race relations and the realities of black life in America through the tropes of the horror film. One of the very few horror movies to receive multiple Oscar nominations, including Best Picture, it frighteningly captures some of the roiling racial tensions within contemporary American society and the problems with what Norman Mailer had controversially labelled 'the white Negro' decades earlier. Peele's follow-up effort *Us* (2019) – as opposed to *Them!* (1954) – shows the same ability to rework the conventions of pop culture forms within the context of horror.

Black photographer Chris Washington (Kaluuya) travels to upstate New York with his white girlfriend, Rose Armitage (Williams), to meet her family – father and neurosurgeon Dean (Whitford), mother and hypnotherapist Missy (Keener), and belligerent brother Jeremy (Jones). Everyone's behaviour, including that of the Black maid and groundskeeper and the guests at the party next day, seems slightly odd, and Peele masterfully builds the suspense with numerous portents until the family's perverse plot is finally revealed. Chris is glad to meet the one Black brother at the party where, unbeknownst to him, his body is being appraised and auctioned off; but, to his surprise, 'Logan King' (Stanfield) acts like the blandest of ofays, 'a black white man', the Stepford husband of an older white woman.

Indeed, the weekend seems ominous from the start, with Rose's parents welcoming Chris as if his skin colour were entirely irrelevant, a nightmarish version of political correctness. Dean boasts of his admiration for Barack Obama and declares he would have voted for him for a third term while criticizing the Third Reich for its 'Aryan bullshit' – but the family are racists in reverse, coveting the physical superiority of Blacks just like the racist Pino in Spike Lee's *Do the Right Thing* (1989), who, as Mookie says, wishes he were Black. As we discover, the family transplants the brains of white folks into the abler, more virile bodies of their Black victims, and Chris is next in line.

Missy hypnotises Chris (a loaded metaphor) so that he is unable to leave because of an implanted trigger she places in his mind which causes him to fall into 'the sunken place', an abstracted darkness in which he can see what is happening but is unable to act of his own free will – a mental marginalization to match the actual marginalizing of non-white Americans. The sunken place thus specifically evokes the oppression of African-Americans as imagined by the nameless narrator of Ralph Ellison's *Invisible Man* (1952), who lives under-

DIRECTOR Jordan Peele
PRODUCER Sean McKitrick, Jason Blum, Edward H. Hamm, Jr., Jordan Peele
SCREENPLAY Jordan Peele
CINEMATOGRAPHY Toby Oliver
EDITOR Gregory Plotkin
MUSIC Michael Abels
PRODUCTION COMPANY Blumhouse Productions, QC Entertainment, Monkeypaw Productions
MAIN CAST Daniel Kaluuya, Allison Williams, Catherine Keener, Bradley Whitford, Caleb Landry Jones, LaKeith Stanfield, Betty Gabriel, Stephen Root

ground, unseen. Here there is literal possession of the Black perspective, as the photographer Jim Hudson (Root) expects to regain his sight from Chris's eyes in the impending operation. In a collaborative act of mental colonization, Missy gets inside the heads of the family's victims, and Dean, who says it's 'a privilege' to experience another person's culture, messes with their brains. Although Chris eventually manages to dispatch his detainers and 'get out' of the evil house, one has to wonder if there really is any escape for him in a nation with a president who boasts at a mostly white rally of 'my African-American over here'.

Further Reading:

Coleman, Robin R. Means. *Horror Noire: Blacks in American Horror Films from 1890s to Present*. New York and Abingdon, UK: Routledge, 2011.

Graves, Stephenie A. '*Get Out* (2017) – Smart Horror'. In *Horror: A Companion*, ed. Simon Bacon, pp. 127–134. Oxford: Peter Lang, 2019.

Keetley, Dawn, ed. *Jordan Peele's Get Out: Political Horror*. Columbus: Ohio State University Press, 2019.

Lloyd, Christopher. '"I Told You Not to Go into That House": *Get Out* and Horror's Racial Politics'. In *Make America Hate Again: Trump-Era Horror and the Politics of Fear*, ed. Victoria McCollum, pp. 109–118. London and New York: Routledge, 2019.

Sobande, Francesca. 'Dissecting Depictions of Black Masculinity in *Get Out*'. In *Gender and Contemporary Horror in Film*, ed. Samantha Holland, Robert Shail, and Steven Gerrard, pp. 237–250. Bingley, UK: Emerald Publishing, 2019.

Gremlins
1984 – 106 mins
Joe Dante

Gremlins is the prime example of family horror – not horror about the family, but horror for the family. Director Joe Dante learned his craft at Roger Corman's New World Pictures, displaying a similar tongue-in-cheek approach to horror as the director of *The Little Shop of Horrors** (1960). Following *Piranha* (1978) and the werewolf film *The Howling* (1981), Dante turned to family-oriented fantastic fare with *Gremlins*, followed by the Spielbergian comedy adventure *Explorers* (1985); *Inner Space* (1987); *Matinee* (1993), a fictionalised version of gimmick filmmaker William Castle (*The Tingler** [1959]) promoting his new film *Mant!* ('half man, half ant') at a Florida movie theatre during the Cuban Missile Crisis; *Small Soldiers* (1998), about action figures that become dangerously sentient through military microchips; and *Gremlins: The New Batch* (1990). Despite the family orientation of *Gremlins*, there are moments of true horror in the film, as when Mrs. Peltzer fights several gremlins in the kitchen, brutally stabbing one, and when Stripe is about to kill Billy. Anyone doubting Dante's serious horror chops should see his two contributions to the *Masters of Horror* television series, 'Homecoming' (2005) and 'The Screwfly Solution' (2006), a chilling adaptation of the short story by James Tiptree, Jr.

Real actions figures were just part of the massive and very successful merchandising campaign that accompanied the release of *Gremlins*, which also included trading cards, novels, audio recordings, and, of course, stuffed animals capitalizing on the cuddly Gizmo, the good little 'mogwai', which became well-publicised high-demand Christmas toys that year. 'I bet every kid in America would like one of these', rightly exclaims eccentric inventor Mr. Peltzer (Axton) when they multiply and he realises their mass produced potential. Gizmo first divides on a pile of comic books, revealing the pop influences at work in the film, as do the movie clips we see on the Peltzers' television, including the 1956 *Invasion of the Body Snatchers* ('they're like huge seed pods'). There are allusions to a number of '50s horror and science fiction movies including Robby the Robot reciting his best lines from *Forbidden Planet* (1956). The casting of Dick Miller as neighbour Murray Futterman nods to the film's awareness that its comic horror is in the tone of *The Little Shop of Horrors*, in which he appeared, as does the presence of other Hollywood stalwarts – Harry Carey, Jr., Kenneth Tobey (Captain Hendry in *The Thing from Another World* [1951]), Scott Brady, and Keye Luke (Charlie Chan's 'number one son').

Gremlins contains numerous sight gags to amuse viewers both young and adult: a gremlin breakdancing, another exposing himself in a trench coat, the elderly Mrs. Deagle flying out of her window in her jimmied chairlift. The gremlins are like mischievous and misbehaving children, proverbial little monsters, so young viewers can readily identify with them even as they embrace the heroic Gizmo, who exposes the evil Stripe to daylight in the climax and causes him to melt. Unlike the more progressive horror films of the same period, *Gremlins* doesn't push a reading of its monsters as a manifestation of the repressed energies within

DIRECTOR Joe Dante
PRODUCER Michael Finnell
SCREENPLAY Chris Columbus
CINEMATOGRAPHY John Hora
EDITOR Tina Hirsch
MUSIC Jerry Goldsmith
PRODUCTION COMPANY Warner Bros., Amblin Entertainment
MAIN CAST Zach Galligan, Phoebe Cates, Hoyt Axton, Polly Holliday, Francis Lee McCain, Keye Luke

the nuclear family, which in this film seems functional, even happy. Rather, Futterman rants about reliable American cars as opposed to the foreign ones that are invading the American market. He identifies the creatures as gremlins and explains that they were introduced into American manufacture for the purposes of sabotage during World War II, and Mr. Peltzer acquires Gizmo in a mysterious-looking China-town of the imagination. When the gremlin army embarks on its eve of destruction, they sabotage traffic lights and streetlights through-out the town, metaphorically compromising America's late-capitalist crumbling infrastructure.

Further Reading

Baksar, Nils, and Gabe Klinger, eds. *Joe Dante*. Vienna: Austrian Film Museum Books, 2013.

Blouin, Michael J. 'The Gizmo Effect: "Japan, Inc.", American Nightmares, and the Fissure of the Symbolic'. *Horror Studies* 2, no. 1 (March 2011): 25–40.

Chute, David. 'Dante's Inferno'. *Film Comment* (June 1984): 22–27.

McDonagh, Maitland. *Filmmaking on the Fringe: The Good, the Bad, and the Deviant Directors*. New York: Citadel, 1995.

McFadzean, Angus. *Suburban Fantastic Cinema: Growing Up in the Late Twentieth Century*. New York: Wallflower Press, 2020.

Halloween
1978 – 91 mins
John Carpenter

Halloween was the commercial breakthrough for director John Carpenter (*In the Mouth of Madness** [1994]), its enormous box-office success setting the template for and spurring a cycle of slasher films (including, for example, Wes Craven's *Scream** [1996]). It was the first in a franchise consisting of eleven films, including eight sequels, a 2018 sequel that ignores the earlier sequels, a remake in 2007 directed by Rob Zombie (*The Devil's Rejects** [2005]), a sequel to that remake in 2009, as well as various merchandising. *Halloween* also established Jamie Lee Curtis as the period's reigning scream queen – she subsequently appeared in *The Fog* (1980), Carpenter's next theatrical feature, and in *Prom Night* (1980), *Terror Train* (1980), and several of the

DIRECTOR John Carpenter
PRODUCER Debra Hill
SCREENPLAY John Carpenter, Debra Hill
CINEMATOGRAPHY Dean Cundy
EDITOR Tommy Wallace, Charles Bornstein
MUSIC John Carpenter
PRODUCTION COMPANY Compass International Pictures, Falcon International Productions, Aquarius Releasing
MAIN CAST Jamie Lee Curtis, Donald Pleasence, Nick Castle, P. J. Soles, Nancy Keyes, Charles Cyphers

Halloween films to follow – and launched a debate regarding the gendered gaze of the camera and its relation to violence, voyeurism, and the victimisation of women.

The famous opening lengthy tracking shot from young Michael Myers's point of view as he comes into the family home after his sister's boyfriend leaves and then kills her suggests a primal trauma that triggers the six-year old's murder spree. Often in the slasher films to follow the killer is motivated by a past trauma activated by the promiscuity of the victims he stalks, and the killings often seem to be a punishment for being sexually active or precocious, as in *Halloween*. Like its imitators, *Halloween* seems to offer such a conservative morality play, with the so-called 'final girl' – in this case, Laurie Strode (Curtis) – who earlier resists temptation (sex, drugs, alcohol) and then survives the killer's murderous rampage.

As in the opening, Carpenter' camerawork – placement, framing, movement – are brilliantly controlled throughout. The film plays with depth of field and the limits of the frame to create the sense that Michael can appear anywhere at any moment, that he is almost supernatural. Tracking shots with the Steadicam (*Halloween* was one of the first films to use it) provide Michael's perspective as he stalks his victims. Yet sometimes these shots, however briefly, are ambiguous as to whether what we are seeing is the film's narration – as in that opening shot, which begins looking like an objective establishing shot but is then revealed to be from Michael's point-of-view – or the perspective of the killer. But Carpenter, characteristically, is less concerned with employing this ambiguity to explore the potentially questionable impulses of the viewer than simply to generate suspense.

The film might also be seen as a comment on suburbia, with its depiction of hedonistic youth, ineffectual and absent parents, and neighbours who turn a blind eye to someone in distress. Dean Cund-ey's cinematography makes even banal residential suburban streets look threatening, with dark shadows from the trees looming overhead in late afternoon and the entire town looking like Halloween night in *Meet Me in St. Louis* (1944). Carpenter's score (according to the end credits, 'the Bowling Green Philharmonic Orchestra') provides an insistently rhythmic soundtrack of a few notes, judiciously placed, that emphasises the discussion in school about the inflexibility of fate – the moment, also, when Laurie Strode (Curtis) first sees Michael through the classroom window. But it is Michael, not metaphysics, that determines destiny. He is mystified as evil by, of all people, his psychiatrist, Dr. Loomis (Pleasence) – the name a reference to John Gavin's character in *Psycho** (1960) – who refers to him as 'it' and describes him as 'pure evil', 'the boogeyman', denying any psychoanalytic or ideological explanation for the killer's murderous madness (unlike *Psycho*).

Further Reading:

Clover, Carol. *Men, Women and Chain Saws: Gender in the Modern Horror Film*. Princeton, NJ: Princeton University Press, 1992.

Conrich, Ian, and David Woods, eds. *The Cinema of John Carpenter: The Technique of Terror*. London and New York: Wallflower Press, 2004.

Dika, Vera. *Games of Terror: Halloween, Friday the 13th, and the Films of the Stalker Cycle*. Rutherford, NJ: Farleigh Dickinson University Press, 1990.

Leeder, Murray. *Halloween*. Leighton Buzzard: Auteur, 2015.

Neale, Steve. '*Halloween*: Suspense, Aggression and the Look'. In *Planks of Reason: Essays on the Horror Film*, revised ed., ed. Barry Keith Grant and Christopher Sharrett, pp. 356–369. Lanham, MD: Scarecrow Press, 2004.

The Hellstrom Chronicle
1971 – 90 mins
Walon Green

The Hellstrom Chronicle (1971) is a mockumentary that combines state-of-the-art microscopic and time-lapse photography with the conventions of both documentary filmmaking and the monster movie to exploit our common fear of insects (entomophobia), a fear invoked in numerous monster movies such as *Them!* (1954) and *Phase IV* (1974). An early entry in the 'revenge of nature' horror cycle (see *The Birds** [1963]), its use of actuality footage and appeal to the 'truth' of documentary anticipates the later cycle of found-footage horror films spurred by the success of *The Blair Witch Project** (1999). *The Hellstrom Chronicle* provided the inspiration for Frank Herbert's science fiction novel *Hellstrom's Hive* (1973), while director Walon Green, who previously had worked on nature documentaries for television, would go on to direct, appropriately, *The Secret Life of Plants* (1978), another documentary that uses similar cinematographic techniques to reveal the behaviour of flora.

DIRECTOR Walon Green
PRODUCER David S. Wolper
SCREENPLAY David Seltzer
CINEMATOGRAPHY Helmuth Barth, Walon Green, Vilis Lapenieks, Ken Middleham
EDITOR John Soh
MUSIC Lalo Schifrin
PRODUCTION COMPANY Wolper Picturess
MAIN CAST Lawrence Pressman

The film is narrated by a fictitious scientist, Dr. Nils Hellstrom (Pressman), an expert speaking to the camera with the frightened, hushed expression of someone who has stumbled onto an elaborate conspiracy that spells the doom of the human race. As Dr. Hellstrom talks, astonishing sequences of wasps, ants, termites, mayflies, and other insects are juxtaposed with occasional clips from monster movies like *Them!* The opening of the later *Empire of the Ants* (1977), about a group of potential home buyers on a real estate junket who are terrorised by giant ants mutated by radioactive waste, begins in a similar pseudo-documentary manner that might have been lifted from *The Hellstrom Chronicle*. As does the narrator of that film, Dr. Hellstrom predicts that insects ultimately will win the battle for survival on Earth because of their adaptability and collective efficiency, unhampered by human individualism, thus invoking that innate fear of the loss of identity, another fear exploited in numerous horror movies. As Hellstrom speaks of evolution's achievement of 'a fetus with the ability to dominate all', we are shown a time-lapse image of a hatching mosquito that makes it seem like the birth of a monster. Numerous big close-ups of insects make them look more frightening than anything produced by Bert I. Gordon, who specialised in movies about giant creatures (in addition to *Empire of the Ants*, he directed *Earth vs. the Spider* [1958], *Village of the Giants* [1965], and *Food of the Gods* [1976]).

Right from the start Hellstrom offers a monstrously melodramatic view of the threat that the insect poses to humanity, explaining that 'He dominates the earth and exploits his dominion well. With each new generation come new experiments in shape and function, transforming him into spectres as limitless as the imagination of the insane.' Accompanying this hyperbolic account is a montage of close-ups of different insects' faces, their expressionless and unblinking gazes blankly returning our own. Viewers are free to read into these impenetrable visages everything their most frightening fantasies can imagine, although Hellstrom happily helps us along by describing insect appetites as 'hideous' and a termite mound as 'a seething house of horrors'.

Another montage shows insects killing, dismembering, and consuming each other, reminiscent of the swarms of undead in *World War Z* (2013). The film also periodically amplifies the sounds of the insects, emphasising the power of their mandibles and making them sound as if they are ominously crushing the earth underfoot as they scuttle along. A shot of insects engaged in a life-and-death battle in the soil tellingly pans away to reveal their battlefield as part of a seemingly serene lawn in a park on which a pair of young lovers are obliviously reclining, suggesting, like the famous opening of David Lynch's *Blue Velvet* (1986), the ever-present dangers that lurk beneath nature's seemingly placid surface and of which we had been blithely unaware – until now.

Further Reading

Chapman, James, and Nicholas J. Cull. *Projecting Tomorrow: Science Fiction and Popular Cinema*. London and New York: I. B. Tauris, 2013.

Lennard, Dominic. *Brute Force: Animal Horror Movies*. Albany: SUNY Press, 2020.

Murray, Robin L., and Joseph K. Heumann. *Monstrous Nature: Environment and Horror on the Big Screen*. Lincoln: University of Nebraska Press, 2016.

Roscoe, Jane, and Craig Hight. *Faking It: Mock-Documentary and the Subversion of Factuality*. Manchester: Manchester University Press, 2001.

Henry: Portrait of a Serial Killer
1986 – 83 mins
John McNaughton

Loosely based on the life of notorious serial killer Henry Lee Lucas, once referred to as the most prolific in the annals of law enforcement, *Henry: Portrait of a Serial Killer* is a gritty, minimalist depiction of a murderer who, with some basic precautionary measures, operates with seeming impunity in an impersonal urban environment. There are several other feature films based on the life of Lucas, including *Confessions of a Serial Killer* (1985) and *Drifter* (2009), as well as two documentaries and several books. *Henry* itself generated a sequel, *Henry: Portrait of a Serial Killer, Part II* (1996), without the involvement of either McNaughton or Michael Rooker, who played Henry in the first film. (This was Rooker's first role in a feature film, the frightening opacity of his character aided by audiences' lack of familiarity with the actor.) The film was shot quickly

DIRECTOR John McNaughton
PRODUCER Lisa Dedmond, Steven A. Jones, John McNaughton
SCREENPLAY Richard Fire, John McNaughton
CINEMATOGRAPHY Charlie Lieberman
EDITOR Elena Maganini
MUSIC Ken Hale, Steven A. Jones, Robert McNaughton
PRODUCTION COMPANY Maljack Productions
MAIN CAST Michael Rooker, Tom Towles, Tracy Arnold

on 16mm on a small budget, its unadorned style and look chillingly reflecting the affectless and alienated personalities of Henry and his friend from prison, Otis (Towles), with whom he is living temporarily in Chicago and who joins him in some of his killings before becoming a victim himself.

Henry Lee Lucas confessed to hundreds of murders, many of which were subsequently discredited, although the evidence indicates that he did kill at least eleven people. McNaughton's film is careful not to claim factual accuracy: it opens with the black-and-white disclaimer that it is 'a fictional dramatisation of certain events. Henry is not intended to be an accurate portrayal of a true story. The film is based partly on confessions of a person named Henry.' The few details we are given about Henry's past, which Henry tells to Otis' sister, Becky (Arnold), are consistent with what is known of Lucas' early life – his mother, a prostitute, forced him to watch her work and to cross-dress – but, then again, these could be more of the lies he tells because this account differs slightly from what he tells Otis (Towles).

Apart from this scene, though, the film refrains from offering any explanation for Henry's murderous motivations, although he is clearly uncomfortable with Becky's amorous advances. At the beginning of the film, we are shown several examples, mostly women, of Henry's grisly work before meeting up with Otis. The first shot is a close-up of a woman's peaceful face, the sun shining benevolently upon it as birds are chirping – but then slowly the camera reverse zooms until we realise that this woman is dead and lying in a field somewhere. A chillingly literal *nature morte*, its visual shift from the apparently blissful to the abhorrently brutal perhaps mirrors Henry's psychopathology while also prodding the viewer to reflect upon the film's own representation of violence.

More understandable is Otis' involvement. Upon first discovering Henry's murderous activities when he kills the two prostitutes they pick up, he seems upset, but quickly taps into his own repressed anger and rising bloodlust. A white man enraged by his own feeling of disempowerment, in frustration he shouts, 'I'd like to kill somebody', and Henry becomes the means for him to act out his rage, telling Otis to 'open his eyes' to the realities of the world in which 'it's either you or them'. Once he randomly shoots a good Samaritan who stops to help them on the side of the road, Otis confesses to 'feeling better'. In the film's most chilling sequence, Henry and Otis arbitrarily break into a family home and kill the three people they find there – stabbing the man, choking and violating the woman, snapping the neck of the teenage son – while videotaping their actions, which are choreographed for the camera. Like them, we see the event as video within the film, which Otis watches repeatedly, replaying the 'good parts', even slowing it down with frame advance. Choosing their victims, they prowl the city in Henry's car (driving to places like Whacker Drive!) and bring their murderous violence from the inner city to the suburbs, anticipating the later cycle of home invasion films (see, for example, *Funny Games US** [2007] and *The Purge** [2013]).

Further Reading:

Freeland, Cynthia A. 'The Slasher's Blood Lust'. In *Dark Thoughts: Philosophical Reflections on Cinematic Horror*, ed. Steven J. Schneider and Daniel Shaw, pp. 198–211. Lanham, MD: Scarecrow Press, 2003.

Hallam, Lindsay Anne. *Screening the Marquis de Sade: Pleasure, Pain and the Transgressive Body in Film*. Jefferson, NC and London: McFarland, 2012.

Kimber, Shaun. *Henry: Portrait of a Serial Killer*. Basingstoke, UK and New York: Palgrave Macmillan, 2011.

Sconce, Jeffrey. 'Spectacles of Death: Identification, Reflexivity, and Contemporary Horror'. In *Film Theory Goes to the Movies*, ed. Jim Collins, Hilary Radner, and Ava Preacher Collins, pp. 103–119. New York and London: Routledge, 1993.

Towlson, John. *Subversive Horror Cinema: Countercultural Messages of Films from Frankenstein to the Present*. Jefferson, NC: McFarland, 2014.

The Hills Have Eyes
1977 – 90 mins
Wes Craven

The Hills Have Eyes was the second horror film for Wes Craven (*A Nightmare on Elm Street* [1984], *Scream** [1996]), made after *The Last House on the Left** (1972), and it continued his focus on the nuclear family as the site of horror. It was one of several horror films in the 1970s, such as *The Texas Chainsaw Massacre** (1974), that explored the monstrous as repression within the family rather than merely an external threat to it, and to imagine that monstrousness in terms of cannibalism. The elegantly simple plot, based in part on the legend of Sawney Bean (as was, in part, *Ravenous** [1999]), follows the Carter family, vacationers who become stranded in the desert and set upon by a primal clan of deformed cannibals who live in the hills. There was a sequel, *The Hills Have Eyes Part II* (1985), also written and directed by Craven, and a remake directed by Alexandre Aja in 2006 and a sequel to it the following year, both also produced by Craven.

The plot follows the Carter family – former police officer Bob (Grieve), his wife Ethel (Vincent), their teenage children Bobby (Houston) and Brenda (Lanier), older daughter Lynne (Wallace), and her husband Doug (Speer) and baby daughter Katie – who are on a road trip vacation from Ohio to Los Angeles. After stopping at a gas station in the Mohave Desert, they drive onto a side road, despite the warnings from Fred (Steadman), the proprietor, to stay on the main highway, where they accidentally break one of their car's axles. As we find out from Fred when Bob walks back to the gas station for help, years ago he had a mutant murderous son named Jupiter (Whitworth) that he left to die in the desert after bashing his head with a tire iron, but Jupiter survived and with an insane prostitute sired three sons, Mars (Gordon), Pluto (Berryman), and Mercury (King), and a daughter, Ruby (Blythe). The killer clan survive in the desert by cannibalizing travelers passing through (they refer with anticipation to Baby Katie as 'tenderloin').

As with the band of psychotic killers in *The Last House on the Left*, the inbred cannibals may be seen as a monstrous version of the seemingly normal family. The car and trailer in which the Carters are travelling serve a similar function to the camper van in *Race with the Devil** (1975), released two years earlier; but whereas in that film the van represents the middle-class generally, in *The Hills Have Eyes* it is primarily an expression of the repressed tensions and denials lurking within the family unit specifically. Both families in *The Hills Have Eyes* are led by a gruff patriarch, with Big Bob Carter (who, as a retired police officer, carries the weight of institutional authority) barking at his family like their two trained attack dogs Beauty and Beast snarl at the unseen killers in the hills.

Some of the Carters survive and manage to outwit and defeat the cannibal clan, but again, as in *Last House*, Craven leaves no room for the comfort of catharsis. Just as Mr. Collingwood's revenge climaxes with his chainsaw mauling of Krug in the earlier film, so in *The Hills Have Eyes* Doug repeatedly stabs Mars's corpse even after he has killed him, absorbed by retributive violence. After this, there is no denouement, and the film fades to red after a shot of Ruby crying. Long before the Carters made that fateful turnoff in the desert, they

DIRECTOR Wes Craven
PRODUCER Peter Locke
SCREENPLAY Wes Craven
CINEMATOGRAPHY
Eric Saarinen
EDITOR Wes Craven
MUSIC Don Peake
PRODUCTION COMPANY
Blood Relations Company,
Vanguard
MAIN CAST Susan Lanier,
Robert Houston, Martin Speer,
Dee Wallace, Russ Grieve,
John Steadman, Michael
Berryman, Virginia Vincent,
Martin Speer, John Steadman,
James Whitworth,
Lance Gordon, Michael
Berryman, Arthur King,
Janus Blythe

were headed, as the song tells us several times in *Last House*, down that 'road to nowhere'.

Further Reading

Muir, John Kenneth. *Wes Craven: The Art of Horror*. Jefferson, NC: McFarland, 1998.

Phillips, Kendall R. *Dark Directions: Romero, Craven, Carpenter, and the Modern Horror Film*. Carbondale: Southern Illinois University Press, 2012.

Robb, Brian J. *Screams & Nightmares: The Films of Wes Craven*. Woodstock, NY: Overlook Press, 1998.

Rodowick, D. N. 'The Enemy Within: The Economy of Violence in *The Hills Have Eyes*'. In *Planks of Reason: Essays on the Horror Film*, revised ed., ed. Barry Keith Grant and Christopher Sharrett, pp. 346–355. Lanham, MD: Scarecrow Press, 2004.

Williams, Tony. *Hearths of Darkness: The Family in the American Horror Film*, revised ed. Jackson: University Press of Mississippi, 2014.

Hostel
2005 – 94 mins
Eli Roth

Written and directed by Eli Roth (*Cabin Fever* [2003]), *Hostel*, along with *Saw** (2004), was one of the formative films of the post-9/11 horror cycle attacked as 'torture porn' for their graphic depiction of bodily violation and often literal torture. Along with such other horror films as *Touristas* (2006) and *The Ruins* (2008), *Hostel* expresses fear at the post-9–11 erosion of the sense of American exceptionalism and the idea that Americans were no longer welcome, much less privileged, anywhere in the world. Playing on the ominous homonym of the less welcoming 'hostile', *Hostel* successfully exploits Americans' typical ignorance of the world, and which Roth repeats with South America in *The Green Inferno* (2013). The film generated two sequels, *Hostel: Part II* (2007), also written and directed by Roth, and *Hostel: Part III* (2011), which relocates the setting of the Elite Hunting Club to the US and with which Roth was not involved.

The plot centres on university students Paxton (Hernandez) and Josh (Richardson), who are backpacking across Europe along with a fellow party animal from Iceland, Óli (Guðjónsson), whom they've met along the way. The trio regard Europe as one big party for their own hedonistic desires. When they get thrown out of a nightclub for causing a disturbance, they loudly protest that they are Americans and therefore have rights – even as a queue of patrons waiting to enter stand patiently behind them. Much uglier Americans than David and Jack in *An American Werewolf in London** (1981), they are lured to Slovakia by a fellow they meet in Amsterdam, Alexei (Bukovy), who tells them their money will buy them all their sexual fantasies. Once there, they become prey of the Elite Hunting Club, a secret organization for wealthy sadists (Japanese filmmaker Takashi Miike is one of them), to live out their most sadistic fantasies on kidnapped tourists, Americans especially prized.

Hostel also offers a topical critique of toxic masculinity. The torture rooms of the Club are monstrous expressions of the rooms in the sex club they visit in Amsterdam, their treatment as torture victims a horrifying variation of their regard for women as commodities to be bought for their pleasure. Once at the hostel, they are seduced by two beautiful women, Natalya (Nedeljáková) and Svetlana (Kaderabkova), like the sirens of Greek myth. *Hostel II* continues the exploration of toxic masculinity and turns the story into an explicit feminist parable complete with castration performed by the heroine in the climax.

Hostel's sense of justice seems as cruel as its scenes of torture. In a twist of fate, it is Paxton, the less admirable character, who by chance survives because he accidentally locks himself into a storage closet after being drugged by the two girls, while Josh, the more sensitive of the two, is brutally mutilated before being killed in the Club. (Roth pulls a similar reversal in *Hostel II*, in which the macho Todd loses his nerve and refuses to kill his victim in the torture room while the seemingly nicer Stuart reveals his repressed violent anger toward women.) Still, the ending seems to lapse into the conventional as Paxton manages to escape his own torture and get out of town, on the way dispatching Natalya, Svetlana, and Alexei. And then, on the train, he

DIRECTOR Eli Roth
PRODUCER Chris Briggs, Mike Fleiss, Eli Roth
SCREENPLAY Eli Roth
CINEMATOGRAPHY Milan Chadima
EDITOR George Folsey, Jr.
MUSIC Nathan Barr
PRODUCTION COMPANY Next Entertainment, Raw Nerve
MAIN CAST Jay Hernandez, Derek Richardson, Eyþór Guðjónsson, Barbara Nedeljáková, Jana Kaderabkova, Jan Vlasák, Jennifer Lim, Lubomir Bukovy, Rick Hoffman

happens to come across the Dutch businessman (Vlasák), torturer of Josh, and kill him too, the individual American hero thus triumphing and meting out justice once again.

Further Reading:

Greven, David. *Ghost Faces: Hollywood and Post-Millennial Masculinity*. Albany: State University of New York Press, 2016.

Kerner, Aaron Michael. *Torture Porn in the Wake of 9/11: Horror, Exploitation and the Cinema of Sensation*. New Brunswick, NJ and London: Rutgers University Press, 2015.

Morris, Jeremy. 'The Justification of Torture-Horror: Retribution and Sadism in *Saw*, *Hostel*, and *The Devil's Rejects*'. In *The Philosophy of Horror*, ed. Thomas Richard Fahey, pp. 42–56. Lexington: University Press of Kentucky, 2010.

Neroni, Hilary. *The Subject of Torture: Psychoanalysis and Biopolitics in Television and Film*. New York: Columbia University Press, 2015.

Wester, Maisha. 'Torture Porn and Uneasy Feminisms: Rethinking (Wo)men in Eli Roth's *Hostel* Films'. In *The Dread of Difference: Gender in the Horror Film*, 2nd edn, ed. Barry Keith Grant, pp. 305–326. Austin: University of Texas Press, 2015.

House of Wax
1953 – 88 min
André De Toth

Sparked by the success of Arch Oboler's *Bwana Devil* (1952), a number of horror and science fiction films were made in 3D in the 1950s, including *It Came from Outer Space* (1953), *Creature from the Black Lagoon** (1954) and its sequel, *Revenge of the Creature* (1955), and *House of Wax*, a 3D remake of Michael Curtiz's *Mystery of the Wax Museum* (1933) with Lionel Atwill, itself based on Charles S. Belden's three-act play, *The Wax Works*. *House of Wax* exploits the 3D format relatively sparingly – most notably, in the scene where a pitchman whacks three paddleballs at the camera simultaneously – perhaps because director De Toth, responsible mostly for routine Westerns, had lost an eye as a youth and so lacked stereoscopic vision. Of greater interest is the film's use of the wax museum setting as a self-reflexive metaphor of horror's affective potential. A similar premise was later employed by Roger Corman in *A Bucket of Blood* (1959) and Herschell Gordon Lewis in *Colour Me Blood Red* (1965), but to different ends, as *House of Wax* is more consciously concerned with the aesthetics of exploitation.

DIRECTOR André De Toth
PRODUCER Bryan Foy
SCREENPLAY Crane Wilbur
CINEMATOGRAPHY Bert Glennon, J. Peverell Marley
EDITOR Rudi Fehr
MUSIC David Buttolph
PRODUCTION COMPANY Warner Bros
MAIN CAST Vincent Price, Frank Lovejoy, Phyllis Kirk, Carolyn Jones, Roy Roberts

Professor Henry Jarrod (Price) is a talented wax figure sculptor in early 1900s New York City who specialises in historical dioramas. A soft-spoken artist absorbed in his work (he refers to his figures as his 'people' and speaks to them), he comes into conflict with his partner, Matthew Burke (Roberts), who argues that their wax museum would be more successful if it emphasised scenes of violence and morbid sensationalism. Burke torches the museum for the insurance money, and Jarrod, seemingly killed in the fire, returns, disfigured and in a wheelchair, with a new attraction, the House of Wax's Chamber of Horrors, giving customers (and, to some extent, film spectators as well) the gruesome content they apparently prefer, with such scenes as the depiction of the deaths of Marat and Anne Boleyn. Jarrod professes an absolute fidelity to realism, and, as we discover, he descended into madness when his 'people' went up in flames, now as twisted mentally as his alter ego is physically, a killer who brings his figures to life by using the bodies of his victims as his raw material. Price's portrayal of Jarrod was important in shifting the actor toward horror roles, particularly those tragic characters in some of the Corman films who have succumbed to evil unwittingly, bringing a pathos to the genre rivalled only by Lon Chaney, Jr.

Relocating the time of the earlier film from the 1930s, when it was made, to the turn of the Twentieth century – the dawn of cinema – contextualises the theme more broadly in terms of a rapidly changing culture that will soon embrace the sensations of the Jazz Age and the horrors of two world wars. The name of Jarrod's theater is the same as the name of the film, and it functions like a proto-cinema of attractions, where the sight of horrible violence recreated in three dimensions is enough to make the genteel young ladies who thrill at them swoon. They come to the House of Wax for the same reasons viewers of *House of Wax* have come to the cinema in which it is being shown: posters for the film proclaimed that its 'half man, half monster who stalks a panic swept city . . . comes off the screen right at you!' At one point the paddle ball huckster breaks the fourth wall and addresses the audience directly ('there's someone with a bag of popcorn') several years before William Castle proffered his punishment poll in *Mr. Sardonicus* (1961).

In Jarrod's monstrous madness he collapses the difference between the thing and its representation – the very spectatorial dynamic that allows for the generation of horror in viewers in the first place. Audiences are put in the same situation as Jarrod when Sue Allen (Kirk), whom Jarrod wants for his Marie Antoinette, is pursued through the House by his mute assistant, Igor (yes, that's right), played by a stolid Charles Bronson. Bronson/Igor stands by a wax figure of William Kemmler, the first man to be legally executed by electric chair (1890), with a head made in his own likeness: spectators have to wonder which is the 'real' Igor even as we realise the question is more complicated than it at first seems. Still, this perceptual problem doesn't hinder the frisson when, shortly thereafter, the face of Jarrod/Price crumbles away as it is struck by Sue to reveal the hideously burned and distorted face underneath.

Further Reading:

Higham, George. *Wax Museum Movies: A Critical Filmography*. Jefferson, NC: McFarland, 2020.

Heffernan, Kevin J. *Ghouls, Gimmicks, and Gold: Horror Films and the American Movie Business, 1953–1968*. Durham and London: Duke University Press, 2004.

Jacobs, Steven, Susan Felleman, Vito Adriaensens, and Lisa Colpaert. *Screening Statues: Sculpture and Cinema*. Edinburgh: Edinburgh University Press, 2017.

Slide, Anthony. *De Toth on De Toth: Putting the Drama in Front of the Camera*. London: Faber and Faber, 1997.

Jones, Nick. *Spaces Mapped and Monstrous: Digital 3D Cinema and Visual Culture*. New York: Columbia University Press, 2020.

The Hunger
UK/US, 1983 – 99 mins
Tony Scott

The first film directed by Tony Scott, the younger brother of director Ridley Scott (*Alien* [1979], *Blade Runner* [1982]), *The Hunger* displays slick and sumptuous production values prefiguring Scott's string of commercial hits inaugurated with *Top Gun* (1986). Although not very successful critically or commercially at the time of its release, *The Hunger* is notable as a postmodern vampire film with stylish visuals and for shifting the vampire story away from its traditional heterosexual and masculinist perspective, as in *Dracula** (1931). *The Hunger* distances itself from the traditional vampire story from the outset, the first scene in the nightclub where The Bauhaus sing 'Bela Lugosi's Dead' ('Undead, undead, undead') in reference to the actor most famous for his portrayal of Bram Stoker's vampire.

The Hunger draws on the tradition of lesbian vampire films (preceded by Joseph Sheridan Le Fanu's novella *Camilla* [1875]) such as *Blood and Roses* (1960), *The Vampire Lovers* (1970) and *Vampyros Lesbos* (1971), although it is more accurate to describe the film's representation of vampiric desire as bisexual. Sarah Roberts (Sarandon), a gerontologist who is researching the causes of ageing in primates, already has a boyfriend, Tom Haver (de Young), when she is drawn to Miriam Blaylock (Deneuve, perfectly cast as the supernaturally obscure object of desire), the vampire who is also supposedly a married woman, when the two have a steamy sexual encounter. It is ambiguous to what extent their mutual attraction is genuine desire or merely the result of Miriam exerting her supernatural influence on Sarah. Certainly, the unyielding logic of 'the hunger', as William Burroughs might put it (see *The Addiction** [1995]), requires that Miriam must come to regard Tom as prey rather than paramour even as she tries to save him.

The inside of Miriam's townhouse is suffused with a soft colour palette shot in soft focus and diffusion filters that, together with the *objects d'art* of classical Western culture and the diaphanous muslin that billows gently throughout, present a world of dreamy eroticism. Miriam and Sarah's sexual encounter looks like soft-core porn, with sensuous shots of female limbs and artfully framed nipples – but no full-frontal nudity. The townhouse is located in the middle of Manhattan, a sensual lure surprisingly close to the beaten path. Miriam represents the monstrous threat of polygamous if not polymorphous perversity. 'I love them all', she protests in the climax, when her past lovers surround her.

Overall, the film's style is consistent with the approach of the contemporary French filmmakers dubbed 'le cinéma du look' (Jean-Jacques Beineix, Leos Carax, Luc Besson) and the coalescing tradition of neo-noir (*Body Heat* was released in 1981; *Blood Simple*, which also features Dan Hedaya, who plays police Lt. Allegrezza in *The Hunger*, in 1984). *The Hunger's* minimal plot is handled elliptically, to some extent the result of studio interference in post-production but also indicative of the emphasis on slick production values over narrative clarity. We see, for example, quick insert shots of Miriam feeding off slaves in ancient Egypt, but we are never explicitly told if she is even older or how she came to be a vampire. And what causes the rumbling in

DIRECTOR Tony Scott
PRODUCER Richard A. Shepherd
SCREENPLAY Ivan Davis, Michael Thomas
CINEMATOGRAPHY Stephen Goldblatt
EDITOR Pamela Power, Peter Honess
MUSIC Howard Blake, Denny Jaeger, Michel Rubini
PRODUCTION COMPANY Richard Shepherd Company, Metro-Goldwyn-Mayer
MAIN CAST Catherine Deneuve, Susan Sarandon, David Bowie, Cliff de Young, Dan Hedaya, Beth Ehlers

the townhouse that releases Miriam's past lovers? Most problematic is the final shots, inserted at the insistence of the studio, showing a somehow resurrected Sarah in Italy with a new lover while Miriam, trapped in a coffin, utters a muffled cry, an ending that seems to contradict all that had come before.

Further Reading:

Ahmed, Aalya, and Murray Leeder. '"You Said Forever": Postmodern Temporality in Tony Scott's *The Hunger*'. In *Dracula's Daughters: The Female Vampire on Film*, ed. Douglas Brode and Leah Deyneka, pp. 253–266. Lanham, MD: Scarecrow Press, 2014.

Creed, Barbara. *The Monstrous-Feminine: Film, Feminism, Psychoanalysis*. London and New York: Routledge, 1993.

Ward, James J. '"You Can Be Young Forever": The Dread of Aging in Tony Scott's Art-Horror Film *The Hunger*'. In *Elder Horror: Essays on Film's Frightening Images of Aging*, ed. Cythia J. Miller and A. Bowdoin Van Riper, pp. 165–178. Jefferson City, NC: McFarland, 2019.

Ní Fhlainn, Sorcha. *Postmodern Vampires: Film, Fiction, and Popular Culture*. London and New York: Palgrave Macmillan, 2019.

I Walked with a Zombie
1943 – 69 mins
Jacques Tourneur

I Walked with a Zombie was the second of nine low-budget horror films made by Val Lewton's production unit at RKO, directed, as was the first film in the series, *Cat People** (1942), and the later *The Leopard Man* (1943, by Jacques Tourneur. (Four other films in the series – *The Seventh Victim* [1943], *The Ghost Ship* [1943], *Isle of the Dead* [1945], and *Bedlam* [1946] – were directed by Mark Robson, who edited *Zombie*.) The film's sensational title, as with the others in the series, was provided by the studio – in this case, from a magazine article by Inez Wallace recounting drugged workers on a Haiti plantation. As in *Cat People*, Tourneur makes fine use of expressionist shadows in a dreamlike evocation of repressed desire while exploiting the zombie vogue that began a decade earlier with *White Zombie** (1932).

DIRECTOR Jacques Tourneur
PRODUCER Val Lewton
SCREENPLAY Curt Siodmak, Ardel Wray
CINEMATOGRAPHY J. Roy Hunt
EDITOR Mark Robson
MUSIC Roy Webb
PRODUCTION COMPANY RKO
MAIN CAST Francis Dee, Tom Conway, James Ellison, Edith Barrett, James Bell, Christine Gordon, Teresa Harris, Sir Lancelot, Darby Jones

The screenplay – written in part by Curt Siodmak, who also wrote some of the Universal horror films including *The Wolf Man** (1941) (his brother Robert directed *Son of Dracula* [1943] for Universal, as well as several canonical film noirs) – is very loosely based on the narrative of Charlotte Brontë's *Jane Eyre*, both featuring the first-person narration of a female protagonist who falls in love with her employer. In voiceover, the entire narrative a flashback (?), Betsy Connell (Dee) tells the story of how she once had 'walked with a zombie'. A Canadian nurse, Betsy accepts a position caring for the wife (Gordon) of a sugar plantation owner, Paul Holland (Conway), on the Caribbean island of Saint Sebastian. According to the local doctor (Bell), the woman, Jessica, who seems in a trance, suffers from an injury of the spinal cord, but eventually we learn that she may in fact be a zombie. Certainly, Paul's mother (Barrett) believes that she was responsible for casting the voodoo spell on Jessica, who doesn't bleed and somehow heeds the calls by the voodoo priest from afar. The climax leaves the truth ambiguous, as Jessica's death may be the result of the voodoo spell or because Paul's half-brother Wesley (Ellison) has killed her in order to free her from her living death.

Throughout the film Tourneur and cinematographer J. Roy Hunt create a menacing atmosphere in a strange place that Paul describes as unhealthy. Shadows lurk everywhere, with enough slatted window patterns for a von Sternberg film, often suggesting not only the unknown and mysterious but also the repression of the proper Betsy's now-awakened illicit desire (she tells Paul she hasn't given much thought to her own 'prettiness'). If the film seems to offer any progressive, postcolonial intent in its depiction of the islanders' world, it nonetheless exoticises that world from the perspective of the white protagonist.

The film's set-piece is the eponymous walk of the title, when Betsy, eager to please Paul by attempting to help cure Jessica, takes her without permission to the houmfort, the gathering place of the local voodoo worshippers, through the cane fields at night. Recalling the nighttime walk through the park in *Cat People*, the camera tracks along with them through the stalks of sugarcane, the unreality of the studio set only adding to our sense of dread of what might lie ahead, out of frame. Tourneur adds to the eerie ambience through sound, as he also does in *Cat People*: as the two women walk, there is the sudden sound of a hooting owl, which turns out to be a dead tree branch with a birdlike shape and the wind whistling through a gourd hanging nearby. Guided by a small circle of illumination from Jessica's flashlight, Betsy comes across the foot of the immobile Carrefour (Jones), and although we are warned about the zombie guard by the maid (Harris), the first sight of him standing motionless in the field, the large whites of his unblinking eyes staring straight ahead, is still unnerving.

Further Reading:

Bowman, Chris. 'Heidegger, the Uncanny, and Jacques Tourneur's Horror Films'. In *Dark Thoughts: Philosophic Reflections on Cinematic Horror*, ed. Steven Jay Schneider and Daniel Shaw, pp. 65–83. Lanham, MD: Scarecrow Press, 2003.

Fujiwara, Chris. *Jacques Tourneur: The Cinema of Nightfall*. Baltimore and London: Johns Hopkins University Press, 1998.

Telotte, J. P. *Dreams of Darkness: Fantasy and the Films of Val Lewton*. Urbana: University of Illinois Press, 1985.

Wood, Robin. *Robin Wood on the Horror Film: Collected Essays and Reviews*, ed. Barry Keith Grant. Detroit: Wayne State University Press, 2018.

I Was a Teenage Werewolf
1957 – 76 mins
Gene Fowler, Jr.

I Was a Teenage Werewolf was the first of four teenage monster movies produced in a two-year period by American International Pictures (AIP), a distribution and production company founded just a few years earlier that specialised in B movies – teen pics, exploitation films, and horror and science fiction movies such as *The She-Creature* (1956), *Terror from the Year 5000* (1958), and *Attack of the Puppet People* (1958) – many of them made for the drive-in market. *I Was a Teenage Frankenstein* (1957) was released just a few months after *Werewolf* and was followed in turn by *Blood of Dracula* (1957) and *How to Make a Monster* (1958). All four films share not only some common actors, dialogue, and sets, but also a common theme of teenagers being victimised and exploited by corrupt adults. But what *Teenage Werewolf*, setting off the cycle, did so

DIRECTOR Gene Fowler, Jr.
PRODUCER Herman Cohen
SCREENPLAY Herman Cohen, Aben Kandel
CINEMATOGRAPHY Joseph LaShelle
EDITOR George Gittens
MUSIC Paul Dunlap
PRODUCTION COMPANY American International Pictures
MAIN CAST Michael Landon, Yvonne Lime, Whit Bissell, Malcolm Atterbury, Barney Phillips, Robert Griffin, Guy Williams, Vladimir Sokolov, Tony Marshall, Louise Lewis

well was to combine the angst of adolescence with the werewolf story, thus providing strong appeal for the baby-boomer generation that had become a significant movie-going demographic at the time. Co-written and produced by B-film producer Herman Cohen, who also produced the other three, it was therefore no surprise that *I Was a Teenage Werewolf* became one of the most successful films ever released by AIP.

In the 1950s, when the concept of the teenager as a transitional period between childhood and adulthood became culturally institutionalised, Tony Rivers (Landon) is a troubled teenager at Rockdale High School with a reputation for fighting and flying off the handle. Alternately courteous and cruel, his girlfriend (Lime) always seems to be walking on eggshells when they are together, afraid his antagonism might explode into violence at any moment. There is much talk between Tony, who insists he wants to do things his own way, and adult authority figures – his father (Atterbury), the school principal (Lewis), the local police detective (Phillips), who has broken up several fights involving the boy – about compromise and playing nicely with others, often couched euphemistically as a matter of 'adjusting'. Director Fowler (*I Married a Monster from Outer Space* [1958]) has little feel for actual teenage life – the scenes at their hangout, the 'haunted house', are painfully stilted – but the refocus of the werewolf myth on teenage rather than adult sexuality resonated with youth audiences. Tony is a monstrous version of the average male teenager's tumultuous feelings, his physical transformation a horrifying exaggeration of his newly manifesting secondary sexual characteristics.

Tony eventually accedes to the chorus of calls from this unofficial adjustment bureau of adults for him to visit the local psychologist, Dr. Alfred Brandon (Bissell), whose hypnotherapy could be just the thing to help him 'adjust'. However, Dr. Brandon instantly assesses Tony as the perfect patient for his regression experiment, babbling on about saving humankind by first destroying it and returning to zero. Using a combination of drugs and hypnosis, he helps an unawares Tony to return to man's primitive state, which he refers to as Tony's true self. Later, just after acting appropriately obsequious with the principal, Tony walks by the school gymnasium where a female student in tights is practicing alone on the parallel bars. Now aroused, he transforms and kills her when a school bell rings near his head. His identity known, he flees into the woods, the pursuing townspeople with their flickering torches a contemporary version of the angry villagers in the classic Universal Frankenstein movies.

Unfortunately, the transformation scenes are relatively poor, consisting of a couple of quick out-of-focus superimpositions in which Tony's face changes rather than transforms. The equally unconvincing makeup (although the similarity between Landon's hairstyle and his werewolf mane is noteworthy) is abetted somewhat in the climax, when in werewolf form Tony turns on and kills Dr. Brandon, foamy white spittle spewing from his mouth. Certainly, horror films such as *I Was a Teenage Werewolf* function as adolescent rites of passage and socialization, and in the end, with Tony's demise, the film endorses the status quo as Detective Donovan utters the standard moral opinion that 'It's not for man to interfere in the ways of God'.

Further Reading:

Doherty, Thomas. *Teenagers and Teenpics: The Juvenilization of American Movies in the 1950s*. Boston: Unwyn Hyman, 1988.

Heffernan, Kevin J. *Ghouls, Gimmicks, and Gold: Horror Films and the American Movie Business, 1953–1968*. Durham and London: Duke University Press, 2004.

Hendershot, Cyndy. *I Was a Cold War Monster; Horror Film, Eroticism and the Cold War Imagination*. Bowling Green, OH: Popular Press, 2001.

Hogan, David J. *Dark Romance: Sexuality in the Horror Film*. Jefferson, NC: McFarland, 1986.

Skal, David J. *The Monster Show: A Cultural History of Horror*. New York and London: Penguin, 1993.

In the Mouth of Madness
1994 – 95 mins
John Carpenter

The third film of John Carpenter's 'Apocalypse Trilogy', preceded by *The Thing* (1982) and *Prince of Darkness* (1987), *In the Mouth of Madness* challenges the very nature of reality itself. A box-office failure upon its release, it combines a story evoking the cosmic horror of H. P. Lovecraft (the film's title invokes Lovecraft's novella *At the Mountains of Madness* [1936], and the titles of writer Sutter Cane's books allude to other Lovecraft titles) with a metafictional narrative about the power of fiction. It succeeds better than many of the actual adaptations of Lovecraft's fiction – *The Dunwich Horror* (1970) and *Re-Animator* (1985), for example – in capturing the lurking dread in his work that what we think of as reality is but a sham ready to be torn away by the revelation of monsters and beings infinitely old and beyond our comprehension. (See also *Colour out of Space** [2019]). Like Poe's poem, the film asks, 'Is *all* that we see or seem/ But a dream within a dream?'

The plot follows John Trent (Neill), an insurance investigator, who has been hired by a publisher (Heston) to investigate the disappearance of his popular horror writer, Sutter Cane (Prochnow), who has disappeared. Trent tells his fantastic story is flashback to a psychiatrist (Warner) in his padded cell ('Oh no, not the Carpenters too' he complains about the music piped into the ward), where he has been committed as insane (another nod to Lovecraft's work). Trent believes that the disappearance of Cane, who combines aspects of Stephen King's popularity with Lovecraft's sensibility, has been staged (which it is!) as a publicity stunt to promote his new novel, *In the Mouth of Madness*.

The film pits Trent's relentless rationality against the mounting and inexplicable horrors he discovers as he travels to the supposedly fictional town of Hobb's End, New Hampshire (Cane's version of King's Castle Rock) to investigate. To get to the town, Trent crosses over a covered bridge that serves as a Yankee equivalent of the Borgo Pass as he seems to enter another plane of existence on the other side. Soon Trent discovers that Cane's horror stories are in fact real, that a race of 'old ones' have been using his work as a conduit to journey back to our world, bringing utter destruction. As he learns that he himself is a fictional character written by Cane, big close-ups of Sam Neill's face graphically capture Trent's sense of the world closing in on him and reality slipping away

Just as the Church is the very source of evil in *Prince of Darkness*, so here it is the epicentre of an evil 'older than mankind and wilder than the known universe'. Its walls drip with an unctuous ooze, the first manifestation of the 'old ones' that recalls the evil slime of that earlier film. But these monsters are enabled by the mass media, its pervasive power manufacturing consent, a theme that also informs Carpenter's *The Fog* (1980) and *They Live* (1988). *In the Mouth of Madness* begins with a montage of endless copies of bestselling paperbacks of Cane's latest horror novel being printed and packaged, recalling the beginning of *Christine* (1983), which shows the demonic car being made on the assembly line. Boasting that he has sold a billion copies of his books and that they have been translated into eighteen languages, Cane explains that

DIRECTOR John Carpenter
PRODUCER Michael De Luca
SCREENPLAY Michael De Luca
CINEMATOGRAPHY
Gary B. Kibbe
EDITOR Edward A. Warschilka
MUSIC John Carpenter,
Jim Lang
PRODUCTION COMPANY
New Line Cinema
MAIN CAST Sam Neill,
Julie Carmen, Jürgen Prochnow,
David Warner, Bernie Casey,
Peter Jason, Charlton Heston

it is his readers' suspension of disbelief in his prose that gives the ancient ones their power. Trent explicitly criticises Cane's novels for all having the same plot involving nameless creatures, people going mad, and eternal monsters – a good description of both Lovecraft's work and the story of *In the Mouth of Madness* itself. We are in the mouth of madness, swallowing ourselves in the mass media, amusing ourselves to death. The television announcer poses the key question: Is Cane 'a harmless pop phenomenon or a deadly mad prophet of the printed page'?

Further Reading

Blyth, Michael. *In the Mouth of Madness*. Leighton Buzzard: Auteur, 2018.

Conrich, Ian, and David Woods, eds. *The Cinema of John Carpenter: The Technique of Terror*. London: Wallflower Press, 2004.

Phillips, Kendall R. *Dark Directions: Romero, Craven, Carpenter, and the Modern Horror Film*. Carbondale: Southern Illinois University Press, 2012.

Smith, Don G. *H. P. Lovecraft in Popular Culture: The Works and Their Adaptations in Film, Television, Comics, Music and Games*. Jefferson, NC: McFarland, 2006.

Interview with the Vampire: The Vampire Chronicles
1994 – 123 mins
Neil Jordan

With high-concept casting, a screenplay written by cult novelist Anne Rice based on her 1976 debut novel, and directed by Neil Jordan as the follow-up to his highly successful *The Crying Game* (1992), *Interview with the Vampire* is a big-budget revisionist take on the vampire movie that, like *The Addiction** (1995), is concerned with the moral and metaphysical implications of vampirism but in this case without the baggage of canonical philosophy. An Irish filmmaker and writer who frequently works in the gothic mode (he returned to the vampire film with *Byzantium* [2012]), and who also often explores questions of sex and gender and guilt (see, for example, *The Company of Wolves* [1984]) and *The Crying Game*), Jordan was a logical choice to direct the author's adaptation. The casting of Cruise as Lestat was controversial, with the author herself initially quite critical, although after the film's release she expressed satisfaction with his performance. (*Queen of the*

DIRECTOR Neil Jordan
PRODUCER David Geffen, Stephen Woolley, Redmond Morris
SCREENPLAY Anne Rice
CINEMATOGRAPHY Philippe Rousselot
EDITOR Mike Audsley, Joke Van Wijk
MUSIC Elliot Goldenthal
PRODUCTION COMPANY Geffen Pictures
MAIN CAST Tom Cruise, Brad Pitt, Christian Slater, Thandi Newton, Kirsten Dunst, Antonio Bandares, Stephen Rea

Damned, based on the third book in Rice's *Vampire Chronicles* trilogy, which also combined elements of the second volume, *The Vampire Lestat*, was released in 1992 but without the involvement of either Jordan, Rice, or any of *Interview*'s principal actors.)

The narrative is framed by an interview in contemporary San Francisco with Louis de Pointe du Lac (Pitt), a vampire who recounts to reporter Daniel Molloy (Slater) his transformation by Lestat de Lioncourt in 1791 and their two centuries together. The frame device recalls that of *Little Big Man* (1970) – except that, in this case, Louis is not aged like Jack Crabbe but, in stark contrast, looks the same as the day he became a vampire. Louis' story spans his life as a young and wealthy plantation owner in Louisiana, when the deaths of his wife and child cause him to sink into despair and welcome the attack by Lestat, Lestat's creation of the child vampire Claudia (Dunst), his European wanderings, and, finally, his disillusioned return to America, all the while emphasising the existential angst and moral guilt he suffers while he tries to come to terms with his unquenchable desire for human blood. Lestat, by contrast, enjoys the hunt and the killing.

As Louis explains, the new technology of the cinema allowed him the opportunity to see the sunrise vicariously, and over the years he has gone to screenings of films from *Sunrise* (1927) to *Tequila Sunrise* (1988). He also has seen the magnificent, colourful dawn at the end of *Gone with the Wind* (1939) – but while for Scarlett O'Hara there is always the hope of tomorrow, for Louis there is only the curse of tomorrow – and tomorrow and tomorrow. Louis praises the glories of cinema, the democratic art of the Twentieth century *par excellence*, while Lestat not only prefers the blood of evildoers because they 'taste better', but also the blood of aristocrats because, as Louis explains, 'the democratic taste doesn't suit Lestat's palette'. The source of evil here may be in the Old World, as in *An American Werewolf in London** (1991), but *Interview with the Vampire* is more concerned with the corruption of the New World.

Stan Winston's makeup effects give the already beautiful actors Cruise, Pitt, and Bandares a sensually heightened quality consistent with Rice's descriptions, while their long, flowing hair and pale, slender fingernails feminise them and add to the homoerotic desire that also suffuses the book. These vampires veer from traditional vampire lore in some ways, but as Louis tells Molloy, the popular depiction of vampires by Bram Stoker in *Dracula* are 'the vulgar fictions of a demented artist'. (Jordan's 2011 novel *Mistaken* is set adjacent to Stoker's home in Dublin.) Accordingly, while *Dracula** (1931) ultimately depicts the containment of the sexual threat represented by the vampire, *Interview with the Vampire*, by contrast, sees the modern world as all too willing to embrace vampirism. At the end of the interview, Molloy fails to understand the point of Louis's story, the warning about the moral morass that comes with such seductive power. The book ends with Molloy fleeing an angered Louis but intending to search for Lestat, while the film, expressing a greater urgency, has Lestat suddenly appear in Molloy's car, taking the wheel from him, and offering him the choice of death or undeath. While this ending may seem unresolved, the film leaves no doubt as to who is in the driver's seat. As Louis remarks at one point, 'a new world had sprung up around us, and we were all Americans now.'

Further Reading

Jordan, Neil. *A Neil Jordan Reader*. New York: Vintage International, 1993.

Pramaggiore, Maria. *Neil Jordan*. Champaign, IL: University Press of Illinois, 2008.

Keller, James R. *Anne Rice and Sexual Politics: The Early Novels*. Jefferson, NC: McFarland, 2000.

Zucker, Carole. *The Cinema of Neil Jordan: Dark Carnival*. London: Wallflower Press, 2008.

Invasion of the Body Snatchers
1978 – 115 mins
Philip Kaufman

Jack Finney's 1955 novel, followed a year later by Don Siegel's original film adaptation, has inspired at least three remakes – Kaufman's in 1978, Abel Ferrara's *Body Snatchers* (1993), and *The Invasion* (2007) – each in its own way interpreting the basic premise of the novel in which people are replaced by alien plants that produce emotionally hollow replicas of them. In Kaufman's, the best of the remakes, the setting is, tellingly, changed from a small imaginary town to an actual big city – San Francisco, one of the major urban destinations of the truckloads of pods being dispersed in the original – to suggest that the general social malaise Siegel's film had warned about is already the characteristic state of affairs in contemporary America. What Miles in the original film version had called 'a malignant disease spreading through the whole country' has now suffused the nation and, as we learn toward the end of Kaufman's film, is already spreading internationally. The screenplay was written by W. D. Richter, who subsequently penned John Badham's similarly revi-

DIRECTOR Philip Kaufman
PRODUCER Robert H. Solo
SCREENPLAY W. D. Richter
CINEMATOGRAPHY
Michael Chapman
EDITOR Douglas Stuart
MUSIC Denny Zeitlin
PRODUCTION COMPANY
Solofilm
MAIN CAST Donald Sutherland,
Brooke Adams, Jeff Goldblum,
Veronica Cartwright, Leonard
Nimoy, Art Hindle

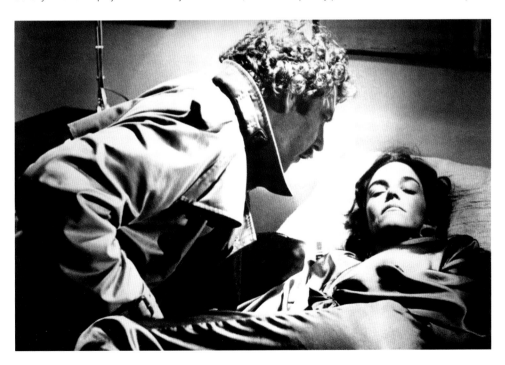

sionist version of *Dracula* (1979) with Frank Langella as the seductive rather than scary Count. Significantly, San Francisco in the previous decade was famous as a countercultural haven serving as a mecca for gays and hippies, thus allowing the film to offer an ironic critique of me-generation hedonism and the culture of narcissism.

In this sense the film is less a remake than a sequel.

As the invasion begins, Elizabeth Driscoll (Adams), who works for the city's Department of Health, wonders to her supervisor Matthew Bennell (Sutherland) about her suddenly distant boyfriend (Hindle), the first person to become a pod. At first shown insulated by his stereo headphones and television sports broadcasts, he seems little different once he becomes a pod, not nearly as obvious as the pod people in Siegel's version. Kaufman uses overlapping dialogue throughout the film to complement the unsettling, oddly framed images, and to show how people fail to hear each other in their self-absorbed routines. The spokesperson for the pods, as in the original, is a psychiatrist, this time played by Leonard Nimoy, famous for his role as the rational and emotionless Vulcan science officer Spock on television's *Star Trek* (1966–69). The further irony here is that Nimoy's stolid onscreen presence means that he, too, appears hardly changed once he becomes a pod.

Kaufman's version is more paranoid than its predecessor. This time we are implicated at the beginning, not merely addressed in the climax ('You're Next!'), as we assume the aliens' pre-pod point of view while they float through space toward Earth. Clearly, the triumph of the pods is more imminent now: Kevin McCarthy, who played protagonist Miles Bennell in Siegel's film, appears here still warning people that 'They're coming! They're already here!' – but then he is struck and killed by a car. Unlike the first version, Kaufman's leaves no doubt about whether humans or pods will win. The shattered windshield through which Matthew looks as he drives is a graphic indication of the irrevocably shattered world beyond. As Matthew's friend Jack Bellicec (Goldblum) observes when still human and trying to escape, 'The

CIA? The FBI? They're all pods already.' The Transamerica Pyramid, the tallest building in the city, looms omnipresently, as if to suggest late capitalism has continued the draining away of humanity that Miles had perceived decades earlier in the original film.

Although Matthew valiantly fights off the pod people, his efforts are in vain. In the film's memorable last shot, the camera zooms into the blackness of the pod Matthew's open mouth, an empty maw, as he emits the eerie pod shriek. This final chilling camera movement ends cinematographer Michael Chapman's frequent use of the zoom in the film, the technique having the effect of flattening the space the characters inhabit as a parallel to what is happening to them physically. The pods first entice people with their beautiful flowers, but this film says that now, a decade after Haight-Ashbury and the Summer of Love, if you're going to San Francisco, definitely do not wear flowers in your hair.

Further Reading

Crowley, Kelley. '"Look, You're in Danger!": Cultural Snapshots of Four Iterations of *Invasion of the Body Snatchers*'. In *The Fantastic Made Visible: Essays on the Adaptation of Science Fiction and Fantasy from Page to Screen*, ed. Matthew Wilhelm Capell and Ace G. Pilkington, pp. 85–100. Jefferson NC: McFarland, 2015.

Grant, Barry Keith. *Invasion of the Body Snatchers*. London: British Film Institute, 2010.

Insdorf, Annette. *Philip Kaufman*. Urbana: University of Illinois Press, 2012.

Loock, Kathleen. 'The Return of the Pod People: Remaking Cultural Anxieties in *Invasion of the Body Snatchers*'. In *Film Remakes, Adaptations, and Fan Productions*, ed. Kathleen Loock and Constantine Verevis, pp. 122–144. London: Palgrave MacMillan, 2012.

It's Alive
1974 – 91 mins
Larry Cohen

Larry Cohen moved from writing and directing for television (he was the creator of *The Invaders* [1967–68], a show that cleverly captured the paranoia of the period) to film, at first with blaxploitation (*Black Caesar* [1973], *Hell Up in Harlem* [1973]) and then a series of horror films beginning with *It's Alive* and including *God Told Me To* (1976), *Q* (1982), and *The Stuff* (1985), that explored the genre's progressive possibilities in the 1970s. In its story of a middle-class couple joyfully expecting their second child who give birth instead to a horribly mutated creature, *It's Alive* is a monster movie that at the same time comments, as Hitchcock said of *The Birds** (1963), on bourgeois 'complacency'. Initially given a limited release by Warner Bros., the movie was rereleased three years later with a new promotional campaign featuring the image of a baby carriage that

DIRECTOR Larry Cohen
PRODUCER Larry Cohen
SCREENPLAY Larry Cohen
CINEMATOGRAPHY
Fenton Hamilton
EDITOR Peter Honess
MUSIC Bernard Herrmann
PRODUCTION COMPANY
Larco Productions
MAIN CAST John P. Ryan,
Sharon Farrell, James Dixon,
William Wellman, Jr., Andrew
Duggan, Guy Stockwell, Michael
Ansara, Daniel Holzman

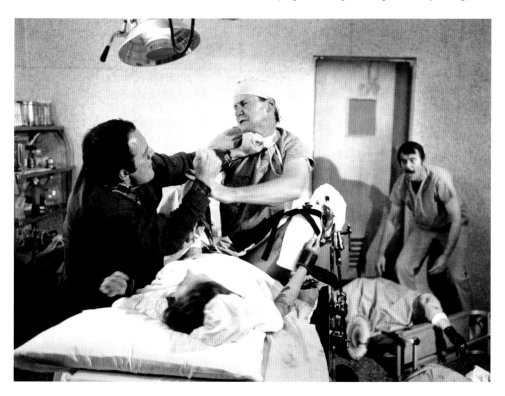

inevitably invoked *Rosemary's Baby** (1968) but promised to be more graphic (a claw protruding from inside the buggy) and an effective tagline ('There's only one thing wrong with the Davis baby. It's Alive.') that helped to build its audience and make it a box-office success sufficient to nurture two sequels, *It Lives Again* (1978) and *It's Alive III: Island of the Alive* (1987), both also directed by Cohen, as well as an inferior remake in 2009.

Frank (Ryan) and Lenore Davis (Farrell), a middle-class Los Angeles couple with their repressed tensions, are about to have their second child as the film begins. But the joyful event that seems already so utterly routine to them (they have been through childbirth once before and have an eleven-year-old son) will quickly turn unpredictably nightmarish. Lenore had been taking contraceptive pills to avoid pregnancy because Frank harboured resentment about the responsibilities of fatherhood. The mutant baby may be a monstrous incarnation of Frank's repressed anger at the constraints of family, but the drug also may have something to do with causing the mutant baby that kills all the medical staff in the delivery room and then escapes – certainly the concerned representative of the drug company that manufactured it thinks so.

The baby, designed by Rick Baker (*An American Werewolf in London** [1981], *The Frighteners** [1996]), has deadly fangs and claws. Although it is never mentioned explicitly, the tragedy of Thalidomide, a drug prescribed for morning sickness for pregnant women before it was discovered in the late 1950s that it caused birth defects, lurks as a subtext. Before the baby's birth Frank sits in the waiting room with the other expectant fathers in a scene indebted to the one in the diner before the attack on the town in *The Birds*. One of the men happens to be an exterminator who explains that pesticides have only succeeded in creating a new breed of cockroach that has adapted to its poisoned environment, an anecdote that might serve as an explanation for the deformed baby and another one that we learn at the end has just been born in Seattle, widening the situation beyond that of one individual couple and at the same time laying the groundwork for sequels.

Big pharma and the police work together with the aim of destroying the baby, and Frank, disavowing the child ('I had nothing to do with this' he insists), joins with them. But then, remembering reading *Frankenstein* and his youthful confusion in thinking that Frankenstein was the name of the monster, not its creator who then rejected his offspring, he decides to accept the baby as his own when he finds it alone and frightened. (The film's title, of course, references Colin Clive's famous cry when his creature first stirs in *Frankenstein* [1931].) The police pursue the baby into the sewer tunnels of the Los Angeles river, as they did with another mutation, the giant ants of *Them!* (1954). But Cohen complicates the typical us versus Them scenario, as the baby kills out of fear not malice and we are put in its perspective through point-of-view shots as it crawls from one place to another. Frank's descent into the tunnels where he finds it becomes a journey of self-discovery as he accepts responsibility for his creation.

Further Reading:

Doyle, Michael. *Larry Cohen: The Stuff of Gods and Monsters*. Albany, GA: Bear Mountain Media, 2016.

Juno, Andrea, and V. Vale. *Incredibly Strange Films*, ed. V. Vale and Andrea Juno, pp. 114–139. San Francisco: RE/search #10, 1986.

Williams, Tony. *Larry Cohen: The Radical Allegories of an Independent Filmmaker*, revised ed. Jefferson, NC and London: McFarland, 2014.

Wood, Robin. *Robin Wood on the Horror Film: Collected Essays and Reviews*, ed. Barry Keith Grant. Detroit: Wayne State University Press, 2018.

Jaws
1975 – 125 mins
Steven Spielberg

In Steven Spielberg's films anything that threatens the family and its routine existence is evil. Such threats arise from the banal as well as the bizarre, like the backyard tree that reaches in the window for the boy in *Poltergeist** (1982). In *Jaws* a normally safe public beach becomes frightening because of a great white shark, a giant 'eating machine', an implacable killing force similar to the semi-truck in the TV-movie *Duel* (1971), Spielberg's first feature film. One of Spielberg's monster movies, along with *Duel*, *Jurassic Park* (1993), *The Lost World* (1997), and his version of *War of the Worlds* (2005), *Jaws*, based on the 1974 novel by Peter Benchley, was his second theatrical feature after *The Sugarland Express* (1974). The film's enormous success at the box office established Spielberg as an important filmmaker and, two years before *Star Wars* (1977) and *Close Encounters of the Third Kind* (1977, also directed by Spielberg), established Hollywood's blockbuster approach to production and release. At once a monster movie, an action film, and a buddy film, *Jaws* was the highest-grossing movie of all time until *Star Wars*. The film spawned three sequels, all without the involvement of either Spielberg or Benchley – *Jaws 2* (1978), *Jaws 3-D* (1983, renamed *Jaws 3* for television), *and Jaws: The Revenge* (1987) – and several theme park rides, videogames, and theatrical adaptations.

Jaws shows Spielberg's ability for manipulating audience response and creating suspense right from the opening scene, when the young woman Chrissie Watkins, going for a late-night swim in the ocean, is pulled under the surface by the shark. Especially unnerving is the later beach scene, when Chief Brody (Scheider) is warily watching for danger while people frolic. In neither scene do we actually see the shark, the sight of which, as in so many monster movies, is reserved for well into the film. In the beach scene, aided by Verna Fields's superb editing (for which she won an Academy Award) and a hint of John Williams' insistently throbbing musical theme, Spielberg conveys to viewers Brody's anxiety and fear about a possible shark attack with several red herrings such as screams on the soundtrack (teenagers playing) and underwater shots of children's dangling legs, emphasising their vulnerability.

The plot of *Jaws* is relatively uncomplicated, but, like the ocean that harbors the giant shark, there is much more going on beneath the surface. The film carries echoes of Hemingway's *The Old Man and the Sea* (1952) and perhaps Henrik Ibsen's *An Enemy of the People* (1882), but its most obvious point of reference is Herman Melville's *Moby-Dick* (1851), with the crusty sailor Quint (Shaw) as obsessed with his hatred of sharks as Ahab is with the white whale. And like Melville's novel, the film has generated a plethora of possible interpretations. From a feminist perspective, the shark embodies a masculine dread of the feminine, its ultimate defeat expressing a reaffirmation of patriarchy. It has also been read as a Freudian parable with Quint (Shaw), Hooper (Dreyfuss), and Brody representing the id, superego, and ego, respectively; and as an eco-horror parable with the shark taking revenge for humankind's destruction of the environment, as in *The Birds** (1964). The three male characters resonate on several levels, clearly touching the pulse of the national psyche at the

DIRECTOR Steven Spielberg
PRODUCER Richard D. Zanuck, David Brown
SCREENPLAY Peter Benchley, Carl Gottlieb
CINEMATOGRAPHY Bill Butler
EDITOR Verna Fields
MUSIC John Williams
PRODUCTION COMPANY Zanuck/Brown Company, Universal Pictures
MAIN CAST Roy Scheider, Richard Dreyfuss, Robert Shaw, Lorraine Gary, Murray Hamilton

time, and so the film also has been understood as an expression of national disillusionment after Watergate and Vietnam (Saigon fell just three months before the film's release). Like the nation, the town of Amity is led by a corrupt government represented by mayor Vaughn (Hamilton), who would sacrifice safety for the potential profits of summer tourism, and in the film's reactionary view it is up to white men of different classes and skills to come together to eliminate the enemy, restore order, and right the ship of state.

Further Reading

Caputi, Jane. 'Jaws as Patriarchal Myth'. *Journal of Popular Film* 6, no. 4 (1978): 305–326.

Hunter, I. Q., and Matthew Melia, eds. *The Jaws Book: New Perspectives on the Classic Summer Blockbuster*. London: Bloomsbury 2020.

Lemkin, Jonathan. 'Archetypal Landscapes and *Jaws*'. In *Planks of Reason: Essays on the Horror Film*, revised ed., ed. Barry Keith Grant and Christopher Sharrett, pp. 321–332. Lanham, MD: Scarecrow Press, 2004.

Quirke, Antonia. *Jaws*. London: British Film Institute, 2002.

King Kong
1933 – 100 mins
Meriam C. Cooper and Ernest B. Schoedsack

The urtext of ape movies, *King Kong* was a box-office smash upon its release and has since become a widely referenced icon of popular culture. Its success inspired a quick sequel, *Son of Kong* (1933), released later the same year and directed by Schoedsack; two remakes also named *King Kong* (1976, 1995), the latter also followed by its own remake, *King Kong Lives* (1986); a reboot entitled *Kong: Skull Island* (2017), and two films from Toho Studios in Japan, *King Kong vs. Godzilla* (1962) and *King Kong Escapes* (1967), both directed by Ishiro Honda. More modest movie monkeys like *Mighty Joe Young* (1949, also directed by Schoedsack) or *Rampage* (2018) inevitably must bow before the King, 'the eighth wonder of the world' as he is described in

DIRECTOR Meriam C. Cooper, Ernest B. Schoedsack
PRODUCER Meriam C. Cooper, Ernest B. Schoedsack
SCREENPLAY James Creelman, Ruth Rose
CINEMATOGRAPHY Edward Linden, Vernon Walker, J. O. Taylor
EDITOR Ted Cheesman
MUSIC Max Steiner
PRODUCTION COMPANY RKO Radio Pictures
MAIN CAST Robert Armstrong, Bruce Cabot, Fay Wray, Frank Reicher

King Kong's opening credits. The franchise also includes novels, comic books, video games, animated television series, and rides at Universal Studios theme parks. Three years in the making, the film resonates with fantasies involving race and sex.

Jungle films had wide appeal for Hollywood, both in fiction and documentary. *King Kong* co-directors Cooper and Schoedsack together had earlier made the documentaries *Grass* (1925) and *Chang: A Drama of the Wilderness* (1927), and Schoedsack had made *Rango* in 1931, the latter two films featuring primates in jungle environments. The duo also co-produced the island thriller *The Most Dangerous Game*, released the year before *King Kong*. In 1930 the faux documentary *Ingagi* boasted of showing native women sacrificed to gorillas. Its box-office success in part motivated RKO to commit to *King Kong*, which combined the adventure and sexual undertones of jungle and ape movies with spectacular special effects by Willis O'Brien. A pioneering stop-motion animator, O'Brien and his team, many of whom worked with him on *Kong*, had animated the animals in *The Lost World* (1925), an adaptation of Sir Arthur Conan Doyle's 1912 novel with a similar premise of a remote land where dinosaurs still exist.

In the plot of *King Kong*, filmmaker Carl Denham (Armstrong), a swaggering showman with echoes of P.T. Barnum and Frank Buck, scans the Depression-era breadlines for the actress he needs for the 'love interest' of his new project. He finds Ann Darrow (Wray) stealing an apple. Desperate for a job, she agrees to join the mysterious voyage to the uncharted territory of Skull Island and is swept away to an exotic, primordial world of monsters where she becomes romantically involved with the ship's first mate, John Driscoll (Cabot), as well as the obscure object of desire for the giant ape, to whom the island's natives are happy to sacrifice her. One might see *King Kong* as a variation on the story of Beauty and the Beast – Denham utters the film's famous final lines as Kong's smashed body lies on the pavement, 'Oh no, it wasn't the airplanes. It was beauty killed the beast' – but it is also an overwrought and horrific inflection of the longstanding racist tradition of representing black people as subhuman primates and a frightening fable of interracial sex. Among the numerous cuts the film endured over the years upon its various re-releases (and now

restored), the most famous is the scene of Kong undressing Ann, the prise for which he, the King, has fought a Tyrannosaurus Rex and won (audibly snapping its jaws), and then provocatively sniffing his fingers. The Freudian implications of the famous shots of Kong leering through the hotel room window at Ann and his giant paw reaching in for her, and the exciting climax in which Kong takes Ann and climbs the Empire State Building, at that point the world's tallest structure, before being brought low by the forces of civilization, hardly need interpretation.

At the same time, the film, released during the depths of the Great Depression, spoke not only to psychological desires and cultural taboos but also to contemporary economic hardships experienced by many of its original viewers. The theme emerges more clearly once the expedition returns to New York City and Kong, on theatrical display like a bound slave for sale in Congo Square, breaks his chains and escapes. Kong's fight with the giant Elasmosaurus is echoed by his destruction of the elevated subway train; the planes strafing Kong atop the Empire State Building are like the pterodactyls. Even on Broadway, in the heart of civilization, it's a jungle out there, and many spectators likely experienced vicarious enjoyment in seeing Kong upset the show for wealthy patrons and leave a path of destruction in his wake.

Further Reading

Carroll, Noël. 'K*ing Kong*: Ape and Essence'. In *Planks of Reason: Essays on the Horror Film*, revised ed., ed. Barry Keith Grant and Christopher Sharrett, pp. 212–239. Lanham, MD: Scarecrow Press, 2004.

Erb, Cynthia. *Tracking King Kong: A Hollywood Icon in World Culture*, 2nd edn. Detroit: Wayne State University Press, 2009.

Goldner, Orville, and George E. Turner. *The Making of King Kong*. New York: Ballantine, 1975.

Gottesman, Ronald, and Harry Geduld, eds. *The Girl in the Hairy Paw: King Konḡ as Myth, Movie, and Monster*. New York: Avon, 1976.

The Last House on the Left
1972 – 84 mins
Wes Craven

The first film by Wes Craven (*The Hills Have Eyes** [1977], *Scream* [1996]), *The Last House on the Left* was loosely based on Ingmar Bergman's *The Virgin Spring* (1960) but lacking any of Bergman's art-cinema credentials. When it was first released, *Last House* was largely vilified as crude exploitation victimising women, filled with gratuitous violence and without any redeeming moral value. Like Sam Peckinpah's *Straw Dogs* (1971), released the year before, it features gruesome scenes of violent retribution; but where Peckinpah proffered a clear perspective (albeit one informed by a patriarchal territorial imperative), Craven's film seemed to provide no particular reason for its horrors or comfort for its viewers. A bogus title at the beginning of *Last House* informs us that the film is based on true events, and its low-budget look gives it an aura of docudrama that heightens the horrors to come. Despite the initial negative reaction of the press, *Last House*'s eventual cult success jump-started the careers of both Craven and the film's producer, Sean S. Cunningham, later responsible for *Friday the 13th* (1980) and several of its ten sequels to date, and, like *Fatal Attraction** (1987), inspired the titles of other movies to follow such as *Last House on Dead End Street* [1972] and *Last House on Hell Street* aka *Beyond Last House on the Left* [2002]).

The plot follows two suburban teenage girls, Mari (Peabody) and Phyllis (Grantham), who are going into the city to attend a rock concert and, looking to buy some marijuana, are kidnapped, tortured, raped, and murdered by a depraved gang of two escaped violent offenders, Krug Stillo (Hess) and 'Weasel' Podowsky (Lincoln), their sadistic friend Sadie (Rain), and Krug's drug-addict younger brother, Junior (Sheffler). By co-incidence, the gang ends up spending the night at the house of Mari's parents, John (Towers) and Estelle Collingwood (Carr), who eventually discover the truth and then exact their revenge, finishing their bloody work just as the police arrive.

Along with Tobe Hooper's *The Texas Chainsaw Massacre** (1974), released just two years later, *Last House* depicts the death of the previous decade's countercultural ideals, replaced by the fear of rising crime rates and resulting urban flight. The girls are going to see the band 'Bloodlust' (foreshadowing the unleashed retribution exacted by the Collingwoods), who, like Alice Cooper, are reputed to have killed chickens on stage. John gives his daughter a peace pendant (later, it tips off Estelle when she notices it around Junior's neck), asking 'Aren't you supposed to be the love generation?' The woods where the two girls are tortured and killed are filmed in saturated greens with dappled golds of autumnal sunlight – a hippie garden turned nightmare – lending it an austere beauty in stark contrast to the frenzied violence and pain of the people in it. Similarly, the film's unfortunate score by Hess (who also plays Krug) clashes discordantly with the onscreen action, suggesting slapstick comedy (in a manner reminiscent of *Bonnie and Clyde* [1967]) rather than horrific and meaningless violence.

DIRECTOR Wes Craven
PRODUCER Sean S. Cunningham
SCREENPLAY Wes Craven
CINEMATOGRAPHY
Victor Hurwitz
EDITOR Wes Craven
MUSIC David Alexander Hess
PRODUCTION COMPANY
Sean S. Cunningham Films,
The Night Company, Lobster
Enterprises
MAIN CAST Sandra Peabody,
Lucy Grantham, David A. Hess,
Fred Lincoln, Jeramie Rain,
Marc Sheffler, Richard Towers,
Cynthia Carr, Marshall Anker

Each of the two mornings of the narrative begins with bucolic images of ducks on a peaceful pond – but the second time the montage is longer as the water moves from the pond to flowing stream to stronger rapids, prefiguring the raging anger about to burst forth later in the day. The perverse gang functions as a dark double of the Collingwood family (Craven employs a similar approach in *The Hills Have Eyes*), with the capture and initial torture of the two girls intercut with Mary's parents at home preparing for Mari's birthday party. The spectre of Freud is raised explicitly by Sadie, who points to Krug's cigars as phallic symbols. Sadie is described by the radio announcer as 'animal-like', but it is the Collingwoods whose repressed animal ferocity emerges in the end, with Estelle biting off Weasel's penis and John repeatedly thrusting a chainsaw into Krug's chest.

Further Reading:

Henry, Claire. *Revisionist Rape-Revenge: Redefining a Film Genre*. London: Palgrave Macmillan, 2014.

Phillips, Kendall R. *Dark Directions: Romero, Craven, Carpenter, and the Modern Horror Film*. Carbondale: Southern Illinois University Press, 2012.

Robb, Brian J. *Screams & Nightmares: The Films of Wes Craven*. New York: Overlook Press, 1998.

Schneider, Steven. *An Auteur on Elm Street: The Cinema of Wes Craven*. London: Wallflower/ New York: Columbia University Press, 2002.

Szulkin, David A. *Wes Craven's Last House on the Left: The Making of a Cult Classic*. Guildford, UK: FAB Press, 2000.

Let Me In
US/UK, 2010 – 116 mins
Matt Reeves

Like *The Ring* (2002), *Dark Water* (2005), *Quarantine* (2008), and several others, *Let Me In* is a remake of a successful foreign horror film, in this case the 2008 Swedish vampire film *Let the Right One In*. Writer-director Matt Reeves (*Cloverfield* [2008], *Dawn of the Planet of the Apes* [2014], *War for the Planet of the Apes* [2017]), makes a few changes from the original but largely respects the sombre tone and unsettling ambiguity of Tomas Alfredson's source film. Reeves resets the story squarely in America in the early 1980s, specifically in Los Alamos, New Mexico, the place where the atomic bomb was first developed – one of several gestures by Reeves to Americanise the story and also, as with the clip of President Ronald Reagan on television asserting that there is evil in the world, to give it specific historical resonance.

The opening teaser scene, in which a man, whom we later learn is Thomas (Jenkins), Abby's helper, jumps to his death from a hospital room window, is achronological and seems to be included at the beginning (we see it again later) for no reason other than to hook an American audience unaccustomed to the slower pace of art cinema. The story then follows Owen (Smit-McPhee), an introverted twelve-year-old boy who, bullied at school and caught in the middle of his preoccupied parents' acrimonious divorce, develops a friendship with a child vampire (Moretz), whom he assumes is a girl. (The other significant change from the original involves the omission of the shot where Owen sees the vampire changing clothes and discovers that the creature has been surgically neutered – again, presumably a concession to the sensibilities of American viewers, especially, one suspects, males.)

On one level, Abby is a wishful embodiment of Owen's frustrations. He is clearly disturbed, indulging in violent fantasies in imitation of and as compensation for what is done to him. Abby first comes to him, Owen inviting Abby into his room, at night, in a semi-awake state, the sleep of reason breeding monsters. Reeves adds the extra element of voyeurism, with Owen looking through the windows of his neighbours' apartments with a telescope, a reference to both Hitchcock's *Rear Window* (1954) and De Palma's *Body Double* (1984), deepening the sense of the boy's loneliness. Abby is, as she says, stronger than she appears, unlike the undersised Owen. The bullies repeatedly refer to him insultingly as a girl, and it is with this monstrous girl-like creature that he bonds. Abby encourages Owen to defend himself and hit back hard when he is bullied, which he does. Abby's climactic revenge on the bully boys who try to drown Owen in the pool is like a nightmare version of all those Charles Atlas ads in which the runt who at first has sand kicked in his face eventually returns after his training to defeat the bully and get the girl.

Yet, *Let Me In*, like the film on which it is based, at the same time establishes a disturbingly ambiguous relationship between Owen and Abby, suggesting something far more sinister than the mere friendship of two misfits. Although some of their moments together do seem genuinely tender, the kind of moments that might pass between two awkward adolescents drawn to each other in a teen coming-of-age drama, the

DIRECTOR Matt Reeves
PRODUCER Donna Gigliotti, Alex Brunner, Simon Oakes, Tobin Armbrust, John Nording, Carl Molinder, Nigel Sinclair
SCREENPLAY Matt Reeves
CINEMATOGRAPHY Greig Fraser
EDITOR Stan Salfas
MUSIC Michael Giacchino
PRODUCTION COMPANY EFTI, Hammer Films, Exclusive Media Group
MAIN CAST Kodi Smit-McPhee, Cloë Grace Moretz, Elias Koteas, Richard Jenkins

entire situation may also be seen as cleverly engineered by Abby to ensnare her next familiar, replacing Thomas. Abby first talks to Owen after overhearing him wish for retaliation against the bullies, quickly sizing up his vulnerabilities, and then comes into his room only after Thomas (who, as Owen discovers, has been with Abby since he was a youth) dies. Even if Abby does genuinely care for Owen, she successfully recruits him at the end.

Further Reading:

Bacon, Simon. 'The Inescapable Moment: The Vampire as Individual and Collective Trauma in *Let Me In* by Matt Reeves'. In *Undead Memory: Vampires and Human Memory in Popular Culture*, ed. Simon Bacon, pp. 263–288. Bern: Peter Lang, 2013.

Billson, Annie. *Let the Right One In*. Leighton Buzzard: Auteur, 2011.

Ní Fhlainn, Sorcha. *Postmodern Vampires: Film, Fiction, and Popular Culture*. London and New York: Palgrave Macmillan, 2019.

Onishi, Brian H. 'Vampires, Technology, and Racism: The Vampire Image in *Twilight* and *Let Me In*'. In *Race, Philosophy, and Film*, ed. Mary K. Bloodsworth-Lugo and Dan Flory, pp. 197–210. London and New York: Routledge, 2014.

The Little Shop of Horrors
1960 – 70 mins
Roger Corman

Roger Corman (*The Masque of the Red Death** [1964]), known as the King of the Bs and the Pope of Pop Cinema, did not earn his reputation for nothing. Corman and his cohorts made *The Little Shop of Horrors* in five days, shooting it in two, with a miniscule budget using the sets still standing from Corman's earlier *A Bucket of Blood* (1959). The middle film of a comic horror trilogy that concluded with *Creature from the Haunted Sea* (1961), the film started as a joke and ended up as a unique blend of horror, black comedy, and ethnic humour. All three films were written by Charles B. Griffith, who in *Bucket of Blood* provides the voice of Audrey, Jr. and appears as the thief. Not very successful at the box-office when released, the film has since

DIRECTOR Roger Corman
PRODUCER Roger Corman
SCREENPLAY Charles B. Griffith
CINEMATOGRAPHY Archie R. Dalzell, Vilis Lapenieks
EDITOR Marshall Neilan, Jr.
MUSIC Fred Katz
PRODUCTION COMPANY The Filmgroup, Santa Clara Productions
MAIN CAST Jonathan Haze, Jackie Joseph, Mel Welles, Myrtle Vail, Dick Miller, Jack Nicholson, John Shaner, Wally Campo, Jack Warford

become a cult favourite, renewed interest in it generated in part by the stage musical *Little Shop of Horrors* (1982), based on the film, which in turn was made into a popular musical film (1986) done in a similar campy spirit.

The plot of Corman's film is as threadbare as the flower shop where the film takes place, basically repeating that of the earlier *Bucket of Blood* with a nerd who desperately seeks acceptance and love through pretense involving killing. The earlier film has a bumbling busboy in a beat café who becomes a celebrated sculptor with the hip cognoscenti by hardening clay over his victims' bodies; in *Little Shop* it's the hapless Seymour Krelborn (Haze, featured in several previous Corman movies), an employee of a failing flower shop who becomes briefly famous for growing a unique plant no one has seen before that relies on human blood for sustenance. Seymour names his plant 'Audrey, Jr.', after Audrey Fulquard (Joseph), his co-worker whose approval he desires, just as in *A Bucket of Blood* the geek Walter (Miller, who appears in *Little Shop* as the kibitzing, fauna-munching Burson Fouch) wants to be liked by café hostess Carla (Barboura Morris, another Corman regular). And in *Bucket*, Walter is exposed when his sculptures crack during his big debut show, while in *Little Shop* Seymour is caught when Audrey, Jr. buds with the faces of the people he has fed to it during an award presentation from the local horticultural society.

The shop itself is said to be located on 'skid row', but apart from a few obligatory exterior shots of Los Angeles streets, the minimalist flower shop seems more like it belongs in New York's Lower East Side given the thick Yiddish accent of its owner, Gavis Mushnick (Welles), and some of his customers. Even the signage in the shop has a Yiddish accent: for example, 'Lots Plants Cheap'. The dialogue in the shop, filled with malapropisms, is often quite witty, but elsewhere the comedy seems extraneous and strained. The business with Seymour's sodden mother (Vail), who drinks liquor for medicinal purposes; Jack Nicholson as Wilbur Force, a masochist who is happy to have his teeth extracted; and the policemen, Sgt. Joe Fink (Wally Campo) and his assistant Frank Stoolie (Jack Warford), parodies of Detective Joe Friday and his partner Frank Smith on the popular television show *Dragnet* (1951–59), all strike one as unrelated filler and more like sketch comedy (although the presence of a young Nicholson has helped to boost interest in the film subsequently).

Still, if *The Little Shop of Horrors* doesn't quite hold together, it does establish a tone that balances the funny with the fearful in a way that looks forward to the humour of later splatstick horror films such as, for example, Sam Raimi's *The Evil Dead** (1981) and Peter Jackson's *Braindead* (aka *Dead Alive*, 1992).

Further Reading

Corman, Roger, with Jim Jerome. *How I Made a Hundred Movies in Hollywood and Never Lost a Dime*. New York: Random House, 1999.

Frank, Alan. *The Films of Roger Corman: 'Shooting My Way out of Trouble'*. London: Batsford, 1998.

McGee, Mark Thomas. *Roger Corman – The Best of the Cheap Acts*. Jefferson, NC: McFarland, 1988.

Naha, Ed. *Brilliance on a Budget: The Films of Roger Corman*. New York: Arco Publishing, 1982.

Nashawaty, Chris. *Crab Monsters, Teenage Cavemen, and Candy Stripe Nurses: Roger Corman: King of the B Movie*. New York: Harry N. Abrams, 2013.

The Lodger
1944 – 84 mins
John Brahm

British author Marie Belloc Lowndes's 1913 novel *The Lodger*, about a mysterious roomer who may be Jack the Ripper, has been filmed multiple times, first in 1927 by Alfred Hitchcock (*Psycho** [1960], *The Birds** [1963]); then by Maurice Elvy in 1932 with Ivor Novello, who also starred in Hitchcock's version); as *Man in the Attic* with Jack Palance, directed by Hugo Fregonese in 1953; and most recently by David Ondaatje in 2009. But the most atmospheric is certainly John Brahm's version featuring Laird Cregar, a compelling young actor who was a rising star but died at the age of thirty after making only a few films, including *Hangover Square* (1945), which reunited Cregar with Brahm, screenwriter Lyndon, and fellow actor George Sanders. Brahm also directed the classic noir *The Locket* (1946), with its complicated flashback structure, *The Undying Monster* (1942), and, for television, twelve episodes (more than any other director) of Rod Serling's original *Twilight Zone* (1959–1964), including perhaps the most memorable, 'Time Enough at Last' (1959). While, on the one hand, the Ripper film *From Hell* (2001) emphasises its stylish atmosphere over character, and, on the other, *Time after Time* (1979) explicitly interprets the infamous serial killer as an emblem of Twentieth century violence generally, in *The Lodger* Brahm brings his ability at ambience to represent at once a mythical moody London and the psychotic state of mind of its main character.

A mysterious and eccentric figure, the portentously named Mr. Slade (Cregar) rents a room in the London home of a kindly couple (Hardwicke, Allgood) amidst the Ripper's killings in Whitechapel. Slade's odd behaviour causes the couple to grow increasingly suspicious that their strange lodger is actually the Ripper – although Kitty Langley (Oberon), a singer who also rooms there, is skeptical. John Warwick (Sanders), a Scotland Yard detective investigating the case, is attracted to Kitty and also suspicious of Slade, with whom Kitty has developed a mutual attraction. In the first version Hitchcock provides the twist of making the lodger, Jonathan Drew, actually innocent, changing Lowndes's novel but thus exploring his favourite themes of guilt and innocence as well as, in typical fashion, implicating the audience, who assumes his guilt like the mob that attacks Drew. But in Brahm's version what little ambiguity there may be about Slade disappears once he attends Kitty's caberet performance.

The opening crane shot beautifully establishes *The Lodger*'s noir-like late-Victorian atmosphere. The film features stairways and shadows aplenty, subjective shots from the killer's perspective, and the inevitable London fog. One shot shows Warwick looking through a magnifying glass examining fingerprints, its Langian sense of fate suggesting that Slade is helpless before his inner drives, like Beckert in *M* (1931), another compulsive serial killer. When Slade, foiled in his plans to kill Kitty, flees the police in the recesses of the theatre in the manner of *The Phantom of the Opera** (1925), he runs down a spiral staircase, suggesting his swirling inner turmoil (and looking forward to the more upscale serial killer treatment in Robert Siodmak's *The Spiral Staircase* two years later). As he crawls along a catwalk high above the stage, its ribbing casts starkly alternat-

DIRECTOR John Brahm
PRODUCER Robert Bassler
SCREENPLAY Barré Lyndon
CINEMATOGRAPHY
Lucien Ballard
EDITOR J. Watson Webb, Jr.
MUSIC Hugo Friedhofer
PRODUCTION COMPANY 20th
Century Fox
MAIN CAST Laird Cregar,
Merle Oberon, George Sanders,
Sir Cedric Hardwicke, Sara
Allgood, Aubrey Mather,
Queenie Leonard

ing light and dark shadows across Cregar's face, a graphic representation of his alternating attraction to and horror of women. Surrounded by police, Slade is at once like a cornered animal and, again, like Peter Lorre's Beckert in *M*, with just his heavy breathing on the soundtrack. The film's emphasis on the details of Slade's psychosis is indicative of the horror film's turn toward Freudian psychology after Word War II, while his need to cut the evil out of women may specifically evoke the horrors of Nazi eugenics.

Further Reading

Colville, Gary, and Patrick Lucanio. *Jack the Ripper: His Life and Crimes in Popular Entertainment*. Jefferson, NC: McFarland, 1999.

Marra, Peter. '"Strange Pleasure": 1940s Proto-Slasher Cinema'. In *Recovering 1940s Horror Cinema: Traces of a Lost Decade*, ed. Mario Degiglio-Bellemare, Charlie Ellbé, and Kristopher Woofter, pp. 27–45. Lanham, MD: Lexington Books, 2015.

Meikle, Denis. *Jack the Ripper: The Murders and the Movies*. Surrey, UK: Reynolds and Hearn, 2002.

Smith, Clare. *Jack the Ripper in Film and Culture: Top Hat, Gladstone Bag and Fog*. London: Palgrave Macmillan, 2016.

Mad Love (The Hands of Orlac)
1935 – 68 mins
Karl Freund

Maurice Renard's 1920 novel *Les Mains d'Orlac* (*The Hands of Orlac*) has been adapted several times, first as *Orlacs Hände* (1924), a silent version that reunited the director (Robert Wiene) and somnambulist star (Conrad Veidt) of *The Cabinet of Dr. Caligari* (1920); then as *The Hands of Orlac* (1960), *Hands of a Stranger* (1962), and *Body Parts* (1991). But *Mad Love* is the most memorable in large part because of Peter Lorre's performance as the increasingly insane Dr. Gogol, a surgeon who becomes obsessed with his object of desire, actress Yvonne Orlac (Drake). It was Lorre's American film debut and the final film to be directed

DIRECTOR Karl Freund
PRODUCER John W. Considine, Jr.
SCREENPLAY Guy Endore,
John L. Balderston
CINEMATOGRAPHY
Chester A. Lyons, Gregg Toland
EDITOR Hugh Wynn
MUSIC Dimitri Tiomkin
PRODUCTION COMPANY MGM
MAIN CAST Peter Lorre,
Frances Drake, Colin Clive,
Ted Healy, Sara Haden,
Edward Brophy

by Karl Freund (*The Mummy** [1932], *Murders in the Rue Morgue** [1932]), cinematographer of several important German expressionist films including Fritz Lang's *Metropolis* (1926). The film imports Universal's expressionist inheritance and adds numerous horror references by writers John L. Balderston, who wrote the play adaptation of *Dracula* on which the 1931 film* is based, as well as the scripts for *The Mummy* (1932) and *The Bride of Frankenstein* (1933), and Guy Endore, author of the 1933 novel *The Werewolf of Paris*, to create a nightmarish stew of psycho-sexual madness.

A shadowy presence, Gogol has attended all of Yvonne Orlac's performances of 'Torturée', a Grand Guignol spectacle one young man in attendance describes as 'a fillip to jaded nerves, a new shudder', and which Gogol watches every night transfixed with sadistic sexual pleasure. He begins to become unhinged when he finally meets her in her dressing room and discovers that this is to be her last performance because she plans to leave the stage with her new husband, concert pianist Steven Orlac (Clive). A man who, as he admits, has 'never known the love of a woman', Gogol cannot understand why if he has conquered science he cannot do so in matters of love.

When Orlac's hands are crushed in a train accident and Yvonne implores Gogol to help, he instead attaches the hands of Rollo (Brophy), a circus knife-thrower just executed for murder – a nice in-joke as Clive, who had played the mad doctor in *Frankenstein* [1931] and *The Bride of Frankenstein** [1933], here reaps what he once sewed, now having body parts attached to him. Orlac's hands still know how to handle blades, and they begin to act aggressively, as if, their new owner says, they have a will of their own. Gogol pushes Orlac to the brink of madness by posing as the ghost of Rollo before descending into total madness himself, while Orlac's mind masters his hands and he uses his new skill to kill Gogol in the climax. The film suggests that it is not Rollo's hands that are the cause of Orlac's recent inclination toward violence but rather, his repressed anger. And certainly, the sight of Gogol in disguise as the dead Rollo – with dark glasses, metal hand, and neck brace keeping his supposedly decapitated head in place – is enough to drive anyone mad. But ultimately Orlac is a triumphant figure of normality, Dr. Gogol the unfortunate embodiment of 'mad love'. His name carries connotations of Russian writer Nikolai Gogol, and wallowing in compulsive obsession, fetishism (the wax statue of Yvonne he keeps), castration anxiety ('If it would help, I'd give my own two hands'), and necrophilia, Dr. Gogol is a 'dead soul', indeed.

The Caligaresque set design of Gogol's world, with its forced perspectives, stark pools of light and shadow, and slightly askew angles, expresses, as in *The Cabinet of Dr. Caligari* (1920), mental breakdown. (Film critic Pauline Kael famously argued that *Mad Love* was an unacknowledged visual influence on Orson Welles's *Citizen Kane* [1941]). Gogol's Freudian diagnosis of Orlac's case as 'arrested wish-fulfillment' more accurately describes his own state, and when, in the operating room, he begins to hear voices, he eyes pop, as if his madness can no longer be contained, like his serial child-killer Beckert in Fritz Lang's *M* (1931).

Further Reading:

Fischer, Dennis. *Horror Film Directors, 1931–1990*. Jefferson NC and London: McFarland, 1991.

Mank, Gregory William. *Hollywood Cauldron: Thirteen Horror Films from the Genre's Golden Age*. Jefferson, NC: McFarland, 1994.

Sevastakis, Michael. *Songs of Love and Death: The Classic American Horror Film of the 1930s*. Westport, CT: Greenwood, 1993.

Smith, Angela M. *Hideous Progeny: Disability, Eugenics, and Classic Horror Cinema*. New York: Columbia University Press, 2011.

The Magician
1926 – 88 mins
Rex Ingram

The films of Rex Ingram, an important filmmaker during the silent era, on occasion touched on the fantastic – see the ending of his version of *The Four Horsemen of the Apocalypse* (1921), for example – but *The Magician* is a milestone of early horror. Based on a 1908 novel of the same name by W. Somerset Maugham, and perhaps also influenced by George du Maurier's earlier *Trilby* (1894), the film is an important link between German expressionism and the Universal horror films soon to follow such as *Dracula** (1931). (Trilby was adapted to film many times, including a version one year after *The Magician* with Paul Wegener, who stars

DIRECTOR Rex Ingram
PRODUCER Rex Ingram
SCREENPLAY Rex Ingram
CINEMATOGRAPHY John F. Seitz
EDITOR Grant Whytock
PRODUCTION COMPANY MGM
MAIN CAST Alice Terry, Paul Wegener, Iván Petrovich, Firmin Gémier, Gladys Hamer, Henry Wilson

as the eponymous evil magician and who also directed, among other films, *The Golem: How He Came into the World* [1920]). Also starring Ingram's wife Alice Terry, *The Magician* is one of the few silent horror films to focus on a woman as main character, albeit one controlled and rescued by men in the narrative.

Margaret Dauncey (Terry) is a sculptor in Paris, where she is working on a large statue of a faun – a work that, as soon becomes clear, embodies her repressed desire. The statue cracks apart, as her world shortly will, falling on her and paralyzing her. The great surgeon who cures her, Arthur Burdon (Petrovich), performs a miracle operation and sculpts her back to health. She and Burdon fall in love, and their blissful days together as she recovers are, like those of the lovers in *Murders in the Rue Morgue** (1932), sappily sentimental – until their happiness is interrupted by the appearance of Oliver Haddo (Wegener), 'hypnotist, magician, and student of medicine', whom we later find out has escaped from a mental institution.

As the couple stroll through a park, Haddo intrudes and plucks a flower despite the sign prohibiting it, immediately associating him with the forbidden. Looking 'as if he stepped out of a melodrama', they first encounter Haddo at a fair – an obvious nod to German expressionism and *The Cabinet of Dr. Caligari* (1920) – a whirlwind of amusements in which the stolid Haddo controls the horned viper, 'the deadliest of all snakes'. His 'stronghold', recalling Nosferatu's *schloss*, looks strikingly phallic. Coming to Margaret at night, he hypnotises her and shows her a Boschian scene of a hellish orgy, tinted red, in which she herself is swept up by one of the satyrs. Her vision of unbridled sexuality is in stark contrast to her relationship with Burdon, who can only express 'affection' for Margaret. When, after the vision,

she takes the initiative and kisses Arthur goodnight, even he admits that 'I have never known you to be so wonderful'.

Haddo, a thinly disguised portrait of the contemporary occultist and magician Aleister Crowley, exerts his hypnotic influence over Margaret from afar, taking off with her on the day she is to marry Burdon with the plan of eventually killing her because he needs the heart blood of a maiden who is white, blonde, and blue-eyed for his experiments in creating life. And so, as Margaret tells Burdon, they have been married in name only – thus allowing the happy resolution of the normative couple in the end. In the climax, Haddo begins the ritual sacrifice, lasciviously advancing toward her and the camera and then cutting away Margaret's dress before Burdon comes to the rescue and Haddo falls into the fire – a shot tinted red and filmed from within the flames, making Haddo look hellish, as in Margaret's orgiastic vision. With Haddo's death, Margaret awakens from her trance, like Mina in *Dracula* (1931), and just as Jonathan Harker leads Mina up a winding staircase from the crypt with the vampire's defeat, so Arthur leads Margaret safely down from the necromancer's tower.

Further Reading

Barton, Ruth. *Rex Ingram: Visionary Director of the Silent Screen*. Lexington: University Press of Kentucky, 2014.

Jones, David Annwn. *Re-envisaging the First Age of Cinematic Horror, 1896–1934*. Cardiff: University of Wales Press, 2018.

O'Leary, Liam. *Rex Ingram, Master of the Silent Cinema*. London: British Film Institute, 1994.

Phillips, Kendall R. *A Place of Darkness: The Rhetoric of Horror in Early American Cinema*. Austin: University of Texas Press, 2018.

Martin
1977 – 95 mins
George A. Romero

George Romero launched another assault on classic horror film conventions with *Martin*, this time focusing on the figure of the vampire rather than the zombie. *Jack's Wife* (aka *Hungry Wives*, *Season of the Witch*, 1972) deconstructs the figure of the witch from a feminist perspective, while *Night of the Living Dead** (1968) and *The Crazies** (1973) undermine the very distinction between 'us' and 'them', the normal and the monstrous, on which the horror film is conventionally built. *Martin*, in turn, explores the deleterious potential of vampire mythology to obscure rather than illuminate reality.

Martin (Amplas) comes to live with his uncle Tateh Cuda (Maazel) in the small town of Braddock, Pa., near Pittsburgh, after the death of his parents. The family, of Lithuanian heritage, believes the Old-World superstitions that there is a curse upon them that turns some of them into vampires. Currently there are three in the family, according to Cuda, Martin being one. The boy, too, believes himself to be a vampire, having been convinced of this by his family, although in fact he is mentally withdrawn and disturbed, acting out what has been told to him as best he can by injecting his victims with a sedative, then slicing their wrists with a razor blade and drinking their blood. He has none of the supernatural traits conventionally ascribed to vampires, such as their ability to change form or to hypnotise their victims, and the conventional means of warding off the vampire that his uncle uses – garlic, crucifixes – have no effect whatever on this very human 'Nosferatu', as Cuda calls him. Martin insists, truthfully, to anyone who will listen that 'there is no magic' in his vampirism.

The film is mostly in colour but interspersed throughout are black-and-white images that evoke the imagery of the classic Universal horror films of the 1930s such as *Frankenstein* (1931) and *Bride of Frankenstein** (1935). These images reconceive Martin's vampiric attacks on his female victims – which are horrific – into sweeping scenarios of Gothic passion and romance, with Martin racing expectantly up magnificent stairways to meet his lover, who eagerly awaits him in her boudoir with open arms; or they transform his guilt and fear after feeding into pictures of pursuit by angry mobs of villagers bearing torches in the night. The ambiguity over whether these images are fantasies or memories is crucial because the film suggests the problem for Martin is that for him, they have become intertwined and confused, just as they have for Cuda, who is reduced to cringing in fear on the ground when Martin surprises him dressed in a cape and wearing greasepaint and false vampire teeth. Father Howard (Romero) is embarrassed by Cuda's superstitions and refers to his own experience of demons, which is limited to seeing *The Exorcist** (1973).

Clearly, the media (a satiric target in *Night of the Living Dead*) have helped shape – and thereby constrain – Martin's mindscape (just as myth has his uncle's) even as he is exploited by the radio talk show host who dubs him 'The Count'. The urban landscapes through which Martin and Cuda walk all suggest the post-industrial decline of the rustbelt, the impoverished spaces mirroring the characters' exhausted imaginations. The ending of *Martin* is as forcefully ironic as that of *Night of the Living Dead*, putting the final nail in the coffin of

DIRECTOR George A. Romero
PRODUCER Richard Rubinstein
SCREENPLAY George A. Romero
CINEMATOGRAPHY Michael Gornick
EDITOR George A. Romero
MUSIC Donald Rubinstein
PRODUCTION COMPANY Columbia Pictures
MAIN CAST John Amplas, Lincoln Maazel, Christine Forrest, Tom Savini, George A. Romero, Elayne Nadeau

classic vampire mythology: as Cuda buries Martin in his backyard after staking him (for a death for which he was in fact not responsible!),
we hear the talk radio show on the soundtrack with people clamoring
for the Count, claiming to be the Count, and elevating the Count to
a cultural icon in a feeding frenzy on Martin's misery.

Further Reading

Abbott, Stacey. *Celluloid Vampires: Life after Death in the Modern
    World*. Austin: University of Texas Press, 2007.

Lippe, Richard. 'The Horror of *Martin*'. In *American Nightmare:
    Essays on the Horror Film*, ed. Andrew Britton et al., pp. 87–90.
    Toronto: Festival of Festivals, 1979.

Phillips, Kendall R. *Dark Directions: Romero, Craven, Carpenter, and
    the Modern Horror Film*. Carbondale: Southern Illinois University
    Press, 2012.

Williams, Tony. *The Cinema of George A. Romero: Knight of the
    Living Dead,* 2nd edn. London: Wallflower, 2015.

The Masque of the Red Death
US/UK, 1964 – 90 mins
Roger Corman

Roger Corman (*The Little Shop of Horrors** [1960]), the King of the Bs, had artistic as well as commercial ambition, and none of his films reveal that tension better than *The Masque of the Red Death*. Shot in England, it is the penultimate of the eight films in Corman's Poe cycle, preceded by *The Fall of the House of Usher* (1960), *The Pit and the Pendulum* (1961), *The Premature Burial* (1962), *Tales of Terror* (1961, based on four Poe stories), *The Raven* (1963), *The Haunted Palace* (1963, actually based on H.P. Lovecraft's *The Case of Charles Dexter Ward* but using the title of Poe's poem), and followed by *The Tomb of Ligeia* (1965) – all starring Vincent Price with the exception of *The Premature Burial*, which featured Ray Milland. *The Masque of the Red Death* is based on Poe's 1842 story but also incorporates a subplot taken from another Poe story, 'Hop-Frog' (1849), which, like 'Masque', also takes place during a masquerade ball. This conflation, whether by screenwriter Charles Beaumont, a prolific writer for television whose many credits include twenty-two episodes of the original *Twilight Zone* (1959–64) and the screenplay of *The Haunted Palace*, or R. Wright Campbell, who finalised the script in England during production, makes sense thematically. And along with the expressive colour cinematography by Nicolas Roeg (who would later employ the colour red in his own horror film, *Don't Look Now* [1973]), *Masque* broaches philosophical questions of good and evil even as it revels in Vincent Price's performance as a sadistic torturer.

In the 'Masque' narrative, Prince Prospero, a cruel oppressor of the local villagers, plans to wait out the plague of the Red Death sweeping the land by staying within his castle walls and indulging in elaborate partying. In both story and film, he ultimately learns that wealth and privilege will not keep disease and death at bay, although the film adds the dimension of satanism and questions of faith. Prospero plucks an attractive peasant girl, Francesca (Asher), from the village as it is about to be ravaged by the plague, intrigued by her uncorrupted innocence. While she is a Christian who believes in God and salvation, he worships the devil because evil and brutality evidently exist in the world, as his own brutal actions make evident. In the climactic masque, an uninvited guest dressed in red moves through the differently coloured rooms of the revels – as far as mainstream cinema could go at the time to show an orgy – and spreads the disease to everyone, including Prospero, while Francesca escapes with her lover, Gino (Weston), who had been imprisoned in the dungeon. Unlike the conclusion of Poe's story, in which 'Darkness and Decay and the Red Death held illimitable dominion over all', in the film the sexually wanton evildoers get their moral comeuppance, thus endorsing Francesca's faith over Prospero's pessimism.

The 'Hop-Frog' story also involves class difference and a moral comeuppance for an oppressive nobleman. In both story and film, a dwarf jester – Hop-Toad (Martin) in the film – talks an arrogant aristocrat (in the story, a king and his seven cruel and corpulent ministers; in the film, the sadistic Alfredo [Magee]) into dressing as an ape for the ball, after which he chains him to a chandelier and burns him alive, to the delight of the amused revellers.

DIRECTOR Roger Corman
PRODUCER Roger Corman, George Willoughby
SCREENPLAY Charles Beaumont, R. Wright Campbell
CINEMATOGRAPHY Nicolas Roeg
EDITOR Ann Chegwidden
MUSIC David Lee
PRODUCTION COMPANY Alta Vista Productions
MAIN CAST Vincent Price, Hazel Court, Jane Asher, David Weston, Nigel Green, Patrick Magee, Skip Martin, John Westbrook

Corman used his larger than typical budget, which enabled him to shoot in colour and widescreen, to expressive advantage. The opulent mix of colours – but no red – in the revellers' costumes, which swirl in a vertiginous, seductive frenzy as the party-goers dance, show their indifference to the plight of the people and their denial of death's dominion. It is probably too much to suggest that the film is self-reflexive to the extent that its sumptuous imagery might appeal to the film spectator for the same reason, but clearly, like Ingmar Bergman's *The Seventh Seal* (1956), the film dabbles in medieval metaphysics, especially in the final scene, an explicit reference to the last shot of Bergman's film, in which the Red Death and six of his 'brothers', each clothed in a different coloured robe, meet on a blasted heath where they express weariness with their appointed tasks.

Further Reading

Butler, Ivan. *Horror in the Cinema*. New York: A. S. Barnes/ London: Zwemmer, 1970.

Corman, Roger, with Jim Jerome. *How I Made a Hundred Movies in Hollywood and Never Lost a Dime*. New York: Random House, 1999.

Frank, Alan. *The Films of Roger Corman: 'Shooting My Way out of Trouble'*. London: Batsford, 1998.

Lowenstein, Adam. '*The Masque of the Red Death*'. In *Books to Film: Cinematic Adaptations of Literary Works*, vol. 1, ed. Barry Keith Grant, pp. 253–256. Farmington Hills, MI: Gale, 2010.

Midsommar
US/Sweden, 2019 – 148 mins
Ari Aster

Midsommar, Ari Aster's follow-up to his impressive debut feature, *Hereditary* (2018), travels down a similarly silvan path as Robin Hardy's *The Wicker Man* (1973, remade by Neil LaBute in 2006), before diverging in the wood to tap into similar post-9/11 fears of the Other and American vulnerability as expressed in, for example, *Hostel** (2005). Set in rural Sweden (although shot in Hungary), the film's title might evoke early Ingmar Bergman melodramas such as *Summer Interlude* (1951); but while there certainly are radiant *Smiles of a Summer Night* (1955) here aplenty, they are more frightening than farcical (although the film has its moments of humour, to be sure) with the communal residents of Hårga looking increasingly enraptured even as the outsiders disappear one by one. The film plays on reversing genre expectations such that its horrors occur in a world of broad daylight rather than cloaked in shadows and night, and with a slowly simmering dread that builds to its memorable climax by adding a feminist twist in its version of the Final Girl.

Dani Ardor (Pugh), a psychology student who has just suffered the the trauma of losing her family, decides to join her boyfriend, anthropology student Christian Hughes (Reynor), and two of his friends, fellow students Josh (Harper) and Mark (Poulter), on a trip to Hälsingland, Sweden at the invitation of their mutual friend Pelle (Blomgren) to attend a midsummer celebration at his traditional commune, the Hårga, that, he explains, occurs only every ninety years. Josh is researching traditional pagan rituals for his thesis, and later the self-centered Christian opportunistically decides to do the same. As in *Candyman** (1992), though, those who presume to parachute into a community with scientific detachment end up becoming part of the phenomenon. Aster shows the students' world literally turning upside down by flipping the image so that they seem to be driving to the commune suspended from the sky. Once they arrive there, they find the place situated in a gorgeous green and sunlit plain suffused with a welcoming calm aided by organic psychedelics that seem to make the flora pulsate and breathe.

The film's lengthy running time befits the holiday it is named for, as Aster provides elaborate anthropological detail about the Hårga and their rituals, including meals, dances, fashion, fertility rites – and, inevitably, human sacrifice. There is even the equivalent of an elaborate Bayeux Tapestry that chronicles some of the rituals we see enacted. Like Dani, who triumphs in the Maypole dance and is crowned May Queen, we are immersed in this strange world. But once these ugly Americans either seek to gain forbidden knowledge or blaspheme by urinating on a sacred tree, they become grist for the communal mill, carefully made part of the bounteous and beautiful natural world that the Hårga celebrate.

As May Queen, Dani is awarded the privilege of choosing the final sacrifice for the Midsummer celebration, either one of the commune members or the now helpless (and appositely named) Christian, paralyzed by a powder he inhaled. Christian's paralysis is first shown from his physical point of view to underscore the horror of what is about to befall him, but then the film emphatically returns us to Dani. Given the self-centered

DIRECTOR Ari Aster
PRODUCER Patrik Andersson, Lars Knudsen
SCREENPLAY Ari Aster
CINEMATOGRAPHY Pawel Pogorzelski
EDITOR Lucian Johnston
MUSIC Bobby Krlic
PRODUCTION COMPANY Square Peg, B-Reel Films
MAIN CAST Florence Pugh, Jack Reynor, William Jackson Harper, Vilhelm Blomgren, Ellora Torchia, Will Poulter, Archie Madekwe

and weak behaviour of Christian throughout, and the commune's sense of family, so strong that its members collectively express each other's pain and joy, what other choice could the recently orphaned Dani be expected to make?

Further Reading

Ingham, Howard David. *We Don't Go Back: A Watcher's Guide to Folk Horror*. Swansea, UK: Room207Press, 2018.

Newman, Kim. 'Demons by Night'. *Sight and Sound* 29, no. 8 (August 2019): 46–49.

Scovell, Adam. *Folk Horror: Hours Dreadful and Things Strange*. Leighton Buzzard, UK: Auteur, 2017.

Misery
1990 – 107 mins
Rob Reiner

Based on Stephen King's 1987 novel of the same name, *Misery* is a masterful exercise in captivity horror, reworking a similar idea of entrapment he used six years earlier in *Cujo* (1981, film adaption 1983) into a fearful fable about how culture consumers take ownership of their beloved texts and how popular culture can constrain creativity. Director Rob Reiner's command of film style to heighten suspense is surprising, given that his sensibility does not seem particularly attuned to the horror genre (although he did direct a fine adaptation of Stephen King's novella 'The Body' as *Stand by Me* in 1986), and he is aided by a fine performance by Kathy Bates, for which she won a Best Actress Oscar. (Bates also starred in *Dolores Claiborne* [1995], based on the King novel of the same name).

In the plot, Paul Sheldon (Caan), the author of a wildly successful series of romance novels featuring the heroine Misery Chastain, crashes while driving in a snowstorm on a remote Colorado mountain road after

DIRECTOR Rob Reiner
PRODUCER Steve Nicolaides, Rob Reiner, Andrew Scheinman, Jeffrey Stott
SCREENPLAY William Goldman
CINEMATOGRAPHY Barry Sonnenfeld
EDITOR Robert Leighton
MUSIC Marc Shaiman
PRODUCTION COMPANY Castle Rock Entertainment, Nelson Entertainment
MAIN CAST Kathy Bates, James Caan, Richard Farnsworth, Frances Sternhagen, Lauren Bacall

finishing his new novel, one that he hopes will take his work in a new direction. Severely injured and unconscious, he is rescued by Annie Wilkes (Bates), a nurse who, as we find out along with Sheldon, is mentally quite unbalanced and wildly obsessed with the Misery books and their author. When he regains consciousness, he finds himself confined in a bed in her home with both legs and a shoulder broken and Annie, who boasts of being his 'number one fan' (King's 'constant reader' as nightmare) nursing him. Annie reads the new *Misery* manuscript and, discovering that Misery dies at the end, keeps Sheldon imprisoned and forces him to burn his manuscript and write a new one in which he somehow resurrects Misery. A variation of Scheherazade's story in *One Thousand and One Nights*, the film then chronicles Sheldon's writing of the manuscript and his attempts to outwit an increasingly insane Annie.

Annie's murderous insanity is fueled by religious fervor, like Mrs. Carmody's in *The Mist** (1980, film 2007), based on another of King's stories. She wears a crucifix prominently displayed at all times, and quotes a line from one of the Misery books, 'There is a justice higher than Man. I will be judged by him', as a justification for her actions. Reiner uses numerous big close-ups of Bates's face, almost always from slightly below eye level, as if putting the viewer into Sheldon's helpless position in bed, while, Joe Peschi-like, she has violent mood shifts, veering unpredictably between cooing sweetly or raging at Sheldon. Her suddenly looming face revealed by a lightning flash as Sheldon wakes up in the night is particularly effective, as is the quick shot of Sheldon's ankle impossibly turned when Annie hobbles him with a sledgehammer. Annie is obsessed with Sheldon and his work because, as she says, Misery made her forget all her problems. In this sense *Misery* explores similar territory to John Carpenter's *In the Mouth of Madness** (1994). 'I love you, Paul. You're mine', she declares, her presumptive sense of fan ownership somewhat self-reflexive in mirroring reaction to King's 1984 novel *The Eyes of the Dragon*, which drew the ire of many fans for straying too far from horror.

But the situation also speaks to masculine anxieties of entrapment and emasculation. Legs broken, Sheldon is dependent on a woman, one who embodies a nightmarish, smothering domesticity. The only copy of his new novel becomes a lump of charcoal embers on the barbecue grill, a vivid indication of his impotence in the face of this powerful and resourceful woman who waves a urine bottle in the air as she prattles on about the sanctity of marriage. It is also significant that the helpless Sheldon is played by James Caan, an actor who established a muscular screen persona as the hothead Sonny Corleone in *The Godfather* (1972), while his immobilization in a wheelchair also recalls his betrayed protagonist in Sam Peckinpah's *The Killer Elite* (1975). Our discomfort at Sheldon's constrained vulnerability is thus heightened, undoubtedly adding to the sense of 'higher justice' when he smashes the face of the 'crazy bitch' during their climactic fight with the typewriter, his tool.

Further Reading:

Berkenkamp, Lauri. 'Reading, Writing and Interpreting: Stephen King's *Misery*'. *The Dark Descent: Essays Defining Stephen King's Horrorscape*, ed. Tony Magistrale and Joseph A. Citro, pp. 203–211. Westport, CT: Greenwood Publishing Group, 1992.

Browning, Mark, editor. *Stephen King on the Big Screen*. Intellect, 2009.

Findley, Mary. 'The Prisoner, the Pen, and the Number One Fan: *Misery* as a Prison Film'. In *The Films of Stephen King: From Carrie to Secret Window*, ed. Tony Magistrale, pp. 91–100. New York and Hampshire, UK: Palgrave Macmillan, 2008.

Keesey, Douglas. '"Your Legs Must Be Singing Grand Opera": Masculinity, Masochism, and Stephen King's *Misery*'. *American Imago: Psychoanalysis and the Human Sciences* 59, no. 1 (2002): 53–71.

The Mist
2007 – 126 mins
Frank Darabont

The Mist, from a 1980 novella by Stephen King included in *Skeleton Crew* (1985), reveals much about contemporary America. Directed by Frank Darabont (producer of TV's *The Walking Dead*, and writer-director of two other Stephen King adaptations, *The Shawshank Redemption* [1994] and *The Green Mile* [1999]), along with Lewis Teague the best interpreter of Stephen King on the big screen, its story involves a group of disparate individuals who find themselves trapped by an invasion of otherworldly monsters in a small-town supermarket. The film's literal monsters are many and varied, and they lurk everywhere out there in the mist, but they are also the monstrous embodiment of the various repressed angers and fears of the people inside the market. Ironically, the bloody tensions between the characters are acted out among the shelves and rows of ample consumer goods, suggesting that these conflicts and animosities are microcosmic of the nation, the American Dream turned to nightmare.

The narrative follows illustrator David Drayton (Jane), who drives into town with his 8-year old son Billy (Gamble) for supplies following a violent thunderstorm, along with his neighbour, Brent Norton (Braugher). Soon a frantic and injured local man named Dan (DeMunn) runs into the market where they are shopping, warning of danger, followed by a thick fog that quickly envelops the store. After Norm the bag boy is snatched away through the shipping bay door by deadly, unnatural tentacles with rows of articulated fangs, the market is attacked by giant mosquito-like insects as staff and customers try to fend them off with the materials at hand, followed by a wave of even larger creatures that look like alien pterodactyls. Unable to communicate with the outside world and faced with the unknown and inexplicable, many of the people trapped in the market rally around a religious fanatic, Mrs. Carmody (Harden), who begins preaching about Judgment Day and a wrathful God. Eventually, she demands that Billy be handed over as a sacrifice. David and a few others escape to his Land Rover, planning to drive as far away as possible in the hope of escaping the bounds of the unearthly mist.

When the car runs out of gas with no end to the mist in sight, the group agree on a final plan: David has enough bullets in his gun to shoot all of them but one. The hero steeling himself to the monstrous task, David proceeds to shoot each of them in the head, including his son, who awakes just in time to register horror on his face as it dawns on him that his father, who has assured him throughout that he will keep him safe, is about to kill him. Afterwards, David exits the car in anguish, waiting to be killed by one of the creatures of the mist, but as he waits, an ominous, barely discernible clanking sound grows louder, becomes recognisable as mechanical, and is followed by the dim headlights of what becomes discernible as the advancing armoured vehicles of the US Army through the now receding mist.

This unremittingly bleak ending, in which the military slowly appears, at first ambiguously, harkens back to the conclusion of Ray Milland's earlier *Panic in Year Zero!* (1962). Milland's film focuses on the

DIRECTOR Frank Darabont
PRODUCER Frank Darabont, Martin Shafer, Liz Glotzer
SCREENPLAY Frank Darabont
CINEMATOGRAPHY Rohn Schmidt
EDITOR Hunter M. Via
MUSIC Mark Isham
PRODUCTION COMPANY Darkwoods Productions
MAIN CAST Thomas Jane, Marcia Gay Harden, Laurie Holden, Andre Braugher, Toby Jones, William Sadler, Jeffrey DeMunn, Frances Sternhagen, Alexa Davalos, Nathan Gamble, Chris Owen

attempt by one family, the Baldwins, to escape the Los Angeles area after it is hit with a nuclear bomb. In the climax, the Baldwins are stopped on the highway by murky headlights which they, and the viewer, at first assume to be from the cars of the hot-rodding youths who earlier were taunting them, but it turns out to be the military, and the film ends happily (despite the obliteration of one of the nation's largest cities) rather than horribly with the family rescued rather than ravaged. *Panic in Year Zero!*'s comfortable closure suggests that despite such an enormous catastrophe, order can and will be restored by government; in *The Mist*, by contrast, the arrival of the military signals a hollow victory, because Drayton is left with the consequences of his monstrous actions. Here the conventional male hero has himself become a monster, the film's ending signaling nothing less than the death of American myths of heroism and regeneration through violence.

Further Reading:

Gresh, Lois H., and Robert E. Weinberg. *The Science of Stephen King: From Carrie to Cell, the Terrifying Truth behind the Horror Master's Fiction*. Hoboken, NJ: Wiley, 2007.

Magistrale, Tony, ed. *The Films of Stephen King: From Carrie to The Mist*. London: Palgrave Macmillan, 2011.

McSweeney, Terence. '"Daddy, I'm Scared. Can We Go Home?" Fear and Allegory in Frank Darabont's *The Mist* (2007)'. In *American Cinema in the Shadow of 9/11*, ed. Terence McSweeney and Alison Landsberg, pp. 227–247. Edinburgh: Edinburgh University Press, 2017.

Burger, Alissa. 'Gazing Upon 'The Daemons of Unplumbed Space' with H. P. Lovecraft and Stephen King: Theorizing Horror and Cosmic Terror'. In *New Directions in Supernatural Horror Literature: The Critical Influence of H. P. Lovecraft*, ed. Sean Moreland, pp. 77–97. London: Palgrave Macmillan, 2018.

The Mummy
1932 – 73 mins
Karl Freund

There had been at least one early short film about mummies (1911), but interest in the subject grew when the opening of Tutankamun's tomb in 1922 received worldwide press coverage, along with the attendant legend of the Curse of the Pharaohs. Producer Carl Laemmle, Jr. had the idea for a horror film to follow the successes of *Frankenstein* (1931) and *Dracula** (1931), and commissioned a story that was subsequently refashioned by John L. Balderston, who wrote the play adaptation of *Dracula* on which the 1931 film is based (among his later credits was the script for *The Bride of Frankenstein** [1933]), and who as a journalist had covered the Tutankamun story for the *New York World*. *The Mummy* was the first American film directed by German

DIRECTOR Karl Freund
PRODUCER Carl Laemmle, Jr.
SCREENPLAY
John L. Balderston
CINEMATOGRAPHY
Charles Stumar
EDITOR Milton Carruth
MUSIC James Dietrich
PRODUCTIONCOMPANY
Universal Studios
MAIN CAST Boris Karloff, Zita
Johann, David Manners, Arthur
Byron, Edward Van Sloan,
Bramwell Fletcher, Leonard
Mudie, Noble Johnson

cinematographer Karl Freund, who had photographed several important German expressionist films including *Der Golem* (1915) and Fritz Lang's science fiction opus *Metropolis* (1926), among others, before coming to Hollywood in 1929 and photographing *Dracula*. His subsequent credits include the memorable *Mad Love** (1935), which introduced Peter Lorre to the American screen, as well as shooting *Murders in the Rue Morgue** (1932) before ending his career directing episodes of the sometimes equally frightening television sitcom *I Love Lucy* for five years [1951–1956]). *The Mummy* transcends its rather plodding plot to achieve a dreamlike, poetic tone about undying love and obsession – another form of 'mad love'.

The story involves a mummy, Imhotep (Karloff), named for the historical Egyptian figure, who is accidentally reanimated in an excavated tomb by British archeologists. Years later, Imhotep, disguised as a modern Egyptian named Ardath Bey, helps Professor Pearson (Mudie) locate the tomb of Princess Ankh-es-en-Amon, the woman he once loved and had sought to resurrect after her death with the Scroll of Toth, a blasphemy for which he was mummified alive. This backstory is shown in Imhotep's misty pool, which possesses not only supernatural qualities but also a very good sense of classic Hollywood narrative style. The plot is essentially a recasting of the narrative of *Dracula* (Edward Van Sloan and David Manners play similar roles in both films) with a patina of Middle-Eastern Orientalism added. In *The Mummy* a similarly stilted hero, Frank Whemple (Manners), fights against a supernatural force that drains people of their will; and where Balderston's *Dracula* becomes fixated on Mina, his Imhotep decides that a young woman, Helen Grosvenor (Johann), Frank's love interest, is the reincarnation of his beloved princess, and so he plans to kill, mummify, and reanimate her so that they may be together for eternity.

Aided by Karloff's effectively desiccated visage as created by makeup artist Jack Pierce (*Frankenstein*), *The Mummy* offers some memorable moments of horror, particularly in the opening scene when Imhotep is reanimated. Despite warnings, impatient archeologist Ralph Norton (Fletcher) opens the box accompanying the sarcophagus and, of course, reads the Scroll of Toth, awakening Imhotep. If the scene recalls the awakening of the somnambulist Cesare in his cabinet, where Conrad Veidt's eyes are wide white orbs staring

vacantly, Karloff's are only partially open, dark pools with the hint of evil intent. Upon seeing Imhotep, Norton turns mad with fright, his insane laughter as disturbing as Dwight Frye's Renfield in *Dracula*, while a close-up shows Imhotep's ragged bandages on the floor slowly disappearing through a doorway as the mummy shambles out.

Unwrapping the Mummy franchise is complicated. Unlike Universal's Frankenstein and Dracula franchises, the studio's subsequent Mummy's movies are not actually sequels to the first film. *The Mummy's Hand* (1940) features different characters (the mummy is now called Kharis) and adds the idea of tana leaves as the secret of reanimation, although the film includes footage from the original. *The Mummy's Tomb* (1942), *The Mummy's Ghost* (1944), and *The Mummy's Curse* (1944) are all sequels to *The Mummy's Hand*, the latter two featuring Lon Chaney, Jr. as the mummy. Of course, there was also the inevitable *Abbott and Costello Meet the Mummy* in 1955, and Universal rebooted the series beginning in 1999 with *The Mummy*, which itself generated two sequels, *The Mummy Returns* (2001) and *The Mummy: Tomb of the Dragon Emperor* (2008), the former itself inspiring several prequels and sequels beginning with *The Scorpion King* in 2002. Hammer Films also rebooted the story, beginning with *The Mummy* in 1959, which was based on *The Mummy's Hand* and *The Mummy's Tomb*, following up with several other discrete mummy movies.

Further Reading:

Feramisco, Thomas. *The Mummy Unwrapped*. Jefferson, NC: McFarland, 2007.

Glynn, Basil. *The Mummy on Screen: Orientalism and Monstrosity in Horror Cinema*. London and New York: Bloomsbury, 2021.

Kawin, Bruce. 'The Mummy's Pool'. In *Planks of Reason: Essays on the Horror Film*, revised ed., ed. Barry Keith Grant and Christopher Sharrett, pp. 3–19. Lanham, MD: Scarecrow Press, 2004.

Sutherland, Doris V. *The Mummy*. Leighton Buzzard: Auteur, 2019.

Weaver, Tom, Michael Brunas, and John Brunas. *Universal Horrors: The Studios Classic Films, 1931–1946*, 2nd edn. Jefferson, NC and London: McFarland, 2007.

Murders in the Rue Morgue
1932 – 61 mins
Robert Florey

French-born Robert Florey, a dependable and prolific B-film director (among his other films is *The Beast with Five Fingers* [1946], from a script by Curt Siodmak), directed this loose adaptation of Edgar Allan Poe's 1841 short story 'The Murders in the Rue Morgue', often credited as the first detective story. (A less interesting, even looser, version relying more on *Phantom of the Opera* was released in 1971.) Photographed by Karl Freund (*The Mummy** [1932], *Mad Love** [1935]), cinematographer of several important German expressionist films including Fritz Lang's *Metropolis* (1926) before coming to Hollywood, it provides sufficient expressionist atmosphere to overcome the flat dialogue by screenwriter John L. Balderston, who also wrote the

DIRECTOR Robert Florey
PRODUCER Carl Laemmle, Jr.
SCREENPLAY Tom Reed, Dale von Every
CINEMATOGRAPHY Karl Freund
EDITOR Milton Carruth
MUSIC Heinz Roemheld
PRODUCTIONCOMPANY Universal Pictures
MAIN CAST Bela Lugosi, Sidney Fox, Leon Ames, Bert Roach, Betty Ross Clark, Brandon Hurst, D'Arcy Corrigan, Noble Johnson, Charles Gemora

play adaptation of *Dracula* on which the 1931 film* (photographed by Freund) is based, as well as the scripts for *The Mummy* (1932) and *The Bride of Frankenstein** (1933). Unlike those other Universal horror films, though, the true monster in *Murders in the Rue Morgue* is all too human.

One year after appearing as Dracula – and the same year he also appeared in *White Zombie** and *Island of Lost Souls* – Bela Lugosi here is Dr. Mirakle, a mad carnival barker who hosts an attraction featuring a violent ape, Erik (Gemora), in mid-Nineteenth-century Paris. Mirakle professes a crackpot version of evolutionary theory which he attempts to put into practice by successfully injecting gorilla blood into young women. (Lugosi would again share the screen with a simian in the horror comedy *The Gorilla* [1939] and become half ape himself in *The Ape Man* [1943].) Pierre Dupin (Ames, credited as Leon Waycoff), a young and naive medical student, uses forensic science (examining the blood of one of Mirakle's victims) and deductive logic (what Poe had called 'ratiocination') to discover the truth, that the murders of the title were committed by an ape, whereupon he and the police hurry to Mirakle's lair to save his fiancée Camille (Fox). Dupin pursues the primate, who, like King Kong the following year, flees clutching his female prise. The ape clambers over the Parisian rooftops after killing his own master in yet another case of poetic justice for a mad scientist transgressing bounds, and in the rather abrupt climax it is shot by Dupin and rolls unceremoniously off the roof into the river below. The climax, like the opening scene in the fairground, reveals the film's expressionist debt to *The Cabinet of Dr. Caligari* (1920).

Although Mirakle wants to create a mate for Erik, the film makes clear that the brutish ape ('the darkness at the dawn of man') represents the untamed desire of its master. Both are instantly taken by Camille when the couple attend Mirakle's sideshow performance. Mirakle is able to converse with the orangutan, and Florey's mise-en-scene often places the two together in the frame. Thanks to the makeup design of Jack Pierce (*Dracula*, *The Mummy*, *Bride of Frankenstein* [1935] *The Wolf Man** [1941]), Lugosi, tellingly, sports a unibrow that gives him a distinctly primatial appearance. The crowd enters Mirakle's show through a hoarding entranceway situated between the legs of a giant painted ape – the libido unleashed. Both ape and Mirakle embody the desire otherwise vociferously denied by bourgeois society. Camille and her friend are scandalised by the sexual allure of the exotic dancers they watch before going on to Mirakle's show, and in the early cornball scene of Dupin wooing Camille he romanticises her as a 'flower' and a 'star'. By contrast, Mirakle's experiments have strong sexual overtones, as is evident in the surprisingly brutal scene in which he injects Erik's blood into a bound streetwalker he has ensnared, killing her and then dumping her body into the Seine (a reference to another of Poe's Dupin stories, 'The Mystery of Marie Rogêt' [1842]).

Further Reading:

Fischer, Dennis. *Horror Film Directors, 1931–1990*. Jefferson NC and London: McFarland, 1991.

Florey, Robert. 'Foreign Atmosphere for the American Screen'. In *Hollywood Directors 1919–1940*, ed. Richard Koszarski, pp. 117–122. New York: Oxford University Press, 1976.

Taves, Brian. *Robert Florey: The French Expressionist*. Metuchen, NJ: Scarecrow Press, 1987.

Weaver, Tom, Michael Brunas and John Brunas. *Universal Horrors: The Studios Classic Films, 1931–1946*, 2nd edn. Jefferson, NC and London: McFarland, 2007.

Wood, Robin. 'An Introduction to the American Horror Film'. In *Robin Wood on the Horror Film: Collected Essays and Reviews*, ed. Barry Keith Grant, pp. 73–110. Detroit: Wayne State University Press, 2018.

Near Dark
1987 – 94 mins
Kathryn Bigelow

Near Dark, Bigelow's second feature, is a generic hybrid of the Western and the vampire film in the venerable tradition of such unassuming genre fare as *Curse of the Undead* (1959) or *Billy the Kid vs Dracula* (1966) but with more serious ambitions. Both the Western and the horror film are structured by binary oppositions that reflect the ongoing tension between individual desire and social responsibility, typically represented in masculine terms. In *Near Dark*, as in her other early films *Blue Steel* (1990), *Point Break* (1991), and *Strange Days* (1995), Bigelow provides the pleasures of genre even as the film questions their traditional and shared ideological assumptions about gender and violence.

Midwestern farm boy Caleb (Pasdar) seemingly falls in love at first bite with an attractive female vampire named Mae (Wright) after a romantic evening together. He is snatched away by her vampire clan, a terrible family reminiscent of those in *The Texas Chainsaw Massacre** (1974) and *The Hills Have Eyes** (1977). Turned into a vampire, Caleb refuses, like Louis in *Interview with the Vampire** (1994), to kill except in self-defence, instead letting Mae do it and then drinking her blood. When Caleb is cured by a blood transfusion performed by his father, he destroys the vampire clan at high midnight on Main Street, literally earning his spurs. In the denouement, Caleb administers the same cure to Mae, who in the film's final shot takes up the traditional domestic role in Caleb's family, which lacks a mother.

Near Dark's narrative closure thus seems emphatically to restore patriarchal gender politics, as the classic horror film tends to do. But given the sexual meanings of vampirism both within generic tradition generally and in *Near Dark* specifically, the film's ending seems somewhat ironic. The sexual allure of the vampire is emphasised throughout and is depicted as destructive to the traditional family by luring Caleb away from home and the world of daylight. Such desire threatens to erupt and destroy bourgeois stability at any moment, as we see when Mae comes back after Caleb's cure, a literal return of the repressed. Unhesitatingly, Caleb rushes to hug Mae, a blue-jean baby as femme fatale, and noticeably exposes his neck to her as they embrace.

The film consistently contrasts Caleb's normal, good family with the undead, evil family of the vampires. But this contrast is more problematic than it at first seems, as in *The Hills Have Eyes*. The vampires are capable of terrible violence, as we see several times in the film and especially in its memorable set piece, their decimation of a roadhouse and all its occupants. This violence is tinged with eroticism and, encouraged by Bigelow's typical skill at the kinetic display of action, is riveting even as it repels, thus dividing the sympathies of the viewer. Further, the film suggests that the sexual and violent allure the vampires represent are fundamental to America: the monstrous patriarch Jesse (Henrikssen) is associated with the violent history of the nation (he claims to have fought for the Confederacy during the Civil War), and they travel across middle America in a generic van, the center of what poet Allen Ginsberg has called the 'heart of the Vortex' out of which American violence emanates.

DIRECTOR Kathryn Bigelow
PRODUCER Mark Allen, Edward S. Feldman, Steven-Charles Jaffe, Charles R. Meeker, Diane Nabatoff, Eric Red
SCREENPLAY Kathryn Bigelow, Eric Red
CINEMATOGRAPHY Adam Greenberg
EDITOR Howard E. Smith
MUSIC Tangerine Dream
PRODUCTION COMPANY F/M, Near Dark Joint Venture
MAIN CAST Adrian Pasdar, Jenny Wright, Lance Henrikssen, Bill Paxton, Jenette Goldstein, Tim Thomerson, Joshua John Miller

Further Reading

Abbott, Stacey. *Near Dark*. London: British Film Institute/
    Bloomsbury, 2020.

Grant, Barry Keith. 'Man's Favourite Sport?': Gender and Action in
    the Films of Kathryn Bigelow'. In *Action and Adventure Cinema*,
    ed. Yvonne Tasker. London and New York: Routledge, 2004:
    371–384.

Jermyn, Deborah, and Sean Redmond, eds. *The Cinema of Kathryn
    Bigelow: Hollywood Transgressor*. London and New York:
    Wallflower Press, 2003.

Philips, Kendall R. 'Liberating the Vampire, but Not the Woman:
    Kathryn Bigelow's *Near Dark* (1987)'. In *Dracula's Daughters:
    The Female Vampire on Film*, ed. Douglas Brode and Leah
    Deyneka, pp. 267–284. Lanham, MD: Scarecrow Press, 2014.

Night of the Living Dead
1968 – 96 mins
George A. Romero

The most commercially successful and influential horror movie ever made outside the studio system, *Night of the Living Dead* single-handedly updated the mythology of the zombie from its colonial Haitian roots to the most resonant horror metaphor of contemporary alienation. (The word 'zombie' is never actually used in the film, the undead referred to instead as 'ghouls'.) No longer merely soulless sleepwalkers, zombies were reimagined by George Romero (*The Crazies** [1973], *Martin** [1977]) as aggressive and cannibalistic. *Night* was followed by five other Living Dead films directed by Romero over the course of many years – *Dawn of the Dead* (1978), *Day of the Dead* (1985), *Land of the Dead* (2005), *Diary of the Dead* (2007), and *Survival of the Dead* (2009) – each responding in a different way to the politics of the day and overall standing as the greatest series in the history of American cinema.

The plot focuses on a disparate group of people – the nominal hero, Ben (Jones), a traumatised woman, Barbra (O'Dea), a middle-class family, and a teenage couple, Tom (Wayne) and Judy (Ridley), all of them white with the exception of Ben, who is black– who come together in a rural Pennsylvania farmhouse (near Pittsburgh, home of the filmmakers) where they are seeking shelter from a sudden and inexplicable phenomenon in which the dead are reanimating and attacking and eating the living. Over the course of one night, the members of the group are killed by the gathering horde of the undead, who finally breach the house and force Ben, at this point the only survivor, to barricade himself in the basement. In the morning, the ghouls have been cleared away by a makeshift militia which, ironically, when they see Ben moving at a window from a distance, shoot him. Now regarded as one of the first midnight movies and a cult classic, *Night of the Living Dead* was attacked upon its release, largely because of its explicit gore – the ghouls are shown scooping up and eating freshly steaming entrails and organs – which opened the door for the more explicit corporeal depredations of the body horror and slasher films to follow.

Night violates numerous conventions of the genre as it was to that point: for example, a military that is inept (an interviewer, played by Romero himself, vainly tries to get answers about the crisis from officials in Washington), the death of the sweet teenage couple (compare, for example, *The Blob* [1958]), and, most disturbing of all, the climactic death of the hero. Its low-budget, grainy black-and-white look gives the film an aura of documentary authenticity, adding to its power. Its unremittingly bleak tone is immediately established in the opening shots of a car on a forlorn country road on its way to a cemetery marked with tombstones and an American flag. As the plot unfolds, the traditional distinction between 'us' and 'them' is complicated by internal divisions involving race, gender, and class differences that threaten the characters' survival as much as the monsters outside. Especially incendiary is the racial tension involving Ben, providing the unsettling ambiguity about whether the redneck militia think he is a threat because he is a zombie or is black.

Night of the Living Dead and Romero's subsequent films in the series generated innumerable other zom-

DIRECTOR George A. Romero
PRODUCER Russell W. Streiner, Karl Hardman
SCREENPLAY John A. Russo, George A. Romero
CINEMATOGRAPHY George A. Romero
EDITOR George A. Romero
PRODUCTION COMPANY Image Ten
MAIN CAST Duane Jones, Judith O'Dea, Karl Hardman, Keith Wayne, Judith Ridley, Marilyn Eastman

bie movies from around the world that have responded to *Night's* basic concepts in some way, from serious to satiric. The 1990 remake, written by Romero, was directed by Tom Savini, a special effects and makeup expert and actor who had worked with Romero on several of his previous films including *Martin** and *Dawn* (he is also a featured actor in the underrated *Knightriders* [1981]). The remake keeps the basic narrative of the original but alters it somewhat so that Barbra (Patricia Tallman) now becomes an active hero rather than an unresponsive damsel in distress, the film now addressing issues of gender (already explored by Romero in *Jack's Wife* (*Hungry Wives*, *Season of the Witch*, 1972), along with race.

Further Reading:

Gagne, Paul R. *The Zombies that Ate Pittsburgh: The Films of George Romero*. New York: Dodd, Mead, 1987.

Hervey, Ben. *Night of the Living Dead*. London: British Film Institute, 2008.

Russo, John. *The Complete Night of the Living Dead Filmbook*. New York: Harmony Books, 1985.

Walters, Jared, and Marco Lanzagorta, eds. *Night of the Living Dead: Studies in the Horror Film*. Lakewood, CO: Centipede Press, 2008.

Office Killer
1997 – 82 mins
Cindy Sherman

Office Killer is to date the only feature film directed by renowned photographer Cindy Sherman. Many of her photographs depict herself in various guises, often characters from movies. At once the subject and object of her photographs, her work is often viewed from a feminist perspective as questioning female stereotypes and their consumption in popular culture by foregrounding their status as representation. In *Office Killer*, she does essentially the same thing, placing an exaggerated version of herself, protagonist Dorine Douglas (Kane), in a serial killer scenario and turning the form toward artistic autobiography.

Dorine is an editor working for *Constant Consumer* magazine, played by Carol Kane at her nerdiest, complete with smudged lipstick, oversised eyeglasses, and completely inept eyebrow pencilling, recalling the heavy makeup Sherman sometimes wears in her photographic work. Because of budget cuts at the office (a financial situation created by the manager, who is actually embezzling corporate funds), Dorine, the butt of office jokes, has to work more from home, where she lives with her invalid mother in a scenario that seems almost as bleak as Arthur Fleck's in *Joker* (2019). And like Fleck, she reaches the breaking point: one night called in to the office, her smug co-worker Gary (Thornton) is accidentally electrocuted trying to fix a computer, and after initially thinking to call the police, she decides to cart Gary's body down the elevator to the parking garage, put him into the trunk of her car, take him home, and install his decaying corpse in a domestic diorama in the basement.

All of her repressed anger and guilt now released, she then sets about deliberately killing some of her other colleagues (and even two girl scouts who happen to knock on her door selling cookies) and bringing their bodies to her basement, where she recreates a gruesome primal scene, as if all her victims are part of her family in past happier times gathered together to watch television (on which flies are now beginning to gather). In the basement, where her invalid mother is unable to go, Dorine rearranges body parts for apparently symbolic purposes (putting the managing editor's fingers, which had annoyingly long fingernail extensions, on the face of a clock; using Gary's hands as toys for her cat), as Sherman often does with mannequins and prosthetic limbs in her photography (see, for example, her *Sex Pictures* series, 1992). Ironically, the one co-worker viewers are most likely to want bumped off, the obnoxious Kim (Ringwald), survives the killing spree.

The plot of *Office Killer* follows the basic narrative pattern of many serial killer films and specifically references such movies as *What Ever Happened to Baby Jane?** (1962). But it is less frightening than funny ('We're working from home now', Dorine tells her assembled corpses), with Sherman less interested in generating fear than in exploring the aesthetic possibilities of her subject. Throughout, she frames her images for expressive purposes like a photographer, cutting off heads (another analogy to Dorine) or juxtaposing foreground and background within the same shot. No doubt some viewers will appreciate the unleashed anger and resentment toward the workplace displayed by Dorine, but those wanting that kind of experienced are better

DIRECTOR Cindy Sherman
PRODUCER Pamela Koffler
SCREENPLAY Tom Kalin, Elise MacAdam, Cindy Sherman
CINEMATOGRAPHY Russell Fine
EDITOR Merril Stern
MUSIC Evan Lurie
PRODUCTION COMPANY Strand, Good Machine, Kardana/Swinsky Films, Good Fear
MAIN CAST Carol Kane, Molly Ringwald, Jeanne Tripplehorn, David Thornton, Barbara Sukowa, Michael Imperioli, Alice Drummond

served by a film like *The Belko Experiment* (2016). And unlike such other movies featuring vengeful nerds as *A Bucket of Blood* (1959) or *Bad Influence* (1990), Dorine doesn't grow less nerdy as the film progresses – not until the end, as she drives off wearing a blonde wig and with the head of Nora (Tripplehorn), the office manager, in her handbag while thinking, like any good office worker, that she has learned to 'accept my limitations while accentuating my strengths'.

Further Reading:

Meagher, Michelle. 'Final Girls: Appropriation, Identification, and Fluidity in Cindy Sherman's *Office Killer*'. In *There She Goes: Feminist Filmmaking and Beyond*, ed. Corinn Columpar and Sophie Mayer, pp. 135–145. Detroit: Wayne State University Press, 2009.

Morris, Catherine. *The Essential Cindy Sherman*. New York: Harry N. Abrams, 1999.

Mulvey, Laura. *Fetishism and Curiosity*. Indiana University Press, 1996.

Schweitzer, Dahlia. *Cindy Sherman's Office Killer: Another Kind of Monster*. Bristol, UK and Chicago: Intellect, 2014.

Sherman, Cindy. *The Complete Untitled Film Stills*. New York: Museum of Modern Art, 2003.

The Omen
UK/US, 1976 – 111 mins
Richard Donner

One of the top box-office hits of 1976, *The Omen* portended a franchise consisting of three sequels – *Damien: Omen II* (1978), the misleadingly titled *Omen III: The Final Conflict* (1981), and *Omen IV: The Awakening* (1991) – several documentaries about the making of the films, a short-lived television show, a series of novels, the first of which was written by screenwriter David Seltzer (*Prophecy* [1979]) and published just before the film's release, and a 2006 remake featuring Mia Farrow (shades of *Rosemary's Baby** [1968], another film with an infernal infant). *The Omen*'s plot of the child antichrist who works his way up the chain of political power is presented with deadly seriousness by director Richard Donner (complemented by the typically wooden acting of Gregory Peck), becoming his breakthrough film before *Superman: The Movie* (1978) and then

DIRECTOR Richard Donner

PRODUCER Harvey Bernhard

SCREENPLAY David Seltzer

CINEMATOGRAPHY
Gilbert Taylor

EDITOR Stuart Baird

MUSIC Jerry Goldsmith

PRODUCTION COMPANY
Mace Neufeld Productions

MAIN CAST Gregory Peck,
Lee Remick, Harvey Spencer
Stephens, David Warner, Billie
Whitelaw, Patrick Troughton

being mired in the *Lethal Weapon* series. Following on the success of *The Exorcist**(1973) – the child in *The Omen* is named Damien, referencing Jason Miller's Father Damien Karras in that film – it is, somewhat ironically, a big-budget, glossy studio production that brought the apocalyptic cynicism of the period squarely into the mainstream.

In a Rome hospital, American diplomat Robert Thorn (Peck) accepts a newborn baby whose mother has died as a substitute for his own child he thinks was stillborn. Only later does he discover the truth that his own child was murdered and that he has been bringing up the antichrist. At first, Thorn, his wife Katherine (Remick), and their little boy (Stephens) are presented as an idyllic family in a montage of family photos and bucolic strolls accompanied by a lush string arrangement on the soundtrack. Their life seems happy and successful, as Thorn is appointed American ambassador to the United Kingdom by his best friend, the president of the United States, and they purchase a grand country estate.

But then the horror begins to unfold, beginning when Damien's nanny, seemingly in a trance, hangs herself from the rafters in public view during the boy's fifth birthday party. Eventually both Thorns die, as foretold in the prophecy – Robert in a church as he is about to kill Damien on hallowed ground. In the famous last shot, at the double funeral for the Thorns, the President is now standing with Damien, who turns and slowly smiles at the camera, at us. The film's Manichean view of good and evil, swathed in Christianity, perhaps speaks to the nation's strong evangelical worldview, in contrast to *The Exorcist*, which seems more focused on its contemporary moment.

Traditional social institutions are unable to stop the rise of the antichrist, the unholy being who will cause conflict among men until 'man is no more'. Indeed, at least two priests are part of the satanic conspiracy to bring the antichrist into the world. One of them, Father Brennan (Troughton), is impaled by a falling lightning rod from the roof a church that is locked to him when he seeks refuge during an unnatural storm. (The most horrific moment, though, is reserved for the photographer Keith Jennings [Warner], who is decapitated by a sheet of glass that accidentally slides off a rolling truck, his head bloodily bouncing over the glass.) Ironic, too, that the police shoot Thorn as he about to plunge a dagger into Damien, thus sealing the world's hellish fate even as they believe they are doing the right thing. In that final funeral scene, the ceremony is replete with state and military honors and American flags. While Damien turns towards the camera, we only see the back of the President's head: his specific identity is irrelevant, for it is the entire system itself that is corrupt and irredeemable.

Further Reading

Duren, Brad L. 'Reckoning the Number of the Beast: Premillennial Dispensationalism, *The Omen* and 1970s America'. In *Divine Horror: Essays on the Cinematic Battle between the Sacred and the Diabolical*, ed. Cynthia J. Miller and Bowdoin Van Riper, pp. 53–63. Jefferson, NC: McFarland, 2017.

Lennard, Dominic. *Bad Seeds and Holy Terrors: The Child Villains of Horror Films*. Albany: SUNY Press, 2014.

Williams, Tony. *Hearths of Darkness: The Family in the American Horror Film*, revised ed. Jackson: University Press of Mississippi, 2014.

Wood, Robin. *Robin Wood on the Horror Film: Collected Essays and Reviews*, ed. Barry Keith Grant. Detroit: Wayne State University Press, 2018.

Paranormal Activity
2007 – 86 mins
Oren Peli

The Blair Witch Project* (1999) spurred a global cycle of 'found footage' horror films in the first decade of the new millennium, including, in the US, Diary of the Dead (2007), Cloverfield (2008), Quarantine (2008, a remake of the Spanish film [Rec] [2007]), and, perhaps most successful of all, Paranormal Activity. Like Blair Witch, it too generated a franchise, in this case consisting of six sequels – Paranormal Activity 2 (2010), 3 (2011), and 4 (2012), Paranormal Activity: The Marked Ones (2014), and Paranormal Activity: The Ghost Dimension (2015). Also like Blair Witch, the film was shot with a home video camera, much of the dialogue was improvised, and the opening acknowledgment and closing titles suggest that the film's footage is real rather than fiction. Paranormal Activity's stripped-down production circumstances demonstrate how horror can be generated effectively onscreen with minimal means, relying more on real time and minimal special effects rather than quick editing and elaborate CGI. Even the room tone picked up by Micah's microphone comes to seem ominous in the film.

Like many found footage films, Paranormal Activity is comprised of scenes that unfold in real time, like observational documentary films, with minimal editing. The camera is often acknowledged within the narrative rather than seemingly invisible, as in classic narrative cinema, and often filmed by one or more of the characters. In this case, the footage was supposedly filmed by Micah (Sloat), who is trying to record evidence of a demon that is apparently haunting his girlfriend Katie (Featherston). The San Diego couple has only recently moved in together, yet when the demon begins to manifest, stresses in their relationship quickly begin to surface. The ineffectual psychic (Fredrichs) who comes to their house is quite right to reiterate that there is 'something going on' here, but it is not simply the presence of the supernatural. Micah insists on dealing with the demon himself, his position at once a claim of masculine control and a comforting trust in technology and reason, while Katie is frightened and wants to seek professional help. Because of Micah's 'strange fascination with electronics', as Katie puts it, more than once he picks up the camera even before rushing to Katie's aid. The more tensions arise between Katie and Micah, and the more frightened they become, the stronger the demon grows until the unsettling climax.

Where Blair Witch exploits the limitations of the frame for frightening effect, Paranormal Activity generates horror by relying on shot duration in a manner that André Bazin, champion of cinematic realism, would have appreciated. The majority of the video footage from Micah's camera is taken from the same place in the couple's bedroom at night while they are asleep. Each night we are placed in the same position, this repetition with possible difference at any moment setting us up for each successive hoary horror, reinvigorating such convention as doors that open and close by themselves. (Comparably, Paranormal Activity 3 exploits visual attention somewhat differently through its reliance on the insistently repeated pan shot.) The couple sleeps on the right side of the frame, while the room's open door is on the left, so that

DIRECTOR Oren Peli
PRODUCER Oren Peli, Jason Blum
SCREENPLAY Oren Peli
CINEMATOGRAPHY Oren Peli
EDITOR Oren Peli
PRODUCTION COMPANY Blumhouse Productions
MAIN CAST Katie Featherston, Micah Sloat, Mark Fredrichs

12:09:07 AM

the viewer is encouraged to study the image, looking for evidence of spectral activity anywhere and everywhere on the screen even while aware of that opening door leading into unknown blackness beyond. The passing seconds as the camera remains in position, emphasised by the time marker in the corner of the image, keeps viewer expectation primed for – something, generating a frightening sense of depth in the image. At one point the couple cringe in fear at what might be behind the door, now closed – a scene that recalls a similar one in Robert Wise's *The Haunting* (1963), another film of the supernatural famous for generating horror more through mood than materialization.

Further Reading:

Grant, Barry Keith. 'Digital Anxiety and the New SF Verité Horror and SF Film.' *Science Fiction Film and Television* 6, no. 2 (Summer 2013): 153–75.

Heller-Nicholas, Alexandria. *Found Footage Horror Films: Fear and the Appearance of Reality*. Jefferson, NC: McFarland, 2014.

Jackson, Kimberly. *Technology, Monstrosity, and Reproduction in Twenty-First Century Horror*. New York: Palgrave Macmillan, 2013.

Raimondo, Matthew J. 'Frenetic Aesthetics: Observational Horror and Spectatorship'. *Horror Studies* 5, no. 1 (April 2014): 65–84.

Turner, Peter. *Found Footage Horror: A Cognitive Approach*. New York and London: Routledge, 2019.

The Phantom of the Opera
1925 – 94 mins
Rupert Julian

The trailer for the 1943 version of *The Phantom of the Opera* with Claude Rains in the title role proclaims 'Here is all you ever wanted in entertainment in one superb show: superb spectacle, splendor, and romance' (also, 'Nelson Eddy in his most vigorous performance'!). The description nicely explains the story's universal appeal since the publication of Gaston Leroux's novel in 1910 and why there have been numerous versions – including the aforementioned glossy 1943 film, Hammer's 1962 remake, variations like *Phantom of the Paradise** (1974) – and, of course, the blockbuster stage musical by Andrew Lloyd Webber, although it has little of the sense of horror conveyed in Rupert Julian's version with Lon Chaney. Atmospherically shot,

DIRECTOR Rupert Julian
PRODUCER Carl Laemmle
SCREENPLAY Raymond Schrock (uncredited), Elliot J. Clawson (uncredited)
CINEMATOGRAPHY Milton Bridenbecker, Virgil Miller, Charles Van Enger
EDITOR Edward Curtiss, Maurice Pivar, Gilmore Walker, Lois Weber
PRODUCTION COMPANY Universal Pictures
MAIN CAST Lon Chaney, Mary Philbin, Norman Kerry, Arthur Edmund Carewe, Gibson Gowland, John Sainpolis, Snitz Edwards, Virginia Pearson, Mary Fabian

Julian's film balances the romance of a monumentally thwarted love with the horror of obsessive compulsion thwarted, perfectly pitched by Chaney's performance. The film's success encouraged Universal's influential horror cycle of the next decade, including *Dracula** (1931), *Frankenstein* (1931), *The Invisible Man* (1933), *The Mummy** (1932), and *The Wolf Man** (1941).

After *The Hunchback of Notre Dame* in 1923, Chaney again created his own makeup for another monstrous yet complex character. Known for his makeup as much as for his acting, in *Phantom*, consistent with the description in Leroux's book, he has a cadaverous appearance – the shock of which is prepared for by the stagehand Buquet's vivid account of him to the dance troupe. To evoke a skull, Chaney painfully pulled his nose up and nostrils back with wire. When Christine Daaé (Philbin), the object of the Phantom's obsession, rips the mask off his face, he is at first facing the camera, not her, his ghastly visage more for the benefit of the spectator ('Feast your eyes – glut your soul on my accursed ugliness!'). Audiences at the time were said to have screamed and even fainted at the Phantom's unmasking. Enhancing the horror, The Phantom casts ominous shadows, sleeps in a coffin, and is associated with the abject dankness of the underground. His lair is hidden down in the 'fifth cellar', accessible only after countless stairways and across a conduit of fetid water – the biggest old dark house of them all.

The film's production was troubled, with several rounds of changes following unenthusiastic preview screenings. Director Julian (*The Cat Creeps* [1930], a sound remake of *The Cat and the Canary** [1927]) was eventually dismissed, with Edward Sedgwick and Chaney himself shooting some sequences. A sound version was also released in 1930. Nevertheless, the film is dreamily evocative, right from the opening scenes of diaphanous dancers flitting about in the mysterious, cavernous spaces of the opera house. Enhancing the mood is the colour tinting – amber, green, blue, red, and yellow – and the Bal Masque sequence, shot in colour. Particularly striking is the scene in which the Phantom, atop a statue on the rooftop, eavesdrops on Christine and Raoul de Chagny (Kerry) planning their escape: his cloak, tinted red, contrasted with the otherwise black-and-white image of the stone that, tinted blue, conveys a sense of passion turned into wrath and despair.

Initially we may feel some sympathy for the Phantom because he has been spurned and abused by society, but soon the film begins to revel in 'the evil that makes my evil face', as he says to Christine. Although we are told that the fashionable opera house is built on top of torture chambers and dungeons, nothing is made of the contrast between the foundation of western culture as symbolised by the opera and those bourgeois patrons enjoying the show (or the audience of the film as well, for that matter). 'If I am the Phantom, it is because Man's hatred has made me so', he tells Christine, who regards the criminally insane escapee from Devil's Island only as 'a monster, a loathsome beast'. But when, in the end, he is tossed into the Seine to drown by an angry mob, prototype for the gathered villagers that inevitably pop up in Universal's later horror films, there is little if any remorse likely to be felt by the spectator, and the final shots of Raoul and Christine on their honeymoon offer no irony.

Further Reading

Hall, Ann C. *Phantom Variations: The Adaptations of Gaston Leroux's Phantom of the Opera, 1925 to the Present* Jefferson, NC: McFarland, 2009.

Hogle, Jerrold E. *The Undergrounds of the Phantom: Sublimation and the Gothic in Leroux's Novel and Its Progeny*. New York and Hampshire, UK: Palgrave, 2002.

Rigby, Jonathan. *American Gothic: Six Decades of Classic Horror Cinema*. Cambridge: Signum, 2017.

Worland, Rick. *The Horror Film: An Introduction*. Malden, MA and Oxford: Blackwell, 2007.

Phantom of the Paradise
1974 – 91 mins
Brian De Palma

Phantom of the Paradise is a musical horror comedy about a devilish rock impresario who sold his soul to the devil and is now a top industry tastemaker. Of the few horror musical hybrids – among them, *The Happiness of the Katakuris* (1981), *Nudist Colony of the Dead* (1991), and, of course, the earlier cult phenomenon *The Rocky Horror Picture Show* (1975) – *Phantom of the Paradise* is the only one whose satiric target is precisely the institution of popular music itself. At first a box-office and critical failure, the film has since acquired a cult following.

Brian De Palma's horror films (*Carrie** [1976], *Dressed to Kill* [1980]) frequently allude to other films, particularly those of Alfred Hitchcock, and *Phantom* is replete with references to horror movies from *The Cabinet*

DIRECTOR Brian De Palma
PRODUCER Edward R. Pressman
SCREENPLAY Brian De Palma
CINEMATOGRAPHER
Larry Piser
EDITOR Paul Hirsch
MUSIC Paul Williams
PRODUCTION COMPANY
Harbor Productions
MAIN CAST Paul Williams,
William Finley, Jessica Harper,
Gerrit Graham, George Memmoli

of Dr. Caligari (1920) to Frankenstein (1931) to Psycho* (1960) in its story of a naïve rock musician, Winslow Leach (Finley, who also plays mad doctor Emile in De Palma's Sisters* [1972]), whose music is stolen (a reference to the 1943 Phantom of the Opera with Claude Rains) and distorted by a towering producer, Swan, ironically played by the diminutive Paul Williams with more than a passing resemblance to Phil Spector. Leach becomes a monster who haunts Swan's new rock palace, The Paradise. The plot is a supernatural stew of elements from Oscar Wilde's The Picture of Dorian Gray (1890), Gaston Leroux's The Phantom of the Opera (1910), and the story of Faust ('Faust? What label is he on?' asks Swan's assistant Philbin [Memmoli]). The latter text, about a scholar who makes a deal with the devil for unlimited knowledge in return for his soul, is a particularly appropriate horror tale in this context, for not only is there an identifiable genre of soul music, but the term 'soul' in music culture generally refers to an artist's ability to translate true emotion into music, to not 'selling out' for commercial appeal.

The film's funniest horror reference comes as Beef (Graham), the untalented glam rocker Swan has perversely hired to perform Leach's music, is showering in preparation for the big show. De Palma constructs the scene like Marion's infamous motel shower in Psycho – but when the Phantom draws open the shower curtain like Mother, instead of stabbing Beef with a knife he unexpectedly sticks a toilet plunger in his face. Warning Beef not to perform, the Phantom removes the plunger from the stunned singer's face with a sickening slurp as he slides down the tiled shower wall like the dying Marion.

Within this playful horror pastiche is a serious message about the power of the culture industries. (See also John Carpenter's In the Mouth of Madness* [1994].) The production numbers mock the history of rock music as little more than changing generic fashion, dic-

tated by the whims of a few. Thus, the same vocal trio appears as the Juicy Fruits, the Beach Bums, and The Undead, in each case employing the expected signifiers of the style (doo-wop, surf music, heavy metal, respectively). Poor Winslow, the aspiring musical artist, is merely a casualty of industry trend. Swan has him imprisoned – in Sing-Sing, of course – on a phony drug charge, where his teeth are extracted for medical experimentation. The involuntary extraction and their creepy silver prosthetic replacement visually suggest how the musical artist's 'voice' is often distorted if not crushed by industrial practices. Later, Winslow's head is caught in the record press at Swan's Death Records factory and literally distorted, his face disfigured like that of his operatic namesake. In the climactic concert, Beef is barbecued onstage by the Phantom and Swan's decayed and dying true self is exposed, the horrifying spectacle merely incorporated into the show by the indifferent and manipulable audience. Swan's body is lifted aloft by the celebrating crowd, which De Palma films from a bird's-eye view, the mosh pit seeming more like a snake pit, the ironically named Paradise now a hellish scenario of swaying, unheeding fans.

Further Reading:

Bliss, Michael. Brian De Palma. Metuchen, NJ and London: Scarecrow Press, 1983.

Dumas, Chris. Un-American Psycho: Brian De Palma and the Political Invisible. Bristol, UK and Chicago: Intellect, 2012.

Keesey, Douglas. Brian De Palma's Split Screen: A Life in Film. Jackson: University Press of Mississippi, 2015.

Hall, Ann C. Phantom Variations: The Adaptations of Gaston Leroux's Phantom of the Opera, 1925 to the Present. Jefferson, NC: McFarland, 2009.

Poltergeist
1982 – 114 mins
Tobe Hooper

Poltergeist began as a Steven Spielberg project, but he was unable to make it while directing *E.T.: The Extra-Terrestrial* (1982), so he chose Hooper to direct based upon his work on *The Texas Chainsaw Massacre** (1974) and the somewhat underappreciated *The Funhouse* (1981). Spielberg based the story in part on his own childhood, but Hooper pushed the film more toward the horrific, a sensibility for which Spielberg himself has shown little affinity, preferring instead science fiction. Accordingly, *Poltergeist* combines the sense of wonder characteristic of Spielberg and the sustained dread more associated with Hooper. The rapt, upward gazes of the Freeling family at the supernatural manifestations in their home might come from *Close Encounters of the Third Kind* (1977) if not for their horrific context. *Poltergeist*'s story of a middle-class suburban fam-

DIRECTOR Tobe Hooper
PRODUCER Frank Marshall, Steven Spielberg
SCREENPLAY Steven Spielberg, Michael Grais, Mark Victor
CINEMATOGRAPHY Matthew F. Leonetti
EDITOR Michael Kahn
MUSIC Jerry Goldsmith
PRODUCTION COMPANY SLM Production Group, MGM
MAIN CAST Jobeth Williams, Craig T. Nelson, Beatrice Straight, Dominique Dunne, Oliver Robins, Hether O'Rourke

ily haunted by spirits from the past is another Spielbergian scenario of the family threatened, as in *War of the Worlds* (2005), but in this case the threat is not aliens. The fact that *E.T.* was released just one week after *Poltergeist* in June 1982 made the contrast between the two filmmakers particularly clear.

One of the highest-grossing films of the year and nominated for three technical Academy Awards, *Poltergeist* generated two lesser sequels, neither of which involved Spielberg or Hooper: *Poltergeist II: The Other Side* (1986) and *Poltergeist III* (1988), directed by Gary Sherman (*Death Line* [aka *Raw Meat*, 1972], *Dead and Buried* [1981]), as well as a remake in 2015 and a narratively unrelated television spinoff, *Poltergeist: The Legacy* (1996–99). The franchise is also known for the widespread legend that it was cursed, like the Freeling family itself, because several of those involved in the making of the films have died, including Dunne, who plays big sister Dana, and O'Rourke, who plays Carol Anne in all three films.

The Freelings are the embodiment of American middle-class family aspiration with their home in the new development of Cuesta Verde filled with all mod cons and the father, Steven (Nelson), a successful real estate salesman selling this particular version of Glengarry Glen Ross. The film begins as a Spielbergian celebration of the family but then, as the haunting progresses, it moves into Hooper territory, with researchers imagining their faces falling off and rotting meat crawling across the kitchen counter. The poltergeists at first seem amusing, bending silverware and moving furniture, merely another diversion for the bourgeois homeowners. But as the spirits become more malevolent than mischievous, they begin to destroy the appurtenances of affluence and separate the family.

Rather than skeletons in the closet, the Freelings find them popping up in their swimming pool and bursting through the ground ('They're here', as Carol Anne says). Steve comes to learn that Cuesta Verde has been built on a cemetery and that actually only the head-stones, not the coffins, had been moved to make way for construction, so that the spirits of those dead souls that have been disturbed are unable to rest in peace. The film thus simultaneously offers a critique of capitalist greed, as in Spielberg's *Jaws** (1975), but redeems the institution of the family, who are innocent. Steve, who on the narrative's first night, is in bed reading a book about Ronald Reagan, then president, is not personally responsible for the defilement of the dead, and mother Diane (Williams) even enters another dimension to keep the family together (this aspect of the film's plot obviously indebted to the 1962 *Twilight Zone* episode 'Little Girl Lost', written by Richard Matheson). Yet if the Freelings' home is filled with the commodities of capitalism, at the same time the rapacious nature of capitalism itself is exposed (Steve proudly tells a prospective buyer that all the houses look the same). Ultimately, the Freelings' home implodes not because of any evil within its occupants, as in the House of Usher, but it is nevertheless a horrifying prospect for any family (compare *The Amityville Horror* [1979], *Dark Skies* [2013])), especially during the recession early in Reagan's presidency at the time of the film's release.

Further Reading:

Kendrick, James. *Darkness in the Bliss-Out: A Reconsideration of the Films of Steven Spielberg*. London and New York: Bloomsbury, 2014.

Mandell, Paul. '*Poltergeist*: Stilling the Restless Animus'. *Cinefex* 10 (October 1982): 4–39.

Muir, John Kenneth. *Eaten Alive at a Chainsaw Massacre: The Films of Tobe Hooper*. Jefferson NC: McFarland, 2003.

Williams, Tony. *Hearths of Darkness: The Family in the American Horror Film*, revised ed. Jackson: University Press of Mississippi, 2014.

Woofter, Kristopher, and Will Dodson, eds. *American Twilight: The Cinema of Tobe Hooper*. Austin: University of Texas Press, 2021.

Psycho
1960 – 109 mins
Alfred Hitchcock

Psycho certainly wasn't the first serial killer film to ascribe the killer's murderous compulsion to psycho-sexual dysfunction: such movies as *The Lodger** (1944), Fritz Lang's *While the City Sleeps* (1956), and Hitchcock's own *Shadow of a Doubt* (1943) preceded it. But these earlier films tended to employ the conventions of film noir and the crime thriller, whereas *Psycho* works squarely in the tradition of horror, as signalled by Bernard Herrmann's screeching violins on the soundtrack and the black and white cinematography (Hitchcock had already worked in colour to excellent effect). The film was based on the 1959 novel of the same name by horror writer Robert Bloch, an acolyte of H. P. Lovecraft whose work moved from the 'cosmic horror' of his mentor to more psychologically driven horror, and inspired in part by notorious real-life serial killer Ed Gein (as was Leatherface in *The Texas Chainsaw Massacre** [1974] and Buffalo Bill in *The Silence of the Lambs** [1991]). It generated a mini-franchise involving several sequels – *Psycho II* (1983); *Psycho III* (1986), directed by Norman Bates himself, Anthony Perkins; and *Psycho IV: The Beginning* (1990) – a television series, *Bates*

DIRECTOR Alfred Hitchcock
PRODUCER Alfred Hitchcock
SCREENPLAY Joseph Stefano
CINEMATOGRAPHY
John L. Russell
EDITOR George Tomasini
MUSIC Bernard Herrmann
PRODUCTION COMPANY
Shamley Productions,
Paramount Pictures
MAIN CAST Janet Leigh,
Anthony Perkins, John Gavin,
Vera Miles, Martin Balsam,
John McIntyre, Patricia
Hitchcock, Simon Oakland,
Mort Mills, Frank Albertson,
John Anderson

Motel, that ran for five seasons on A&E (2013–2017); a supposedly shot-for-shot remake in 1998 by Gus Van Sant; and the inevitable merchandising (action figures, T-shirts). The most crushing depiction of a clinging mother ('He was never all Norman, but he was often only mother', explains the psychiatrist [Oakland]) and a progenitor of the slasher film along with the contemporary British film *Peeping Tom* (1960), *Psycho* has influenced numerous other movies ranging from comedies such as Mel Brooks' *High Anxiety* (1977) to Brian De Palma's horror homage *Dressed to Kill* (1980).

The plot involves a secretary in a real estate office, Marion Crane (Leigh), who steals $40,000 from her employer in order to marry her indebted fiancé, Sam Loomis (Gavin), and her random, fateful meeting with a schizophrenic motel operator named Norman Bates (Perkins) when she stays at his inn overnight on her way to meet Sam. When she arouses the lonely Norman's sexual desire, his vengeful and jealous mother kills Marion. After Arbogast (Balsam), a dogged private detective hired by Mary's employer, also is killed when he trails her to the Bates motel, Sam and Marion's sister Lila (Miles) check in posing as motorists. After a struggle with Norman in which he is subdued, the truth is learned by the characters and the audience: Norman had killed his mother, had stolen and preserved her corpse, and had given over part of his personality to her in order to create the illusion that she was still alive. It was he who, as if in a trance, had killed Marion and buried her body (and, it is suggested, several other women as well) in the swamp of repression behind the motel.

Just as the plot is bifurcated, with the first part following Marion and the second part focusing on Norman, the two main characters are also split, both possessing secret selves masked by respectable exteriors: Marion is a career woman who is also a thief, while Norman seems a pleasant young fellow but is in fact a psychotic murderer. Hitchcock conveys this psychic split in his characters by frequently including doubling images in the mise-en-scène, the characters literally reflected by mirrors or mirrored in two-shots within the frame. In the key scene in Norman's parlor, when Marion suggests that Norman put his ailing mother in a mental institution, he protests that 'We all go a little mad sometimes'. His observation about the universal potential for monstrous madness gives voice to Hitchcock's view of the duality of human nature, a theme he consistently explored in his films. Hitchcock takes this idea furthest in *Psycho* through his deft manipulation of audience response, most powerfully when Marion, the apparent protagonist, is killed halfway through, and viewers are then encouraged to identify with Norman as he cleans up his mother's mess in a scene that extends well beyond the time required merely to advance the plot.

In the film's opening shots, the camera moves from the airy openness of a sunny midafternoon to the dark, enclosed interior of a hotel room, alighting on the sill like a bird – the first of many avian references in the film (see also *The Birds** [1963].). The blind is partially drawn for privacy, but the camera peers in nonetheless. The occupants clearly have something to hide, but as the camera looks into the room, the lens aperture opens, letting more light in and showing us the clandestine extramarital affair of Sam and Marion. This opening thus functions as a microcosm of the movement of the film as a whole, from nondescript normality to the heart of darkness it covers over but which the film sheds light on.

Further Reading

Durgnat, Raymond. *A Long Hard Look at Psycho*. London: British Film Institute, 2002.

Kolker, Robert, ed. *Alfred Hitchcock's Psycho: A Casebook*. Oxford and New York: Oxford University Press, 2004.

Rebello, Stephen. *Alfred Hitchcock and the Making of Psycho*. New York: St. Martin's Griffin, 1998.

Rothman, William. *Hitchcock – The Murderous Gaze*. Cambridge, MA and London UK: Harvard University Press, 1982.

Wood, Robin. *Hitchcock's Films Revisited*, revised ed. New York: Columbia University Press, 2002.

The Purge
2013 – 85 mins
James DeMonaco

In *The Purge*, the home invasion movie meets religious fundamentalism in a dystopian future with echoes of Shirley Jackson's short story 'The Lottery' (1948) and Margaret Atwood's *The Handmaid's Tale* (1985). Like Atwood's novel, which spun off a very successful television series, *The Purge* struck a chord with audiences, generating several sequels – *The Purge: Anarchy* (2014), *The Purge: Election Year* (2016), *The First Purge* (2018), and *The Forever Purge* (2021) – and, again like Atwood's novel, a television series, *The Purge* (2018–19). The premise of the film and its sequels is that in the near future the New Founding Fathers in their wisdom established a nationally recognised and sanctioned twelve-hour period one night each year when murder, rape, torture, arson, and other violent and normally illegal acts are allowed and first responders are not available to help. This contemporary Saturnalia is a modern version of the frontier, as hypothesised by Frederick Jackson Turner – a 'safety valve' for siphoning off social discontent, in a world in which the frontier no longer exists and society is instead imploding. The film depicts the horror of the unleashed collective id in the context of a socially sanctioned ritual ('Release the beast, boys. Let the killing commence.')

The plot follows the Sandins – James (Hawke) and Mary (Headey) and their two children, Zoe (Kane) and Max (Burkholder) – who try to survive Purge Night in their upscale gated-community home in suburban Los Angeles with its high-end security system. They expect to spend the night in quiet safety, but the crisis comes when Max briefly admits a wounded black man (Hodge) who has been targeted for purging. The group of young purgers demands that he be returned to them or else they will kill everyone inside the house. Their leader (billed in the credits as the 'polite stranger') speaks to the Sandins through the doorbell security camera, giving his face a slight anamorphic distortion and exaggerating his chillingly false smile. At first James and Mary will do whatever is necessary to survive, including subduing the stranger and surrendering him, but then they have a moral reawakening and decide to protect the man and their own family at whatever cost ('This is our home. Our kids live here', asserts James).

The Purge raises issues of class and racial tensions within American society, as well as a promising exploration of repression and violence within the nuclear family and American culture's foundational violence, but collapses into yet another action movie in which the white patriarch must defend the familial home as he blasts the interlopers one after another. The polite stranger introduces his group as consisting of 'five young, educated guys and gals', and they understand purging as a form of entitlement. Their target is a black man, a 'homeless swine', a black life that doesn't matter. The Sandins' neighbours, so polite before the Purge begins, come in to finish the job for the young purgers because, jealous of the Sandins' upward mobility, they see an opportunity to 'cleanse' themselves. They surround the bound Sandins like a coven, doing their 'duty as Americans'.

On the family's television at the beginning of the evening, a criminologist expounds that the Purge ritual is actually about the elimination of the poor ('unburdening the economy'), but it is left to the sequels to explore

DIRECTOR James DeMonaco
PRODUCER Jason Blum, Michael Bay, Andrew Form, Brad Fuller, Sébastien K. Lemercier
SCREENPLAY James DeMonaco
CINEMATOGRAPHY Jacques Jouffret
EDITOR Peter Gvosdas
MUSIC Nathan Whitehead
PRODUCTION COMPANY Blumhouse Productions, Why Not Productions, Platinum Dunes, Dentsu, Overlord Productions
MAIN CAST Ethan Hawke, Lena Headey, Adelaide Kane, Max Burkholder, Arija Bareikus, Dana Bunch, Chris Mulkey, Rhys Wakefield, Edwin Hodge

this idea further. Perhaps taking its premise from the Two Minutes Hate in George Orwell's *Nineteen Eighty-Four* (1948), *The Purge* prefigures the rise of the Trump rally with their chants of 'lock 'em up' and assaults on journalists, but is more interested in this 'one night of American rage', and while the neighbours spout patriotic nonsense about America, 'a nation reborn', the film ends up as another iteration of the American family reunited through violence, thus providing viewers, ironically, with the very pleasures it wants to critique.

Further Reading

Briefel, Aviva, and Sam J. Miller, eds. *Horror after 9/11: World of Fear, Cinema of Terror*. Austin: University of Texas Press, 2011.

Kerner, Aaron Michael. *Torture Porn in the Wake of 9/11: Horror, Exploitation and the Cinema of Sensation*. New Brunswick, NJ and London: Rutgers University Press, 2015.

McCollum, Victoria. *Make America Hate Again: Trump-Era Horror and the Politics of Fear*. New York and London: Routledge, 2019.

Race with the Devil
1975 – 88 mins
Jack Starrett

Directed by exploitation actor and director Jack Starrett (*Cleopatra Jones* [1973], *Final Chapter: Walking Tall* [1977]), who also has a cameo in the film as the ominously odd gas station attendant of convention, *Race with the Devil* manages to rise above its minimal ambitions to express a frighteningly paranoid vision of an embattled and besieged America. Like *The Devil's Rain*, released the same year, *Race with the Devil* suggested that the American heartland is suffused with evil.

The story concerns two married couples who begin a long-awaited vacation in the American southwest in a new state-of-the-art mobile camper and encounter an extensive coven of Satanists along the way. Roger Marsh (Fonda) and Frank Stewart (Oates) own a motorcycle dealership in San Antonio, Texas – which allows for two scenes of Fonda riding his bike, a nod by the director to the genre he worked in as both actor (the appositely named *Hells Angels on Wheels* [1967], *Angels from Hell* [1968] and *Hell's Bloody Devils* [1970] among them), and director (*Run, Angel, Run* [1969], *Nam's Angels* [1970]), as did Fonda (*The Wild Angels* [1966]). Along with their wives Kelly (Parker) and Alice (Swit), they head out on the highway looking for adventure – and, unfortunately, find it on the first night in the form of Satanists performing a sacrificial ritual. From then on, they have to fight their way through what seems like a conspiracy in which everyone else, including the police, is involved. The remainder of the film depicts their attempt to reach the interstate highway which leads to Amarillo and the attacks upon them and the motor home by the pursuing Satanists, who seem to be everywhere.

Race with the Devil taps into the expectations of the road movie with a glorious image of a highway winding away into the western distance like a golden ribbon as the foursome begin their holiday. The image invokes Walt Whitman's 'Song of the Open Road', the poem's very title having become a metaphor for the American Dream – although in the film it turns out to be a highway to Hell. The film's major metaphor is that of the mobile camper, which is portrayed as having all the luxuries and conveniences of the modern home, including colour TV, microwave oven, and a fully equipped bar. Frank emphasises that he has waited five years for this vacation from the pressures of his job, and the motor home is the physical embodiment of the fundamental yet paradoxical desire of the men to escape the constraints and demands of middle-class life while retaining the perks of civilization.

Traveling from city to rural America, the film's protagonists are in one sense fleeing from their regular lives, evoking the contemporary phenomenon of 'urban flight' and fear of rising crime in the inner city, both at their height in the 1970s. But the rural America the four discover is both strange and estranging. In one memorable scene, Starrett nicely infuses the commonplace with creepiness when Kelly feels that everyone is watching her in the crowded campground swimming pool in midafternoon. The home is transformed into a nomadic fortress, always on the move fighting off the terrible demons that threaten to invade and

DIRECTOR Jack Starrett
PRODUCER Wes Bishop, Paul Maslansky
SCREENPLAY Wes Bishop, Lee Frost
CINEMATOGRAPHY Robert Jessop
EDITOR John F. Link
MUSIC Leonard Rosenman
PRODUCTION COMPANY 20th Century Fox
MAIN CAST Warren Oates, Peter Fonda, Loretta Swit, Lara Parker, R. G. Armstrong

overwhelm it, a modern equivalent of the floating castle in James Fenimore Cooper's *The Deerslayer* (1841), which moves about a lake to prevent attack by another group of Others, Indians. The hidden rattlesnakes that burst forth from the camper's cupboards suggest that the killer cultists who planted them represent, as the Indians do for Cooper, primal energies that have been repressed by bourgeois culture. In embodying these bourgeois anxieties, *Race with the Devil* anticipates the later cycles of yuppie horror films such as *Pacific Heights* (1990) and *The Hand that Rocks the Cradle* (1992) and home invasion movies such as *You're Next* (2011) and *The Purge** (2013).

Further Reading

Scovell, Adam. *Folk Horror: Hours Dreadful and Things Strange.* Leighton Buzzard, UK: Auteur, 2017.

Williams, Tony. *Hearths of Darkness: The Family in the American Horror Film*, revised ed. Jackson: University Press of Mississippi, 2014.

Wood, Robin. *Robin Wood on the Horror Film: Collected Essays and Reviews*, ed. Barry Keith Grant. Detroit: Wayne State University Press, 2018.

Ravenous
UK/US/Czech Republic, 1999 – 100 mins
Antonia Bird

British theatre, film, and television producer and director Antonia Bird was hired to replace original director Milcho Manchevski, who was fired shortly after filming began, on this horror Western. Although production got off to a shaky start, Bird brought a darkly satiric tone to the film and understood its central premise of cannibalistic wendigos in the American west as a critique of westward expansionism and American capitalism.

The story takes place in a remote army outpost in the Sierra Nevada mountains in the late 1840s during the Mexican-American War. Captain John Boyd (Pearce) is assigned to Ft. Spencer, where there are only a handful of troopers and guides. Soon a nearly dead settler named Colqhoun (Carlyle) staggers into the fort with a story about how his wagon train was headed west but became lost in the mountains, where his party spent three months in a cave and eventually resorted to cannibalism to survive. Although the native scouts George (Runningfox) and Martha (Tousey) recognise that Colqhoun has become a wendigo, a cannibalistic spirit that consumes the essence of the one it eats (the film's advertising tagline was 'You are who you eat'), Colqhoun succeeds in entrapping them all by luring a rescue party away, killing them, and returning to the fort posing as the expected Col. Ives with a secret plan to make the fort his base of operations for feeding on future pioneers travelling through.

Ravenous becomes increasingly gory in its second half yet leavens the grisly bloodletting with some wry humour, giving the film an unsettling tone. So, for example, as the rescue party sets out from the fort, commanding officer Col. Hart (Jones) stumbles over stones and must be reminded to take his cap – hardly like, say, John Ford's noble cavalry roaming the landscape in mythic silhouette. When Ives is preparing a cauldron of stew and Dr. Knox (Spinella) asks if he can help, Ives replies that 'Perhaps later you might contribute', while Col. Hart, turned by Ives, admits to Boyd that 'It's lonely being a cannibal. It's tough making friends.' At the same time, though, the film is quite serious, as signalled by the first shot, an American flag, which also appears prominently in the background during the scene toward the end when Colqhoun explicitly ties his wanton consumption and killing to Manifest Destiny and westward expansion. He compares himself to the nation, 'stretching out its arms, consuming all we can'. Colonialist predation is implicit in the names of the native scouts, George and Martha, obviously renamed by the Whites for whom they work. The fate of Colqhoun's party recalls that of the infamous Donner Party, similarly trapped in the Sierra Nevadas in the 1840s, and of Alferd Packer, 'the Colorado Cannibal', yoking this horror tale to the actualities of American history.

Boyd, like Louis in *Interview with the Vampire** (1994), resists the cannibalistic impulse because he deems it wrong, but he cannot escape the violence of American history, of which he is a part. Twice in the film he is 'reborn' from the dead, but ultimately, he embraces Colqhoun in mutual death. Tellingly, the film begins with Nietzsche's famous warning that he who fights monsters may become one in the process. Martha, the

DIRECTOR Antonia Bird
PRODUCER Adam Fields,
David Heyman, Tim Van Rellim
SCREENPLAY Ted Griffin
CINEMATOGRAPHY
Anthony B. Richmond
EDITOR Neil Farrell
MUSIC Michael Nyman,
Damon Albarn
PRODUCTION COMPANY
Heyday Films
MAIN CAST Guy Pearce,
Robert Carlyle, Jeffrey Jones,
David Arquette, John Spencer,
Neal McDonough, Steven
Spinella, Sheila Tousey,
Joseph Runningfox

lone survivor, throws open the fort door and leaves in the end, like Chief Bromden fleeing the mental hospital at the end of Ken Kesey's *One Flew Over the Cukoo's Nest* (1962). But really, where can she go to escape from this American madness? After all, visiting General Slauson (Spencer) has already tasted approvingly of the simmering 'stew a la Major Knox'.

Further Reading

Brottman, Mikita. *Meat is Murder: An Illustrated Guide to Cannibal Culture*. London and New York: Creation Books, 1998.

DiMarco, Danette. 'Going Wendigo: The Emergence of the Iconic Monster in Margaret Atwood's *Oryx and Crake* and Antonia Bird's *Ravenous*'. *College Literature* 38, no. 4 (2011): 134–155.

Donnelly, K. J. 'Europe Cannibalises the Western: *Ravenous*'. In *Music in the Western: Notes from the Frontier*, ed. Kathryn Kalinak, pp. 148–164. New York and London: Routledge, 2012.

Green, Paul. *Encyclopedia of Weird Westerns*, 2nd edn. Jefferson, NC: McFarland, 2016.

Rosemary's Baby
1968 – 136 mins
Roman Polanski

Director Roman Polanski found the ideal source material with Ira Levin's best-selling novel *Rosemary's Baby*. His earlier films *Repulsion* (1965) and *The Fearless Vampire Killers* (1967) already showed Polanski's ability to work his particular demons involving fate and paranoia, borne of his traumatic experiences as a child in Poland during World War II, in the horror genre. His sensibility fit perfectly with that of author Levin, whose other horror/science-fiction thrillers, like *Rosemary's Baby* (1967), also have contemporary urban settings and also have been adapted to film, including *The Stepford Wives* (1972, film adaptations 1975, 2004),

DIRECTOR Roman Polanski
PRODUCER William Castle
SCREENPLAY Roman Polanski
CINEMATOGRAPHY
William Fraker
EDITOR Sam O'Steen,
Bob Wyman
MUSIC Krzystof Komeda
PRODUCTION COMPANY
Paramount Pictures
MAIN CAST Mia Farrow,
John Cassavetes, Ruth Gordon,
Sidney Blackmer, Ralph Bellamy,
Maurice Evans, Charles Grodin

Sliver (1991, film adaptation 1993), also set within a New York City apartment building, and *The Boys from Brazil* (1976, film adaptation 1978). With *Rosemary's Baby* – his American breakthrough and the second in his so-called 'apartment trilogy', along with *Repulsion* and *The Tenant* (1976), in which he casts himself as the paranoid protagonist Trelkovsky – Polanski, who also wrote the screenplay, leavens Levin's tale of a satanic cult in contemporary New York with anxieties regarding the family and childbirth during the height of second wave feminism.

Like Polanski's *Chinatown* (1974) and *Macbeth* (1971), *Rosemary's Baby* suggests society is permeated by evil. Struggling actor Guy (Cassavetes) and Rosemary Woodhouse (Farrow) move into Manhattan's prestigious Bramford apartment building (the exteriors were filmed at the Dakota, the famous 19th-century building where John Lennon was murdered in 1980) and are quickly befriended by their eccentric and oddly intrusive neighbours, Roman (Blackmer) and Minnie Castevet (Gordon). Polanski makes Rosemary's every encounter seem ominous as she tries to establish a sense of home in their apartment. As we discover later along with Rosemary, Guy has entered into a pact with Roman and Minnie's coven, agreeing to let the Devil sire her child in return for a successful career. Rosemary gradually learns the extent of the conspiracy, which includes her obstetrician, the respected Dr. Saperstein (Bellamy), but, in her weakened state, is kept a virtual prisoner until she delivers the baby.

In his adaptation Polanski remained remarkably close to the book – indeed, much of the dialogue comes directly from the novel – including Levin's strategy of balancing the supernatural with real-world details. For example, as in the novel, so in the film Rosemary, while in Dr. Hill's office, picks up the famous April 1966 issue of *Time* magazine with its cover asking, portentously, 'Is God Dead?' The location shooting at recognisable Manhattan exteriors works similarly. Several familiar Hollywood faces anchor the two younger leads, both of whom are perfectly cast: Cassavetes as the callow careerist, Farrow as the fragile female of melodrama overlaid with connotations of Twiggy in the swinging 60s. Still, Gordon steals her scenes and deservedly received an Academy Award for Best Supporting Actress. (Gimmick exploitation filmmaker William Castle [*The Tingler** (1959)], who produced the film, has a cameo waiting outside a telephone booth containing a frantic Rosemary, where at first his indistinct, hulking form could be a stalking Saperstein. Attuned to the horrors of the real world, Polanski eschews special effects, except for one brief optical effect toward the end, preferring instead to emphasise little details like muffled sounds through apartment walls and the placement of wardrobes.

Further Reading:

Fischer, Lucy. 'Birth Traumas: Parturition and Horror in *Rosemary's Baby*'. In *The Dread of Difference: Gender in the Horror Film*, 2nd edn, ed. Barry Keith Grant, pp. 439–458. Austin: University of Texas Press, 2015.

Newton, Michael. *Rosemary's Baby*. London: British Film Institute, 2019.

Orr, John, and Elzbieta Ostrowska, eds. *The Cinema of Roman Polanski: Dark Spaces of the World*. London and New York: Wallflower Press, 2006.

Wexman, Virginia Wright. 'The Trauma of Infancy in Roman Polanski's *Rosemary's Baby*'. In *American Horrors: Essays on the Modern American Horror Film*, ed. Gregory A. Waller, pp. 30–43. Urbana and Chicago: University of Illinois Press, 1987.

Saw
US/Australia, 2004 – 103 mins
James Wan

Perhaps no post-9/11 horror film to be labelled 'torture porn' (see, for example, Eli Roth's *Hostel** [2005]) deserves the title more than *Saw*. It initiated one of the most successful American horror franchises ever, with nine films to date – the imaginatively named *Saw II* (2005), *Saw III* (2006), *Saw IV* (2007), *Saw V* (2008), *Saw VI* (2009), *Saw 3D* (2010), *Jigsaw* (2017), and *Spiral* (2021) – and a range of merchandising and other media tie-ins. It was the first feature for director James Wan, whose subsequent credits include *Insidious* (2010), *The Conjuring* (2013), and *Aquaman* (2018). *Saw* centres on a terminally ill cancer patient, John Kramer, the 'Jigsaw Killer' (although he is killed in *Saw III*, his prearranged ploys influence the plots of the later films). Jigsaw does not kill his victims himself but instead ensnares them in elaborate, potentially deadly situations that he refers to as 'games' or 'tests' that, he believes, will help them find themselves and make them truly grateful for their lives – if they survive. ('Psychopath teaches sick life lessons' blares a newspaper headline we see.) The premise allows for the presentation of a series of ingenious torture scenarios, thinly veiled as a kind of vigilante justice that taps into the same mix of helplessness and rage characteristic of contemporary America and exploited in other films like *The Purge** (2013).

Each of Jigsaw's games involves potential death or dismemberment for the unwilling players that ironically reflects in a loose way the sin or flaw of which they are, at least according to Kramer, guilty. So, for instance, he imprisons a man who cuts himself for attention in a series of razor-wire cages that he must crawl through if he is to survive. Of course, he doesn't. As the film begins, photographer Adam Stanheight (screenwriter Whannell, who also wrote *Insidious* for Wan) and Dr. Lawrence Gordon (Elwes) awaken on opposite sides of an abandoned and filthy industrial washroom with their ankles chained to pipes, between them a bloody corpse on the tile floor holding a pistol and a cassette player. The place is convincingly repulsive, and we cannot but agree with Adam when, searching for clues, he realises too late that he should have checked inside the water tank first before reaching his hand into the exceedingly foul toilet bowl. As Jigsaw's infernal and complicated game unfolds, it encompasses not only these two men, but also Gordon's wife and daughter; Zep Hindle (Emerson), an orderly at the hospital where Gordon is a surgeon; and Amanda (Smith), the only survivor of one of Jigsaw's games.

Jigsaw is in command of impossibly impressive technologies in his games, including surveillance, while his victims are helpless, any strategy they might devise already countered in advance by the seemingly omniscient and masterful maniac who forces them to turn on each for survival. Here and in the sequels an animated puppet ('Billy') appears on a tricycle to deliver messages to victims, its mechanical obedience a metaphor for the victims' own helplessness and manipulability. In that awful space where Dr. Gordon comes to consciousness – a stark reminder of America's industrial decline – he begins as the model of rationality, determined to find a way to escape through calm logic. But eventually he completely breaks down, like the razor-wire victim

DIRECTOR James Wan
PRODUCER Gregg Hoffman, Oren Koules, Mark Burg
SCREENPLAY Leigh Whannell
CINEMATOGRAPHY David A. Armstrong
EDITOR Kevin Greutert
MUSIC Charlie Clouser
PRODUCTION COMPANY Evolution Entertainment, Twisted Pictures
MAIN CAST Cary Elwes, Leigh Whannell, Danny Glover, Michael Emerson, Ken Leung, Tobin Bell, Shawnee Smith, Monica Potter, Makenzie Vega

whom Jigsaw describes as 'a perfectly sane middle-class male' now desperate to escape his cage. As Gordon frantically explains to Adam before taking action, 'You have to die...my family', summing up the philosophy of much of Hollywood cinema.

And what was Adam's horrible sin? He was, says Jigsaw, a voyeur – not unlike, presumably, the film viewer.

Further Reading:

Aston, James, and John Walliss, eds. *To See the Saw Movies: Essays on Torture Porn and Post-9/11 Horror*. Jefferson, NC and London: McFarland, 2003.

Hills, Matt. 'Cutting into Concepts of 'Reflectionist' Cinema?: The *Saw* Franchise and Puzzles of Post-9/11 Horror'. In *Horror after 9/11: World of Fear, Cinema of Terror*, ed. Aviva Briefel and Sam J. Miller, pp. 107–23. Austin: University of Texas Press, 2011.

Kerner, Aaron Michael. *Torture Porn in the Wake of 9/11: Horror, Exploitation and the Cinema of Sensation*. New Brunswick, NJ and London: Rutgers University Press, 2015.

Poole, Benjamin. *Saw*. Leighton Buzzard: Auteur, 2011.

Sharrett, Christopher. 'The Problem of *Saw*: Torture Porn and the Conservatism of Contemporary Horror Films'. *Cineaste* 35, no. 1 (Winter 2009): pp. 32–37.

Scream
1996 – 111 mins
Wes Craven

Scream was instrumental in launching the cycle of postmodern horror films wherein the characters, like the film itself, are aware of the genre conventions at work in the world they inhabit. Directed by Wes Craven (*The Last House on the Left** [1972], *The Hills Have Eyes** [1977]) and written by Kevin Williamson (*I Know What You Did Last Summer* [1997], *The Faculty* [1998]), *Scream* satirises what the film's characters refer to as the 'rules' of the slasher subgenre as established in *Halloween** (1978) and continued in such other slashers as *Friday the 13th* (1980) and Craven's own *A Nightmare on Elm Street* (1984), among others. The film plays its moments of horror straight, with killings that violate generic expectation, even as it knowingly satirises its own conventions, thus having it both ways. One of the most commercially successful of slasher films, it was followed by three sequels – *Scream 2* (1997), *Scream 3* (2000), *Scream 4* (2011), the second and fourth also written by Williamson – and a television series (2015-), as well as subsequent films inspired by its success, such as *Scary Movie* (2000) and *The Final Girls* (2015).

The plot of *Scream* is typical – 'This is *Prom Night* [1980] revisited, man', observes movie geek Randy Meeks (Kennedy). A high school student, Sidney Prescott (Campbell), along with her friends, is being targeted and slaughtered by an unknown killer, in this case wearing a Halloween costume (an actual one purchased by Craven) with a mask (after *Halloween*'s Michael Myers, every mass killer had to have one), one based on Edvard Munch's iconic 1893 painting popularly referred to as 'The Scream'. Like the comical casting of Henry Winkler – known for his iconic portrayal of the rebellious high-school dropout Fonzie on television's *Happy Days* (1974–84) – as the school principal, the 'Ghostface' reference to Munch announces the film's awareness of its intertextual traditions. The characters, immersed in California teen culture, frequently discuss actual movies, often framing their own lives as if they were in a movie, and, as the bodies begin to pile up, referencing the conventions of horror movies, particularly slashers, even as they are about to happen.

The killer taunts his victims on the telephone, asking 'What's your favourite scary movie?' and forcing them to answer trivia questions about horror movies. When asked about his motives, Billy (Ulrich) repeats Norman Bates's famous line from *Psycho** (1960), 'We all go a little mad sometimes', and then cites his reference. Although Billy obligingly provides a possible reason for his murderous rampage, one involving a past family trauma (surprise), while his collaborator Stuart (Lillard) merely cites 'peer pressure', ultimately motives are irrelevant in this self-conscious genre exercise ('It's the millennium – motives are incidental').

While the gang watch *Halloween* on television, *Scream* literally interacts with its intertextual inspiration in several ways as it builds toward Sidney's climactic confrontation with the killer. Deputy Dewey (Arquette) bursts into the house to rescue the teens, but, mistaking Jaimie Lee Curtis's screams on television for the real thing, is overcome by the killer. Sidney topples the television set onto the prone Stuart, electrocuting him, the image of

DIRECTOR Wes Craven
PRODUCER Cathy Konrad, Cary Woods
SCREENPLAY Kevin Williamson
CINEMATOGRAPHY Mark Irwin
EDITOR Patrick Lussier
MUSIC Marco Beltrami
PRODUCTION COMPANY Woods Entertainment
MAIN CAST Neve Campbell, David Arquette, Courteney Cox, Matthew Lillard, Jamie Kennedy, Rose McGowan, Skeet Ulrich, Drew Barrymore, W. Earl Brown

Jaimie Lee defending herself from Michael Myers with a knife on the screen at that moment so that the blade seems to be attacking Stuart. Randy explains the rules for surviving in a horror movie, the first being that you should never have sex when a mass killer is on the loose. Yet Sidney, who gives in to her 'sexual anorexia' and loses her virginity to Billy earlier in the evening, becomes the Final Girl when she finishes off the killer, rewriting the script and altering the convention.

Further Reading

Greven, David. *Ghost Faces: Hollywood and Post-Millennial Masculinity*. Albany: State University of New York Press, 2016.

Muir, John Kenneth. *Wes Craven: The Art of Horror*. Jefferson, NC: McFarland, 1998.

Phillips, Kendall R. *Projected Fears: Horror Film and American Culture*. Westport, CT and London: Praeger, 2005.

Tudor, Andrew. 'From Paranoia to Postmodernism? The Horror Movie in Late Modern Society'. In *Genre and Contemporary Hollywood*, ed. Steve Neale, pp. 105–116. London: British Film Institute, 2002.

West, Steven. *Scream*. Leighton Buzzard: Auteur, 2019.

The Shining
UK/US, 1980 – 146 mins
Stanley Kubrick

Apart from the horrors that people inflict upon each other in his films, *The Shining* is Kubrick's only actual horror film (his sensibility was more attuned to science fiction), yet it remains not only one of the most well-known of the many adaptations of Stephen King's fiction – despite the significant changes from the author's 1977 novel and his stated disapproval of it – but also one of the most famous horror movies of all time, polarising viewers. A sequel, *Doctor Sleep* (2019), based on King's own 2013 sequel and focusing on Danny Torrance as an adult struggling with his trauma and 'shine'-sucking vampires, was a box-office disappointment; but the documentary film *Room 237* (2012), named for the guest room in the Overlook Hotel that Danny (Lloyd) is warned by chef Hallorann (Crothers) not to enter, demonstrates the extent to which *The Shining* has fascinated viewers and entrapped them in Kubrick's maze of meanings, generating interpretations ranging from the genocide of Native Americans to the Holocaust. Ultimately, though, while there is some

DIRECTOR Stanley Kubrick
PRODUCER Stanley Kubrick
SCREENPLAY Stanley Kubrick, Diane Johnson
CINEMATOGRAPHY John Alcott
EDITOR Ray Lovejoy
MUSIC Wendy Carlos, Rachel Elkind
PRODUCTION COMPANY The Producer Circle Company, Peregrine Productions, Hawk Films
MAIN CAST Jack Nicholson, Shelley Duvall, Danny Lloyd, Scatman Crothers, Barry Nelson, Philip Stone, Joe Turkel

supernatural stuff involving the ability of people and places to 'shine', or communicate telepathically, *The Shining* is most compelling as a petrifying portrait of a family, like so many in King's oeuvre, riven and torn apart by underlying psychic tensions of guilt, repression, denial, anger, and violence.

A former schoolteacher, Jack Torrance (Nicholson) accepts a job as winter caretaker at the isolated Overlook Hotel in the Colorado Rockies, closed for the season, where he will live with his wife Wendy (Duvall) and son Danny while he writes (we never learn what his 'project' might be). But not long after they take up residence, things begin to unravel. Jack, a recovering alcoholic, becomes increasingly erratic and violent, and Danny is so traumatised he disassociates as 'Tony' ('the one who lives in my mouth'). Wandering into the Gold ballroom, Jack meets the ghost of Grady, a previous caretaker who had gone mad and killed his family before taking his own life, and Jack's resentment and guilt over dislocating Danny's arm when he was drunk several years ago now explodes like the red sea of blood that, in one of the film's most memorable shots, bursts through the hotel elevator doors and floods the hotel lobby.

Along with Wendy, we discover that Jack, supposedly writing, has in fact been typing the same phrase over and over again: 'All work and no play makes Jack a dull boy.' But this Jack is hardly dull as, now completely insane, he attacks Wendy with a sharp axe and with mad glee announces 'Heeere's Johnny' (ad-libbed by Nicholson) as the blade splinters her locked door and she cowers in terror. Referring to the ritual introduction of former host Johnny Carson on television's popular *Tonight Show*, Jack's comment, along with the family discussion about the cannibalism of the Donner Party (see also *Ravenous** [1999]) as they are driving up to the hotel, contextualise the Torrance family's psychic torrents within American culture more broadly despite their physical isolation for almost the entire film.

The Shining, like *Halloween* (1978)*, was one of the first horror films to make use of the Steadicam, a harness device that permits smooth tracking of the camera even when it is handheld. The Steadicam shots of Danny riding his tricycle through the empty corridors of the Overlook, the camera very low to the ground, were startling at the time and heighten the viewer's sense of anxiety, even today. The surreal quality of the Overlook's vast yet claustrophobic spaces – described by Wendy alternately as a maze and a ghost ship – mirror the emerging madness of Jack (Kubrick twice shows him in the hotel as a mirror reflection first), a man obviously frustrated by his own failures as a father and husband, and make the hotel one of horror cinema's most memorable terrible houses.

Further Reading

Donelly, Kevin J. *The Shining*. London: Wallflower Press, 2018.

Luckhurst, Roger. *The Shining*. London: British Film Institute, 2013.

Mee, Laura. *The Shining*. Leighton Buzzard: Auteur, 2017.

Olson, Danel, ed. *The Shining: Studies in the Horror Film*. Lakewood, CO: Centipede Press, 2015.

The Silence of the Lambs
1991 – 118 mins
Jonathan Demme

The Silence of the Lambs, based on the 1988 novel by Thomas Harris, won five top Academy Awards, including Best Director, Best Actor and Actress, and Best Picture – the only horror film to have done so – and launched the intense popular and scholarly interest in serial killers and their representation in popular culture. Michael Mann's *Manhunter* (1986, adapted from Harris's 1981 novel *Red Dragon*), the first film to feature Harris's character of Hannibal 'the Cannibal' Lecter, was not a box-office success, but *Silence of the Lambs* was one of the biggest grossing films of the year. It was followed by a sequel, *Hannibal* (2001), in which Hopkins reprised his Oscar-winning role as Lecter, and two prequels, *Red Dragon* (2002) and *Hannibal Rising* (2007). While the film generated some controversy because of protest from gay and feminist groups, *Silence of the Lambs* may be read as a critique of dominant masculine power.

FBI trainee Clarice Starling (Foster) is assigned to interview Lecter, an imprisoned former psychiatrist and cannibalistic serial killer, because her superior, Jack Crawford (Glenn), thinks he might help them find another serial killer, 'Buffalo Bill', who murders young women and flays sections of their skin. Dr. Frederick Chilton (Heald), the sadistic warden of the Baltimore maximum security facility where Lecter has been imprisoned for the past eight years when the story begins, describes Lecter as 'a monster, a pure psychopath', and the iconic mask Lecter wears when he is brought to meet Senator Martin certainly gives him a predatory, animalistic look. But the film's take on good and evil is somewhat more complex: for even while Lecter is a vicious murderer (he tells Starling he ate an annoying census-taker's liver 'with some fava beans and a nice chianti'), he metes out (so to speak) a not entirely unjust punishment to Chilton ('I'm having an old friend for dinner') and not only provides helpful clues to Starling but also lays bare the truth about the gendered power imbalance in the world at large.

As the film opens, Starling is training on an FBI obstacle course, and the film soon shows us the patriarchal power with its hurdles and pitfalls through which she must routinely navigate, like a starling flitting through danger. The idea is literalised with the gauntlet of incarcerated men she must walk through, trying to ignore their taunts (one of them shouts 'I can smell your cunt') to reach Lecter's cell at the end of the corridor. The various law enforcement officers seen throughout the film are overwhelmingly male, and at one point, in an elevator with other trainees, all of them men, she is literally surrounded, hemmed in by them. One of the entomologists who helps her identify the moths shoved into the throats of Buffalo Bill's victims brazenly hits on her, making explicit the tensions underlying everything she does as a professional woman in a man's world. She seems a pawn being played by men, whether it is Lecter, Chilton, Crawford, or, in the climax, Buffalo Bill.

An actual cannibal, Lecter also feeds off Starling's personal trauma with his demand for a quid pro quo, information on Buffalo Bill in exchange for personal details about her nightmares as a child after witnessing lambs being slaughtered. Lector makes the thematic connection when providing a clue about

DIRECTOR Jonathan Demme
PRODUCER Kenneth Utt, Edward Saxon, Ron Bozman
SCREENPLAY Ted Tally
CINEMATOGRAPHY Tak Fujimoto
EDITOR Craig McKay
MUSIC Howard Shore
PRODUCTION COMPANY Strong Heart/Demme Productions
MAIN CAST Jodie Foster, Anthony Hopkins, Scott Glenn, Ted Levine, Anthony Heald, Kasi Lemmons,

Bill, asking Starling, 'Don't you feel eyes moving over your body?' Men are shown doing exactly this periodically, a daily occurrence taken to horrific extreme in Bill's stalking of Starling in the dark basement of his terrible house with his night goggles. Unlike, say, Michael Myers in *Halloween** (1978), who his psychiatrist describes as the devil incarnate, Lecter explains that Buffalo Bill is the product of years of abuse, presumably doled out by the patriarchal and homophobic society directly addressed in the famous 'anti-money' shot of Buffalo Bill with full frontal nudity but penis lacking, hidden between his thighs.

Further Reading:

Forshaw, Barry. *The Silence of the Lambs*. Leighton Buzzard: Auteur, 2013.

Halberstam, Judith. *Skin Shows: Gothic Horror and the Technology of Monsters*. Durham and London: Duke University Press, 1995.

Persons, Dan, et al. 'Silence of the Lambs'. *Cinefantastique* 22, no. 4 (February 1992): 16–39.

Seltzer, Mark. *Serial Killers: Death and Life in America's Wound Culture*. London: Routledge, 1998.

Tasker, Yvonne. *The Silence of the Lambs*. London: British Film Institute, 2002.

Sisters
1972 – 92 mins
Brian De Palma

Sisters was Brian De Palma's first horror film (see also Carrie* [1976] and Phantom of the Paradise* [1974]) and perhaps his most penetrating meditation on the relation of the gaze to horror as well as his most sustained reworking of tropes from Alfred Hitchcock, the filmmaker who has influenced him more than any other. Sisters, like De Palma's later Dressed to Kill (1980), takes its premise of a schizophrenic murderer from Psycho* [1960] – the film to which it was compared in publicity material when it was released – and also, like Psycho, uses horror to explore questions of morality in film spectatorship. Mapping horror's privileged

DIRECTOR Brian De Palma
PRODUCER Edward R. Pressman
SCREENPLAY Brian De Palma, Louisa Rose
CINEMATOGRAPHY Gregory Sandor
EDITOR Paul Hirsch
MUSIC Bernard Herrmann
PRODUCTION COMPANY American International Pictures
MAIN CAST Margot Kidder, William Finley, Jennifer Salt, Charles Durning, Lisle Wilson, Dolph Sweet, Mary Davenport

form of the double onto biological Siamese twins, it follows *Psycho* in morally implicating the spectator even as it depicts its doppelgangers as actually conjoined.

Sisters immediately establishes the relation of the gaze to the audience's own questionable desires in the opening scene in which Phillip (Wilson) finds himself in a locker room where a blind woman comes in, unaware of his presence, and begins to undress. The situation is suddenly interrupted as we discover that this is a pre-recorded setup for a *Candid-Camera*-type television game show, 'Peeping Toms' – the title of course evoking Michael Powell's *Peeping Tom* (1960), released the same year as *Psycho* and exploring similar themes of voyeurism and violence – and the contestants have to guess what Phillip will do under the circumstance. This is the same question film viewers likely have already asked themselves, before the interruption, because of the dynamics of spectatorship and identification already mobilised in this opening scene. Phillip chooses to be chivalrous, which makes his murder later all the more shocking.

After the television show, Phillip and the blind woman, actually a model, Danielle Breton (Kidder), spend the night together in her apartment, and the next morning Grace Collier (Salt), a local reporter, sees Phillip being murdered by her there from her own apartment window. She later watches Danielle in her apartment through her binoculars, recalling *Rear Window*, another of Hitchcock's most probing meditations on voyeurism and the cinematic experience. During Phillip's murder we see the action within Danielle's apartment and Grace watching from her kitchen simultaneously via split screen, a technique of which De Palma is so fond and that is perfectly appropriate here, given that the film, again like *Psycho*, is about a violent psychopath with a split personality, the presence of the second personality taken on as a way of coping with guilt over the death of the other (Mother in *Psycho*, conjoined sibling Dominique in *Sisters*).

Grace follows Danielle and her doctor/lover Emil (Finley, who also plays Winslow Leach/the eponymous *Phantom of the Paradise*) to his clinic, where she is discovered and finds herself suddenly transformed from distanced spectator to active participant, from observer of horror to its object. Emil accuses her of wanting to know all their secrets without paying a price and says he will 'share' them with her anyway. He drugs her, and there follows a surreal dream sequence evoking Fellini, complete with nuns and priests, in which Grace imagines herself as Dominique about to be surgically separated (that is, killed) by Emil so that he can be with Danielle, with whom he has fallen in love. The sequence's editing places us in Grace/Dominique's perspective, so that, just like Danielle, we 'become' Dominique, watching as the meat cleaver is passed to Emil and he swings it toward the twins like a butcher. As with the famous verité-style 'Be Black, Baby' sequence of De Palma's earlier *Hi, Mom!* (1970), the intent is to make us experience the events rather than merely witness them.

Further Reading

Dumas, Chris. *Un-American Psycho: Brian De Palma and the Political Invisible*. Bristol, UK and Chicago: Intellect, 2012.

Graham, Allison. "The Fallen Wonder of the World': Brian De Palma's Horror Films'. In *American Horrors: Essays on the Modern American Horror Film*, ed. Gregory A. Waller, pp. 129–144. Urbana and Chicago: University of Illinois Press, 1987.

Keesey, Douglas. *Brian De Palma's Split Screen: A Life in Film*. Jackson: University Press of Mississippi, 2015.

Mackinnon, Kenneth. *Misogyny in the Movies: The De Palma Question*. Newark: University of Delaware Press, 1990.

Wood, Robin. *Robin Wood on the Horror Film: Collected Essays and Reviews*, ed. Barry Keith Grant. Detroit: Wayne State University Press, 2018.

Targets
1968 – 90 mins
Peter Bogdanovich

A movie about the changing nature of horror in contemporary culture and an homage to classic cinema, *Targets* was the first film directed by Peter Bogdanovich, a film historian and critic who championed the work of classic Hollywood filmmaking. Bogdanovich got the chance to make *Targets* when Roger Corman (*The Little Shop of Horrors** [1960], *The Masque of the Red Death** [1964]) realised that Boris Karloff contractually owed him two days› work and told the aspiring director he was free to make whatever film he wanted with the horror star as long as he stayed within budget and included clips from Corman's own 1963 movie *The Terror*. Despite these constraints, Bogdanovich produced a smart horror movie that served as the perfect swan

DIRECTOR Peter Bogdanovich
PRODUCER Roger Corman, Peter Bogdanovich
SCREENPLAY Peter Bogdanovich
CINEMATOGRAPHY Laszlo Kovacs
EDITOR Peter Bogdanovich
MUSIC Ronald Stein
PRODUCTION COMPANY Saticoy Productions
MAIN CAST Boris Karloff, Tim O'Kelly, Peter Bogdanovich, Nancy Hsueh, James Brown, Sandy Baron, Arthur Peterson, Tanya Morgan

song for Karloff's career in Hollywood. Sold to Paramount, *Targets*, with a plot involving a mass killer, was given only limited release by the studio after the assassinations of Martin Luther King and Bobby Kennedy two months later.

The clever narrative (with uncredited help from Samuel Fuller) alternates between two stories, one involving the old and disillusioned horror star Byron Orlok – a reference to Max Schreck's vampire Count Orlok in *Nosferatu* (1922) – played by Karloff, who has suddenly decided to retire; the other following Bobby Thompson (O'Kelly), a disturbed Vietnam veteran who calmly goes ballistic and kills his wife and mother (and grocery boy), after which he fires on drivers on a crowded freeway from atop an oil storage tank (echoes of Raoul Walsh's *White Heat* [1949]) before going behind the screen of a drive-in theatre where he snipes at people in their cars. Bobby's character was inspired by Charles Whitman, who in 1966 stabbed his wife and mother to death and then ascended the University of Texas at Austin tower where he shot 45 people, killing 14 of them. The two stories come together as the film being shown at the drive-in is 'The Terror', where Orlok is making his last public appearance.

Like Hitchcock, Bogdanovich builds audience identification through the alternation of point-of-view and tracking shots, frequently putting the viewer in Bobby's perspective but, interestingly, never in Orlok's, who, because he is also Karloff, is as much a myth as a man. Bobby, though, is one of us, and although the film provides no explicit answers for his killing spree, it is strongly implied that Bobby is one of those pure products of America who has gone crazy. Actor Tim O'Kelly's all-American looks resemble Whitman's; the gun store owner where Bobby buys his ammo observes that he has 'an honest face'. Even as popular culture pervades Bobby's world, from the Baby Ruth candy bars he eats and Kool cigarettes he smokes to the radio that continually blares inane pop music when he drives, it always bespeaks serious repression. His clothes are perfectly pressed and pale, like the colour scheme of his family home, bleached out like his lack of emotional affect.

Bogdanovich inserts homages to one of his favourite auteurs, Howard Hawks, as boy wonder Sammy Michaels (played by the director) and Orlok watch with admiration a scene from *The Criminal Code* (1931) on television, and when Orlok walks with determination to confront Bobby behind the drive-in screen in the climax, he is grazed in the forehead with a bullet just as John Wayne's Dunson is in the climax of *Red River* (1948). (*Red River* is the film referred to in the title of Bogdanovich's breakthrough follow-up to *Targets*, *The Last Picture Show* [1971].) Orlok views himself as outdated in the context of actual world events ('No one's afraid of a painted monster anymore'), but his climactic confrontation with Bobby in conjunction with his towering screen image confuses the killer and negates his threat, suggesting that Hollywood classic horror movies, mythic in stature, still retain their spectatorial power. At the same time, though, the impersonality and randomness of Bobby's killings anticipates later postmodern horror films about the waning of affect, such as *Henry: Portrait of a Serial Killer** (1986), and seems as relevant today, in an era when mass shootings at soft target public gatherings have become commonplace.

Further Reading:

Dixon, Wheeler Winston. *Cinema at the Margins*. London and New York: Anthem Press, 2013.

Henderson, Brian. '*Targets*: An Unshielding Darkness'. In *Focus on the Horror Film*, ed. Roy Huss and T. J. Ross, pp. 152–161. Englewood Cliffs, NJ: Prentice-Hall, 1972.

Lager, Mark. 'Peter Bogdanvich's *Targets*'. *Film International* 16, no. 4 (2018): 13–15.

Yule, Andrew. *Picture Shows: The Life and Films of Peter Bogdanovich*. New York: Limelight, 1992.

The Texas Chainsaw Massacre
1974 – 83 mins
Tobe Hooper

One of the most influential and frightening of American horror films, *The Texas Chainsaw Massacre* set a precedent for John Carpenter's *Halloween** (1978) and the slasher cycle (see *Scream** [1996]) that soon followed. For some viewers it is merely a particularly vivid example of exploitation cinema's execrable treatment of women, although many see it as a comment on and product of the crisis of American society in the wake of Watergate and Vietnam. Independently financed and made on a small budget by a group of filmmakers based in Austin, including director Tobe Hooper – who would go on to direct, among others, the television miniseries *Salem's Lot* (1979), *The Funhouse* (1981), and *Poltergeist** (1982) – the film was followed by three sequels – *The Texas Chainsaw Massacre 2* (1986), also directed by Hooper; *Leatherface: The Texas Chainsaw Massacre III* (1990); and *Texas Chainsaw Massacre: The Next Generation* (1995) – a remake in 2003; two prequels, *The Texas Chainsaw Massacre: The Beginning* (2006) and *Leatherface* (2017); and a sequel, *Texas Chainsaw 3D* (2013), and influenced other redneck horror movies to follow such as the *Wrong Turn* series (2003–2014) and *The Devil's Rejects** (2005).

The film begins in a way that suggests documentary actuality, with its opening title (including a precise date, August 18, 1973 – only the first of a number of connections to Hitchcock's *Psycho** [1960]) – and a promise to provide an account of 'one of the most bizarre crimes in the annals of American history'. The minimal plot follows a group of five friends who fall victim to a family of cannibals while on a road trip to visit the old, abandoned family homestead of two of them, Franklin Hardesty (Partain) and his sister Sally (Burns). There they encounter the neighbours, a clan of psychotic cannibals, one of whom, Leatherface (named only in the credits), wearing a mask of human skin, kills them all but Sally, who is imprisoned in the house and tortured throughout the course of an evening before she manages to escape. The film ends with the pursuing Leatherface crazily waving his smoking and buzzing chainsaw in crazy arcs in the air as the sun rises behind him, the dawn of a new and violent post-hippie era. The character of Leatherface was in part inspired by the infamous killer Ed Gein, as were both *Psycho* and *The Silence of the Lambs** (1991), but the film's plot is largely fictional.

The final third of *Massacre* is devoted entirely to the torture of Sally. There is little dialogue, the soundtrack filled mostly with her continuous screams, Leatherface's ominously whirring chainsaw, and an unsettling score. There are big close-ups of Sally's frightened eyes staring in incomprehension and utter fear, like those of animals in a slaughterhouse, and her mouth contorted by screams. The opening of the film suggests a cosmic disturbance or evil of some kind, with images of exploding sunspots accompanying the credits, and Pam (McMinn), who ends up first on a meat hook and then stuffed in a freezer, reading from her astrology book that 'Saturn is in Retrograde'. But rather than being about some form of Lovecraftian cosmic evil, the film focuses on the horrors of a quotidian American civilization that has imploded, metaphorically feeding

DIRECTOR Tobe Hooper
PRODUCER Tobe Hooper
SCREENPLAY Tobe Hooper, Kim Henkel
CINEMATOGRAPHY Daniel Pearl
EDITOR Sallye Richardson, Larry Carroll
MUSIC Tobe Hooper, Wayne Bell
PRODUCTION COMPANY Vortex
MAIN CAST Marilyn Burns, Paul A. Partain, Allen Danziger, Edwin Neal, Jim Siedow, Gunnar Hansen, Teri McMinn, William Vail

upon itself. It presents a blighted, post-industrial landscape that belies the promise of the American west – after the credits the first image is of a dead armadillo in the middle of the road, the blistering and oppressive heat visibly rising off the asphalt – with the family home now displaced by horror's archetypal terrible house. Like *The Last House on the Left** (1972), the film offers no explanations, no narrative closure, no heroic protagonist, and, as Pam quotes from Franklin's horoscope, 'The events of the world are not doing much either to cheer one up'.

Further Reading

Clover, Carol. *Men, Women and Chain Saws: Gender in the Modern Horror Film*. Princeton, NJ: Princeton University Press, 1992.

Lanza, Joseph. *The Texas Chainsaw Massacre and Its Terrifying Times: A Cultural History*. New York: Skyhorse, 2019.

Rose, James. *The Texas Chain Saw Massacre*. Leighton Buzzard: Auteur, 2013.

Sharrett, Christopher. 'The Idea of Apocalypse in *The Texas Chainsaw Massacre*'. In *Planks of Reason: Essays on the Horror Film*, revised ed., ed. Barry Keith Grant and Christopher Sharrett, pp. 300–320. Lanham, MD: Scarecrow Press, 2004.

Wood, Robin. 'The American Family Comedy: From *Meet Me in St. Louis* to *The Texas Chainsaw Massacre*'. In *Robin Wood on the Horror Film: Collected Essays and Reviews*, ed. Barry Keith Grant, pp. 171–179. Detroit: Wayne State University Press, 2018.

The Tingler
1959 – 82 mins
William Castle

A flamboyant producer and director known as 'The Abominable Showman', William Castle (who also produced Roman Polanski's *Rosemary's Baby** in 1968) made a series of gimmicky horror films beginning with *Macabre* (1958), for which patrons could purchase a $1,000 life insurance policy against 'Death by Fright' (such a death certificate appears in *The Tingler*). The original *House on Haunted Hill* (1959) featured 'Emergo', a skeleton on wires that came out from above the screen and flew above the audience at appropriate moments, while spectators watching *13 Ghosts* (1960) were treated to the process of 'Illusion-O', which required them to don a pair of special glasses to see the ghosts on the screen. And in *Mr. Sardonicus* (1961), Castle (the basis for the flamboyant Lawrence Woolsey [John Goodman] in Joe Dante's *Matinee* [1993]) himself interrupts the plot just before the climax with a 'punishment poll' in which he asks the audience to vote on whether the title character, who has been forced to live by drinking the blood of virgins, should receive a merciful fate or not. The third of five collaborations between Castle and writer Robb White (the other two being *House on Haunted Hill* (1959) and the *Psycho* (1960)*-inspired *Homicidal* [1960]), *The Tingler*, featuring the gimmick of 'Percepto', is at once his most absurd and most interesting film.

The nonsensical premise posits the existence of a parasite that, resembling a cross between a lobster and a mutated caterpillar that might have been imagined by David Cronenberg, actually lives in the base of the human spine and is, in the words of its discoverer, Dr. Warren Chapin (Price), the 'force of fear' incarnate. The tinger is formed when one experiences fear and dissipated only with a cathartic scream – otherwise it would ascend the spine and snap it, causing death. The tingler is ugly because man's fear is ugly, Chapin explains to his young assistant, David (Hickman). Although no surgeon or medical examiner has ever noticed this phenomenon before, Chapin soon manages to extract one alive from a mute woman (Evelyn) who has just died, deliberately scared to death, as we later find out, by her husband (a plot point perhaps borrowed from Henri-Georges Clouzot's 1957 thriller, *Les Diaboliques*).

The creature eludes Chapin and escapes into an adjacent movie theater, as *The Blob* (1958) had done a year earlier, and at this point in the film's initial run, the electrically wired random seats in select theatres were switched on, providing some patrons (and audience shills) with surprise vibrations. Castle appears at the beginning of the film, like Edward Van Sloan in *Frankenstein* (1931), to warn us that we might feel a tingling sensation during the movie and that if we do, we should feel free to scream for our lives. Now the film's projection seems to stop as the silhouette of the tingler crawls across the screen and Price's voice is heard on the soundtrack warning the audience to scream.

The cinema into which the tingler escapes, which specialises in silent films, is showing Henry King's *Tol'able David* (1921), and *The Tingler*, recalling *House of Wax** (1953) before it, suggests a distinction between the older form of melodrama and the newer cinema of sensation, with 'Percepto' an attempt to achieve

DIRECTOR William Castle
PRODUCER William Castle
SCREENPLAY Robb White
CINEMATOGRAPHY
Wilfred M. Cline
EDITOR Chester W. Schaeffer
MUSIC Von Dexter
PRODUCTION COMPANY
William Castle Productions,
Columbia Pictures
MAIN CAST Vincent Price,
Judith Evelyn, Darryl Hickman,
Philip Coolidge, Patricia Cutts,
Pamela Lincoln

a rudimentary form of interactive cinema. Also, *The Tingler* offers a clever metaphor for the therapeutic function of horror, which provides a release, a catharsis, of our collective and individual fears – literally enacted by the collective scream the film explicitly elicits. Earlier in the film, Chapin, conducting research into fear, tries to scare himself by taking a double dose of LSD (*The Tingler* was the first film to depict the effects of the drug, prefiguring Roger Corman's 1967 *The Trip* by almost a decade), and the otherwise black-and-white film inserts a few colour images of a blood-filled sink and bathtub with a hand reaching up from it. This is, like, far out, but the film reveals its conservative perspective when Chapin, unlike the traditional mad scientist, decides that knowledge of the tingler should remain undisclosed and reinserts it into its dead host's body (apparently a simple procedure of shoving it in), a resonant image of repression that is downright disturbing.

Further Reading

Brottman, Mikita. *Offensive Films*. Nashville: Vanderbilt University Press, 2005.

Castle, William. *Step Right Up! I'm Gonna Scare the Pants off America*. New York: Putnam's Sons, 1976.

Heffernan, Kevin J. *Ghouls, Gimmicks, and Gold: Horror Films and the American Movie Business, 1953–1968*. Durham and London: Duke University Press, 2004.

Leeder, Murray, ed. *ReFocus: The Films of William Castle*. Edinburgh: Edinburgh University Press, 2018.

Twentynine Palms
France/Germany/US, 2003 – 119 mins
Bruno Dumont

In *Twentynine Palms* Bruno Dumont brings New French Extremism to the American West. These films, such as Catherine Breillat's *Fat Girl* (À *ma soeur*, 2001) and Gaspar Noé's *Irreversible* (2002), are all horrifying but not necessarily horror films like *Haut Tension* (High Tension [*Switchblade Romance*], 2003), *Frontiere(s)* (2007), and *Martyrs* (2008). Characterised by graphic sexuality and violence, often presented together, they have much in common with the most radical of horror movies in their extraordinary meditation on masculine power, repression, and the fate of women in contemporary society. They also show, often by juxtaposing horrific imagery within seemingly banal contexts, that horror is less the supernatural than the standard, merely a pervasive part of everyday life. In *Twentynine Palms*, as in *Midsommar** [2019], the horrors take place in broad daylight rather than hidden in the dark, but they seem relatively routine until they explode into violence.

Breillat's À *ma soeur* proceeds at a leisurely pace until blindsiding the unsuspecting spectator with a burst of violence in the climax, violence that clearly lay beneath the surface, but which is surprising in its intensity when it manifests nonetheless. *Twentynine Palms* works in a similar fashion, precipitated by a literal blindsiding. The film's story involves a location scout, David (Wissak), and his girlfriend Katia (Golubeva), who drive from Los Angeles to explore the California desert. They proceed in the most leisurely, meandering manner, occupying most of the film's running time, until the shocking conclusion. Dumont follows the couple's activities once they arrive in the town of Twentynine Palms, showing their scouting forays into the desert, driving, lovemaking, eating, and arguing. The language barrier between them – he speaks little Russian, she little English, so they both talk in French, in which neither seems fluent – expresses the emotional distance between them. The languorous images of them naked among the desert rocks are ambiguous, making them seem at once harmonious with nature and starkly opposed to it.

During their final drive through the desert, they are accosted by a trio of men who suddenly appear and ram their truck, pull them from it, beat them, and sodomise David. After this traumatic event, the couple return to their motel room, alive but badly injured. David refuses to call the police, presumably because of his shame, and sends Katia to fetch dinner. When she returns, he emerges suddenly from the bathroom, head shaved, pins her to the bed, and stabs her to death. While these two scenes come as a startling surprise, and are starkly different in tone than all that has come before, they may be understood in retrospect as a more extreme expression of the power dynamics between the couple from the very beginning of the film, where David drives his muscular Hummer while Katia sleeps in the passenger seat. Throughout the film the camera shows in subtle ways how David transforms sex and intimacy into assertions of masculine power.

As in a classic Western, the savages seem to come from nowhere, emerging from the landscape like Indians. David and Katia are unaware of their menacing truck until it appears behind them and forces them to a stop. The look on David's face during the attack echoes his expressions during his sexual climaxes, which

DIRECTOR Bruno Dumont
PRODUCER Rachid Bouchareb
SCREENPLAY Bruno Dumont
CINEMATOGRAPHY
Georges Lechaptois
EDITOR Dominique Petrot
PRODUCTION COMPANY
3B Productions, The 7th Floor,
Thoke Moebius Film Company
MAIN CAST Yekaterina
Gulobeva, David Wissak

are shown to be fiercely animalistic. If David's Hummer, now resembling a mere toy beside the attackers' inexplicably huge pickup truck, is an extension of his masculinity, it is rear-ended, just as he is by his attackers. The inevitable reference here is to the male rape of Bobby in *Deliverance* (1972), the violation similarly destroying the victim's sense of masculine identity. In the deliberately downbeat ending, the police find David's dead (limp) body by the Hummer.

Further Reading

Horeck, Tanya, and Tina Kendall, eds. *The New Extremism in Cinema*. Edinburgh: Edinburgh University Press, 2011.

Palmer, Tim. *Brutal Intimacy: Analyzing Contemporary French Cinema*. Middletown, CT: Wesleyan University Press, 2011.

Taylor, Alison. *Troubled Every Day: The Aesthetics of Violence and the Everyday in European Art Cinema*. Edinburgh: Edinburgh University Press, 2017.

West, Alexandra. *Films of the New French Extremity*. Jefferson, NC and London: MacFarland, 2016.

Two Thousand Maniacs!
1964 – 87 mins
Herschell Gordon Lewis

In the 1960s Herschell Gordon Lewis, 'the Godfather of Gore', made a range of exploitation films including nudies (*The Adventures of Lucky Pierre* [1961], *Goldilocks and the Three Bares* [1963], the first nudie musical) and horror, most notably a series of three films retrospectively referred to as 'The Blood Trilogy': *Blood Feast* (1963), *Two Thousand Maniacs!*, and *Colour Me Blood Red* (1965), his last film before parting ways with producer David F. Friedman. With an alternate career in marketing and advertising, Lewis found a niche in the drive-in and grindhouse market before the mainstreaming of hardcore porn and splatter, to which he contributed significantly. Roger Corman had *A Bucket of Blood* (1959) – clearly an inspiration for the plot

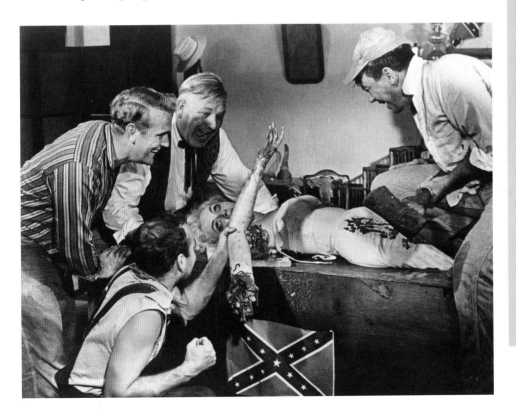

DIRECTOR
Herschell Gordon Lewis
PRODUCER David F. Friedman
SCREENPLAY
Herschell Gordon Lewis
CINEMATOGRAPHY
Herschell Gordon Lewis
EDITOR Robert Sinise
MUSIC Larry Wellington
PRODUCTION COMPANY
Jacqueline Kay, Friedman-Lewis
Productions
MAIN CAST Connie Mason,
William Kerwin ('Thomas
Wood'), Jeffrey Allen, Gary
Bakeman, Ben Moore,
Jerome Eden, Shelby Livingston,
Michael Korb, Yvonne Gilbert,
Vincent Santo

of *Colour Me Blood Red* – but Lewis unabashedly went for 'gouts of blood' (quoting from Macbeth – before his film career Lewis was a professor of English literature), troweling it on and colouring his images bright red with saturated tones and bold colour contrasts (Lewis was his own cinematographer in addition to scoring his films and occasionally producing and editing them as well). In *Two Thousand Maniacs!* (remade in 2005 as *2001 Maniacs*), the middle film of the Blood Trilogy, Lewis exploits the regional tensions between North and South that have existed since the Civil War – tensions heightened, certainly, by contemporary confrontations in the Civil Rights movement – in a story of jes' plain folks who offer unsuspecting Yankees a grisly version of Southern hospitality.

The premise of *Two Thousand Maniacs!* is taken from the 1947 Broadway musical *Brigadoon* (film version, 1954), about two Americans on a hunting trip in Scotland who stumble upon a village that materialises for one day every one hundred years. In Lewis's film, six motorists from the North (Lewis shows the Illinois license plate of the car of the two married couples with its 'Land of Lincoln' motto) are deliberately diverted while driving in the South to the town of Pleasant Valley (the film was actually shot in St. Cloud, Florida), where they are oddly welcomed as 'guests of honor' by the entire town for its centennial celebration. Only later do we discover that the celebration is intended as a 'blood Centennial' wherein all the residents of the ironically named Pleasant Valley, which apparently is automatically modernised when it appears, who were killed when some renegade Union soldiers razed the town (perhaps a reference to General Sherman's March), participate in the gruesome public torturing, dismemberment, and killing of their Yankee 'guests'.

Clearly, this isn't just another Pleasant Valley Sunday. Paving the way for redneck horror that would reach its apotheosis with *The Texas Chainsaw Massacre** (1973), the film's Southern stereotypes are as thick as its occasional dollops of movie blood. The mayor (Allen) is the most unctuous of Southern politicians, while his sidekicks Rufus (Bakeman) and Lester (Moore) are like Homer and Jethro gone mad. With the townsfolk as extras waving Confederate flags everywhere and grinning broadly as the killings take place, it is as if the cast of *Hee Haw* had become *The Crazies** (1973). The Centennial celebration consists of a 'horse race' in which one of the victims is drawn and quartered, a 'barrel roll' in which another is forced down a hill in a barrel with nails in it, and a 'tetterin' rock' game of skill in which a third is crushed by a boulder. Apart from the shocking dismembering of Bea (Livingston), much of the violence is presented with some humour, as when a pan shot of one of John's severed legs is followed by the Pleasant Valley Boys singing 'Look Away, Dixieland' or when they sing 'Roll in My Sweet Baby's Arms' while Bea's severed arm roasts on the barbecue.

Further Reading:

Crane, Jonathan. 'Scraping Bottom: Splatter and the Herschell Godon Lewis Oeuvre'. In *The Horror Film*, ed. Stephen Prince, pp. 150–166. New Brunswick, NJ and London: Rutgers University Press, 2004.

Juno, Andrea, Mark Pauline, and Boyd Rice. 'Herschell Gordon Lewis'. *Incredibly Strange Films*, ed. V. Vale and Andrea Juno, pp. 18–36. San Francisco: RE/Search #10, 1986.

McCarty, John. *Splatter Movies: Breaking the Last Taboo of the Screen*. New York: St. Martin's Press, 1984.

Mendik, Xavier. '"Gouts of Blood": The Colourful Underground Universe of Herschell Gordon Lewis'. In *Underground U. S. A.: Filmmaking beyond the Hollywood Canon*, ed. Xavier Mendik and Steven Jay Schneider, pp. 204–220. London and New York: Wallflower Press 2002.

The Unknown
1927 — 50 mins
Tod Browning

Silent film star Lon Chaney, American cinema's first horror icon, made a series of ten films with director Tod Browning (*Dracula** [1931], *Freaks** [1932]), beginning with *The Wicked Darling* in 1919 and concluding with *Where East is East* (1929). Some of these films have been lost, but of those that have survived, *The Unknown* is the most remarkable. In Wallace Worsley's *The Penalty* (1920), Chaney played a criminal whose legs had been amputated, and in Browning's *West of Zanzibar* (1928) his character's legs are paralyzed; *The Unknown* does the same for his upper limbs. Based on a story by Browning, the film is thick with overtones of masochism, emasculation, and self-debasement in the context of sexual desire. It depicts an *l'amour fou* even more

DIRECTOR Tod Browning
PRODUCER Irving G. Thalberg
SCREENPLAY Waldemar Young
CINEMATOGRAPHY
Merritt B. Gerstad
EDITOR Henry Reynolds,
Errol Taggart
PRODUCTION COMPANY MGM
MAIN CAST Lon Chaney,
Norman Kerry, Joan Crawford,
Nick De Ruiz, John George,
Frank Lanning

fou than *Mad Love** (1935). There is nothing supernatural about the film, despite the title; monstrousness exists only in the twisted mind of one whose obsessive love is unrequited and so turns bitter.

Chaney plays Alonzo the Armless, a circus entertainer who fires pistols and tosses knives with his feet at the fetching Nanon Zanzi (Crawford, in one of her first important roles), literally stripping her clothing as he does so. As we learn, Alonzo actually has arms – it isn't long before we see his diminutive assistant Cojo (George) help him out of his constraining corset – but he uses his supposed lack of limbs as a cover so no one will suspect him of the robberies he pulls in places where the circus travels. Nanon has a phobia about men's hands touching her, and so she resists the advances of Malabar, the strongman (Kerry, co-star with Chaney in *The Phantom of the Opera** [1925]), befriending the seemingly unthreatening Alonzo, who is secretly in love with her. Alonzo mistakes her little gestures of friendship as signs of love and, against the sage advice of Cojo, decides to have his arms amputated for real so that he can be with Nanon without her recoiling in disgust. But while he is away recuperating from the surgery, Nanon and Malabar fall in love, and she overcomes her antipathy to arms. In the excruciating scene that follows, Alonzo joyfully returns to Nanon only to discover that she is happily planning to marry Malabar and all too eager to demonstrate how she loves when his hands caress her body in a way that Alonzo's no longer ever can. Chaney's face marvellously registers the radical shift from coming bliss to consuming rage as he begins to plot his revenge. He contrives to speed up the treadmills on either side of Malabar, each of which is tethered to one of his arms and powered by a horse; but in the act Alonzo finds himself incapable of doing anything that would harm Nanon, and intervening to subdue the horses, the armless man ironically is trampled underfoot.

Some scenes in which Chaney handles cigarettes and knives were done with an armless double, Paul Desmuke, hiding in the shot. In his films with Browning, Chaney often played deformed characters, but *The Unknown* is the darkest of their collaborations in psychosexual terms. The film depicts sexuality as a circus arena, as if it were a grotesque game. In a primal scene, Alonzo kills Nanon's father, the circus owner, when he discovers Alonzo's secret, and seeks to replace him. Alonzo's double thumb signifies a potential phallic potency that, however, is unrealisable when compared to the bulging limbs of Malabar. His sexual inadequacy translates into self-emasculation that is mocked by a cruel world. What is no longer 'unknown' in *The Unknown* is the dark depths to which a person might sink in order to fulfill their desire.

Further Reading:

Herzogenrath, Bernd, ed. *The Cinema of Tod Browning: Essays of the Macabre and Grotesque*. Jefferson City, NC: McFarland, 2008.

Rosenthal, Stuart. 'Tod Browning'. In Stuart Rosenthal and Judith M. Kass, *The Hollywood Professionals*, vol. 4. New York: A. S. Barnes/ London: Tantivy Press, 1975.

Skal, David J. *Dark Carnival: The Secret World of Tod Browning, The Master of the Macabre*. New York: Doubleday, 1995.

Worland, Rick. *The Horror Film: An Introduction*. Malden, MA and Oxford: Blackwell, 2007.

Weird Woman
1944 – 63 mins
Reginald Le Borg

Weird Woman is the second of six 'Inner Sanctum' B films produced by Universal from 1943 to 1945, all of them starring Lon Chaney, Jr. (*The Wolf Man** [1941], *Bud Abbott and Lou Costello Meet Frankenstein** [1948]). The series was inspired by the radio series *Inner Sanctum Mystery* (1941–1952), one of serval horror and fantasy radio shows popular during the medium's 'golden age'. Another film titled *Inner Sanctum*, inspired by the radio series and directed by Lew Landers (director of *The Raven* [1935] with Boris Karloff and Bela Lugosi) was released in 1948, and there was also a television series in 1954. Episodes of the radio show were based on books published in the Simon & Shuster book series of the same title. The first three films in the series – *Calling Dr. Death* (1943), *Weird Woman*, and *Dead Man's Eyes* (1944) – were directed by Reginald

DIRECTOR Reginald Le Borg
PRODUCER Ben Pivar, Oliver Drake
SCREENPLAY Brenda Weisberg
CINEMATOGRAPHY Virgil Miller
EDITOR Milt Carruth
MUSIC Paul Sawtell
PRODUCTIONCOMPANY Universal Pictures
MAIN CAST Lon Chaney, Jr., Anne Gwynne, Evelyn Ankers, Ralph Morgan, Elisabeth Risdon, Lois Collier, Harry Hayden, Elizabeth Russell, Phil Brown

Le Borg (*Voodoo Island* [1956, with Karloff], *The Black Sleep* [1957, again with Chaney]). All three display an efficient mix of horror, mystery, and film noir, tilting decidedly toward the latter two as the possibility of the paranormal or supernatural is more often than not revealed to be the result of mortal machinations. *Weird Woman*, based on Fritz Lieber's celebrated novel of contemporary witchcraft, *Conjure Wife* (1943) – adapted again later as *Night of the Eagle* (*Burn, Witch, Burn!* [1962]) and the comedy *Witches' Brew* (1980) – is typical in the way it compromised the novel's supernatural aspect.

Weird Woman begins, as do all of the films in the series except for the last (*Pillow of Death* [1945]), with the head of actor David Hoffman in a crystal ball on a table in a library, his face distorted by the curved glass and accompanied by ominous organ music as he speaks to us of our common potential for 'murrrrder'. The introduction is a carryover from the radio series (Raymond Edward Johnson's sardonic host of the radio series was the model for many others, both on radio and later on television), as is the clumsy occasional voiceover of the protagonists' thoughts. The film's dramatic tension, as in Lieber's novel, involves a conflict between reason and superstition, with Norman Reed (Chaney), a sociology professor who prides himself on rationality, coming to wonder whether his new wife Paula (Gwynne), whom he had met and married while on vacation on an unnamed Pacific island, is actually a witch. The fact that Reed is a professor foregrounds the importance of his rational worldview and the horror of its impending collapse when confronted with the possibility of magic after his scoffing at Paula's voodoo talismans and burning them is quickly followed by a series of calamitous events including two deaths.

After a brief uncanny uncertainty, it is revealed, unlike the novel, that there is in fact nothing of the supernatural at work, only jealousy, with Norman's colleague Ilona Carr (Ankers) exposed as, in the words of the Dean of Women (Risdon), merely 'a woman scorned'. By contrast, the novel plays on male fears of women, as our professor learns that the women around him are all secret conspirators battling spells and shaping the destiny of their husbands, who are busy thinking and doing research. The film also firmly associates the masculine with reason and science ('I'm a man of reason or I'm nothing', Reed declares) and femininity with mysticism and magic, and then dismisses voodoo as, in Reed's patronisingly patriarchal words, the strange beliefs of a 'superstitious child'. Accordingly, Paula's island culture is reduced by the film to a hodgepodge of Hollywood 'South Seas' signifiers, which for Reed is comforting because, as he says to Paula, 'Now it's evil that we can understand'.

Further Reading:

Ellbé, Charlie. 'Making Visible the Sonic Threat: The *Inner Sanctum Mysteries* Radio Series and Its Universal Studios Film Adaptations'. In *Recovering 1940s Horror Cinema: Traces of a Lost Decade*, ed. Mario Degiglio-Bellemare, Charlie Ellbé, and Kristopher Woofter, pp. 129–145. Lanham, MD and London: Lexington Books, 2015.

Grams, Martin, Jr. *Inner Sanctum Mysteries: Behind the Creaking Door*. Churchville, MD: OTR Publishing, 2003.

Hand, Richard J. *Terror on the Air!: Horror Radio in America, 1931–1952*. Jefferson, NC and London: McFarland, 2006.

Meehan, Paul. *Horror Noir: Where Cinema's Dark Sisters Meet*. Jefferson, NC: McFarland, 2011.

Weaver, Tom, Michael Brunas, and John Brunas. *Universal Horrors: The Studios Classic Films, 1931–1946*, 2nd edn. Jefferson, NC and London: McFarland, 2007.

What Ever Happened to Baby Jane?
1962 – 133 mins
Robert Aldrich

A psychological horror thriller about two sisters, Jane (Davis) and Blanche (Crawford), both aging Hollywood stars from a bygone era, locked in their past and the traumas created by their fraught relationship, *What Ever Happened to Baby Jane?* is notable in large part for the controversial portrayal of the title character as a slovenly psychopath by an actual older Hollywood star in a performance marked by grotesque excess. A box-office success (a well-publicised feud between the two stars helped) that garnered five Academy Award nominations, including Best Actress for Davis, the film generated a cycle of similar 'hag horror' movies featuring melodramatic madwomen played by aging Hollywood actresses whose careers were on the decline,

DIRECTOR Robert Aldrich
PRODUCER Robert Aldrich
SCREENPLAY Lukas Heller
CINEMATOGRAPHY
Ernest Haller
EDITOR Michael Luciano
MUSIC Frank DeVol
PRODUCTION COMPANY
Seven Arts Productions
MAIN CAST Joan Crawford,
Bette Davis, Victor Buono,
Bert Freed, Anna Lee, Maidie
Norman

as well as a made-for-television remake starring real-life sisters Lynn and Vanessa Redgrave in 1991. Sometimes referred to as 'psycho-biddy' films, the subgenre includes Aldrich's follow-up to *Baby Jane* two years later, *Hush … Hush, Sweet Charlotte* (1964), this time combining Davis and Olivia de Havilland (after Crawford dropped out); Crawford again in William Castle's *Straight-Jacket* (1964); *What Ever Happened to Aunt Alice?* (1969) with Geraldine Page and Ruth Gordon; Curtis Harrington's *Who Slew Auntie Roo?* (1971) with Shelley Winters, and *What's the Matter with Helen?* (1971), this time pairing Winters with Debbie Reynolds.

Baby Jane begins in 1917, when 'Baby Jane' Hudson is a child vaudeville star, adored by her parents and audiences while her sister is brushed aside. In 1935, Jane has faded into obscurity, and Blanche is now a famous movie star. One night, coming home from a party Blanche is paralyzed from the waist down in an accident for which Jane, we learn later, has taken the blame, complicating our assumptions about victim and victimiser. Now, in the present, Blanche and Jane live together in a comfortable home purchased with the income of the former, who is confined to a wheelchair in the upstairs part of the house. Jane, now a resentful and unstable alcoholic, is pushed over the edge when she learns that Blanche is intending to sell the house and commit her to an institution. She keeps Blanche isolated from the outside world and begins to torment and torture her as she slowly starves her to death.

After killing the cleaning lady Elvira (Norman) with a hammer when she discovers Blanche imprisoned and disposing of the body, Jane flees, taking Blanche with her to the beach where Blanche, weak and near death, confesses that it was she who drove the car in the accident with the intent of hurting Jane but broke her own spine instead. Jane, seemingly now unburdened of years of guilt and anger, dances happily before a crowd of surprised beachgoers, completely lost in her own fantasy world. In the last shot, as two policemen rush toward the prone figure of Blanche on the beach, the image is so distant that is remains ambiguous whether she has survived.

Some regard the performances of the two leads as little more than grotesque caricatures of themselves. Certainly, Crawford's quiet suffering contrasts with the extravagant madness of Davis, who dominates the film with scenes like the one in which she warbles her childhood hit 'I've Written a Letter to Daddy' in its excruciating entirely. Jane looks monstrous in her thick makeup (created by Davis herself), emphasising her sagging but extraordinarily expressive face as she tries to look impossibly young. The film has its memorable scares (it originally received a X rating in the UK) – most memorably, one involving Blanche's pet parakeet – but perhaps the most frightening thing about the film is its critique of youth culture as enacted by Davis. *Baby Jane* also depicts the entertainment industry as indifferent to individuals after their fifteen minutes of fame, a theme director Robert Aldrich, who preferred to work outside the studio system, also explored in *The Big Knife* (1955), *The Legend of Lylah Clare* (1968), and *The Killing of Sister George* (1968).

Further Reading

Derry, Charles. *Dark Dreams 2.0: A Psychological History of the Modern Horror Film from the 1950s to the 21st Century.* Jefferson, NC: McFarland, 2009.

Russell, Lorena. 'Queering Consumption and Production in *What Ever Happened to Baby Jane?*' In *Horror Film: Creating and Marketing Fear*, ed. Steffen Hantke, pp. 213–226. Jackson: University Press of Mississippi, 2004.

Shelley, Peter. *Grande Dame Guignol Cinema: A History of Hag Horror from Baby Jane to Mother.* Jefferson, NC: McFarland, 2009.

Williams, Tony. *Body and Soul: The Cinematic Vision of Robert Aldrich.* Lanham, MD: Scarecrow Press, 2004.

White Zombie
1932 – 73 mins
Victor Halperin

Inspired by the 1929 novel *The Magic Island* by William Seabrook and having the distinction of being the first American feature film to depict zombies, the independently made *White Zombie* exploited the recent popularity of Bela Lugosi, who had starred in *Dracula** (1931) the year before and *Murders in the Rue Morgue,** released the same year and just a few months before *White Zombie*. Director Victor Halperin, together with his producer-brother Edward, made several B-films in the 1920s and 30s (his other horror credits include *Supernatural* [1933] and *Torture Ship* [1939]), of which *White Zombie* is the most well-known. Indeed, it helped spark a cycle of voodoo movies and the first zombie craze with such subsequent films as Dwain Es-

DIRECTOR Victor Halperin
PRODUCER Edward Halperin
SCREENPLAY Garnett Weston
CINEMATOGRAPHY
Arthur Martinelli
EDITOR Harold McLemon
MUSIC Guy Bevier Williams
(Chant) and pre-existing music
by Modest Mussorgsky, Hugo
Riesenfeld, Gaston Borch, Franz
Liszt, Richard Wagner, and H.
Maurice Jacquet
PRODUCTION COMPANY
Halperin Productions,
United Artists
MAIN CAST Bela Lugosi,
Madge Bellamy, Joseph
Cawthorn, John Harron, Robert
Frazer, Brandon Hurst, George
Burr MacAnnan

per's *Maniac* (1934), Michael Curtiz's *The Walking Dead* (1936) with Boris Karloff, and Halperin's own *Revolt of the Zombies* (1936), which was initially conceived as a sequel to his earlier film. Remade in 2014 – and the inspiration for the name of Rob Zombie's (*The Devil's Rejects** [2005]) band – *White Zombie*, with its languorous pacing and lugubrious atmosphere, marks a bridge between the contemporary Universal horror cycle and Val Lewton's more moody movies in the next decade.

Here Bela Lugosi as sinister voodoo master 'Murder' Legendre sports an impressive widow's peak, bushy eyebrows to match those of his Dr. Mirakle in *Murders in the Rue Morgue*, and a forked beard, makeup to which Jack Pierce, responsible for, among others, the look of Karloff's monster in Universal's *Frankenstein* (1931) and *The Bride of Frankenstein** (1935), contributed. (Made on a very small budget, *White Zombie* was filmed in part at Universal at night, employing sets from several of the studio's movies.) Eyes are emphasised throughout the film, almost from the beginning when the betrothed Madeline Short (Bellamy) and Neil Parker (Harron) are traveling by coach to the plantation of Charles Beaumont (Frazer) and are met by the creepy Legendre. In this scene and elsewhere Legendre's staring eyes are superimposed over the action, as if he has the ability, like Fritz Lang's Dr. Mabuse, to see and to influence action remotely. Because the eyes are the window to the soul, Beaumont feels tormented by the zombified Madeleine, whom he comes to possess as his own after she seems to die, is buried, and resurrected by Legendre's supernatural powers. With the transfixed gaze that has marked movie zombies ever since, her eyes are, he says, 'lifeless'.

The zombie was initially a horrifying image of the enslavement of blacks in America and their consequent loss of identity, until George Romero updated them in *Night of the Living Dead** (1968) as monstrous metaphors of contemporary alienation. The earlier meaning is invoked in *White Zombie* explicitly at Legendre's sugar mill, worked entirely by plodding undead workers. When one of them stumbles and falls into the blades of the giant cane-shredder, the rest unflinchingly carry on unperturbed in their tasks with that blank stare, grist for the mill of capitalist exploitation. 'They work faithfully – they are not worried about long hours', Legendre explains – a proposition that was particularly frightening in the depths of the Depression. Yet *White Zombie* is less interested in critiquing the racial and class depredations of capitalist exploitation than, as the title suggests, in the sensationalism of a captivity narrative involving a bourgeois white woman, one whom at one point we get to see provocatively dressed in lingerie and wedding veil.

Further Reading:

Jones, David Annwn. *Re-envisaging the First Age of Cinematic Horror, 1896–1934*. Cardiff: University of Wales Press, 2018.

Lowry, Edward, and Richard de Cordova. 'Enunciation and the Production of Horror in *White Zombie*'. In *Planks of Reason: Essays on the Horror Film*, revised ed., ed. Barry Keith Grant and Christopher Sharrett, pp. 172–211. Lanham, MD: Scarecrow Press, 2004.

Peirse, Alison. *After Dracula: The 1930s Horror Film*. London: I. B. Taurus, 2013.

Rhodes, Gary D. *White Zombie: Anatomy of a Horror Film*. Jefferson, NC: McFarland, 2002.

Sevastakis, Michael. *Songs of Love and Death: The Classic American Horror Film of the 1930s*. Westport, CT: Greenwood, 1993.

The Wind
2019 – 73 mins
Emma Tammi

The title of Emma Tammi's gothic Western inevitably invokes Victor Sjöström's 1928 silent masterpiece of the same name with Lillian Gish. Both films involve women who have come west to face the hard conditions of the frontier, and both use the unforgiving landscape metaphorically as the pioneer women are driven to the brink of madness. But while Sjöström's film ends with the restoration of the couple's marriage, here the family is destroyed. And while the woman in the earlier film is threatened by an all too familiar male predator, there are no hints of a supernatural entity inhabiting a cursed land, as in Tammi's film, which depicts the traumatic experiences of many women on the frontier.

The film's plot is told achronologically, cutting between scenes in the past and the present, and between fantasy and reality. Lizzy (Gerard) and Isaac Macklin (Zukerman), who had come from St. Louis, live on an isolated New Mexico farm when another couple, Gideon (McTee) and Emma (Julia), move into an abandoned cabin nearby. Already traumatised by her stillborn child some time earlier and feeling intruded upon by the newcomers, Lizzy grows more paranoid as the relationship between the two couples becomes more intertwined, and her belief that there is an evil entity lurking somewhere out there in the desert asserts itself more strongly. The narrative's jumbled time frame is appropriate, expressing Lizzy's delirium as her paranoia deepens (at one point she has a literal fever). Indeed, throughout, as in Anne Radcliffe's 1794 archetypal gothic novel *The Mysteries of Udolpho*, which Lizzy reads to Emma, '… whether the terror of her mind gave her ideal sounds or that the real ones did come, she thought footsteps were ascending the private staircase.' Like the novel, the film dwells in the uncanny space between the real and the imaginary, with Lyn Moncrief's cinematography and the natural lighting effectively turning the small cabin into a menacing haunted house.

For Lizzy, the frontier is a place where one abandons all hope. When her baby dies, Lizzy denies God, burying her bible with the baby ('He'll use it more than I will') and preferring the pamphlet 'Demons of the Prairie' instead. Her growing paranoia is echoed by the gathering clouds and lightning on the expansive horizon, landscape shots worthy of a good Western. Several times Lizzy is photographed in the cabin as a mirror reflection, its bevelled glass creating a ghostly double image of her that graphically suggests her loosening grip on reality. The sympathetic Isaac thinks that her hysteria may be the result of female impressionability to sensational fiction, betraying an unexamined sexism that may in part have contributed to her mental condition in the first place.

Still, the passage Isaac reads to her from *Frankenstein*, in which the creature demands a mate and envisions the two of them as isolated monsters who in their loneliness 'shall be more attached to one another', seems more applicable to the couple's worsening situation. Lizzy insists to the end that 'There's something out there', but Isaac is adamant that she is delusional. Emma, too, feels that the place is 'wrong', that 'we're not supposed to be here', a response that may seem an acknowledgment of the American genocide of native

DIRECTOR Emma Tammi
PRODUCER Christopher Alender, David Grove Churchill Viste
SCREENPLAY Teresa Sutherland
CINEMATOGRAPHY Lyn Moncrief
EDITOR Alexandra Amick
MUSIC Ben Lovett
PRODUCTION COMPANY Divide/Conquer, Soapbox Films
MAIN CAST Caitlin Gerard, Ashley Zukerman, Julia Goldani Telles, Dylan McTee, Miles Anderson

Americans that accompanied westward expansion. But the focus of the film remains on Lizzy, her mental breakdown capturing the terrors of women on the frontier and effectively giving voice to an aspect of western history that had been largely overshadowed by the masculine myths of the West.

Further Reading:

Fine, Kerry, Michael K. Johnson, Rebecca M. Lush, and Sarah L. Spurgeon, eds. *Weird Westerns: Race, Gender, Genre*. Lincoln: University of Nebraska Press, 2020.

Green, Paul. *Encyclopedia of Weird Westerns*, 2nd edn. Jefferson, NC: McFarland, 2016.

Miller, Cynthia J., and Bowdoin Van Riper, eds. *Undead in the West: Vampires, Zombies, Mummies, and Ghosts on the Cinematic Frontier*. Lanham, MD: Scarecrow Press, 2012.

Miller, Cynthia J., and Bowdoin Van Riper, eds. *Undead in the West II: They Just Keep Coming*. Lanham, MD: Scarecrow Press, 2013.

The Witch
US/Canada, 2015 – 93 mins
Robert Eggers

The characteristic narrative ambiguity of supernatural horror is beautifully exploited in Robert Eggers' debut feature, *The Witch*, a tale of possible witchcraft and sorcery set in 17th-century New England. The strange events that occur in the film can be read as literally happening or as the overheated imagination of devout Christians living in a strange new world and unsure whether events are divine signs of election or damnation.

William (Ineson), his wife Katherine (Dickie), and their children Thomasin (Taylor-Joy), Caleb (Scrimshaw), and fraternal twins Mercy (Grainger) and Jonas (Dawson), are banished from a Puritan community because of theological differences. The family departs into the wilderness and establishes their own farm. Katherine soon gives birth to her fifth child, Samuel, who mysteriously vanishes while being watched by Thomasin. The family then begins to spiral into mutual and self-destructive recrimination and fear. Caleb wanders lost in the forest while hunting and comes upon a beautiful and seductive young woman in a hut; the woman may be a

DIRECTOR Robert Eggers
PRODUCER Rodrigo Teixeira, Daniel Bekereman, Lars Knudsen, Jodi Redmon, Jay Van Hoy
SCREENPLAY Robert Eggers
CINEMATOGRAPHY Janin Blaschke
EDITOR Louise Ford
MUSIC Mark Korven
PRODUCTION COMPANY Parts and Labor, RT Features, Rooks Nest Entertainment, Maiden Voyage Pictures, Mott Street Pictures, Code Red Productions, Scythia Films, Pulse Films, Special Projects
MAIN CAST Anya Taylor-Joy, Ralph Ineson, Kate Dickie, Harvey Scrimshaw, Ellie Grainger, Lucas Dawson

witch who enchants Caleb, making him ill and eventually killing him, or his own unbearable guilt at the awakening of adolescent sexuality. Soon the fear of God's displeasure and the possibility of the devil's influence result in the parents becoming afraid of their own children and boarding them up in the goat stable.

In Nathaniel Hawthorne's classic short story 'Young Goodman Brown' (1835), clearly a major influence on Eggers (as Melville is on his subsequent film, *The Lighthouse* [2019]), the eponymous young Puritan must leave his wife, the aptly named Faith, and travel through the woods in the dark of night for a reason never stated, although on a metaphorical level it may be understood as a spiritual journey into that dark place where faith and doubt are in conflict. In the forest, Brown comes upon a witches' coven that includes several respectable citizens of the town. Hawthorne never makes it clear whether Brown experiences a vision or actuality, constantly qualifying his descriptions of events, and Brown himself is not sure. But the ambiguity has crushed his youthful, naïve optimism: 'My Faith is gone!' he cries, and his fate is to become 'a distrustful, if not a desperate man' whose 'dying hour was gloom' because he could no longer be certain of distinguishing good and evil again when he looked in the faces of others. In the conclusion of *The Witch*, William is gored to death by their goat 'Black Philip', and Thomasin in self-defence is forced to kill her mother, who has attacked her in a superstitious frenzy. Then 'Black Phillip' reveals itself to Thomasin as Satan in disguise. He invites her into the forest, where, wandering naked, she discovers a firelit coven in the blackness of night like the one Goodman Brown stumbles upon. She joins them, laughingly levitating herself in the dark forest night in the film's eerie final shot. Yet, as in Hawthorne's story, even this uncanny event may not be actually happening, but instead may be the feverish delusion of a now overwhelmingly guilty and likely insane girl who has just committed matricide.

The key to reading the film's supernatural occurrences as subjective visions is the scene in which Katherine, grieving over her lost baby, seems to have found him and taken him to her breast. She is shown suckling him in close-up, but then the film cuts to a long shot – distanced, hence more objective – showing her with a raven plucking at her breast instead of the baby, and we realise, in retrospect, that the shots of her holding the baby were her imagination. The next morning, as William arises from the conjugal bed, Katherine is briefly seen remaining prone, pretending to be asleep, but carefully concealing the blood stains on the front of her white shift. The shot is brief, thus requiring viewers to be attentive to the film's details, just as the Puritans needed vigilance to determine and decipher God's signs.

Further Reading:

Grafius, Brandon. 'Securing the Borders: Isolation and Anxiety in *The Witch*, *It Comes at Night*, and Trump's America. In *Make America Hate Again: Trump-era Horror and the Politics of Hate*, ed. Victoria McCollum, pp. 119–128. New York and London: Routledge, 2019.

Madden, Victoria. '"Wouldst Thou Like to Live Deliciously?": Gothic Feminism and the Final Girl in Robert Eggers' *The Witch*'. In *Final Girls, Feminism, and Popular Culture*, ed. Katarzyna Paskiewicz and Stacy Rusnak, pp. 135–151. New York and London: Palgrave Macmillan, 2020.

Prasch, Thomas. '"What Went We Out in This Wilderness to Find": Supernatural Contest in Robert Eggers' *The Witch: A New-England Folktale* (2015)'. In *Divine Horror: Essays on the Cinematic Battle between the Sacred and the Diabolical*, ed. Cynthia J. Miller and Bowdoin Van Riper, pp. 11–28. Jefferson, NC: McFarland, 2017.

Russell, Sharon. 'The Witch in Film: Myth and Reality'. In *Planks of Reason: Essays on the Horror Film*, revised ed., ed. Barry Keith Grant and Christopher Sharrett, pp. 63–71. Lanham, MD: Scarecrow Press, 2004.

The Wolf Man
1941 – 70 mins
George Waggner

Universal Pictures made *Werewolf of London* with Henry Hull in 1935, but it's Lon Chaney, Jr.'s memorable performance as the unfortunate Lawrence Talbot in *The Wolf Man* that established the hirsute horror as a monstrous equal of Universal's Dracula and Frankenstein's monster. The film generated four sequels by the studio – *Frankenstein Meets the Wolf Man* (1943, also written by Curt Siodmak), *House of Frankenstein* (1944), *House of Dracula* (1945) and, of course, *Bud Abbott and Lou Costello Meet Frankenstein** (1948). Chaney played Talbot/The Wolf Man in all of them, the only classic Universal monster to be played by the same actor. *The Wolf Man* was remade in 2010 with Benicio del Toro, but Chaney brought to the role a sense of pathos, if not tragedy, that no other actor has managed.

The story follows Larry Talbot (Chaney), who returns to his ancestral home in Wales to reconcile with his estranged father, Sir John Talbot (Rains). He becomes romantically interested in Gwen Conliffe (Ankers), the proprietor of a local antique shop, from whom he buys a silver-headed walking stick decorated with a silver wolf while flirting with her. That night, Larry kills what he insists was a wolf attacking Gwen's friend Jenny with the walking stick but is bitten in the fight. A gypsy fortune teller (Ouspenskaya) explains to Larry that the creature he killed was actually her son Bela (Lugosi). Talbot scoffs at her superstitious beliefs but himself transforms into a werewolf and stalks through Universal's wonderfully expressionist sets, killing the local gravedigger. He remembers his transformations and the murderous impulses they bring, pleading with his father to help, but Sir John refuses to believe, like his son before him. However, in the end his father is forced to beat Larry to death with the silver walking stick when the creature the townspeople are hunting attacks Gwen.

Competently directed by Waggner, who had earlier directed Chaney, Jr. in *Man Made Monster* (1941), *The Wolf Man* was a breakthrough in Hollywood for writer Curt Siodmak (brother of Robert Siodmak, director of *The Spiral Staircase* [1946]). Siodmak, whose novels (*Donovan's Brain* [1942], *Riders to the Stars* [1954], both of which were adapted to film) and screenplays (*I Walked with a Zombie** [1943], *The Magnetic Monster* [1953], *Earth vs. the Flying Saucers* [1956]) were often exercises in horror and science fiction, invented in *The Wolf Man* several enduring aspects of werewolf mythology, such as the victim being marked by a pentagram, the famous verse about 'Even a man who is pure in heart' (which every villager in the film seems to know), and the idea that the creature can only be killed with silver objects. The film is unclear about werewolves transforming with exposure to the full moon, leaving it to *Frankenstein Meets the Wolf Man* to make explicit, implying instead that it happens in autumn when the wolfbane blooms.

The trademark series of lap dissolves that show Talbot's transformation is largely absent from this, the first film in the series, which shows his feet changing rather than his face. But as with many horror narratives involving men who metamorphose into animals, *The Wolf Man* may be read as being about the beast within – specifically, the beast of phallic masculinity. Gwen is already engaged, but the wolfish Larry aggressively

DIRECTOR George Waggner
PRODUCER George Waggner
SCREENPLAY Curt Siodmak
CINEMATOGRAPHY Joseph Valentine
EDITOR Ted J. Kent
PRODUCTION COMPANY Universal Pictures
MAIN CAST Lon Chaney, Jr., Claude Rains, Warren William, Ralph Bellamy, Patric Knowles, Bela Lugosi, Evelyn Ankers, Maria Ouspenskaya

pursues her anyway. He spies on her in her own rooms with his father's telescope, violates her privacy, and seems to be indifferent to
the existence of her fiancé, Frank (Knowles). Because Larry is unable
to channel his desire into socially acceptable behaviour, he meets his
inevitable end (until the sequel) at the hands of the Father, bludg-
eoned, significantly, with his own cane.

Further Reading:

de Blécourt, Willem, ed. *Werewolf Histories*. Basingstoke, UK and
    New York: Palgrave Macmillan, 2015.

Fischer, Dennis. *Horror Film Directors, 1931–1990*. Jefferson, NC and
    London: McFarland, 1991.

Mann, Craiglan. *Phases of the Moon: A Cultural History of the
    Werewolf Film*. Edinburgh: Edinburgh University Press, 2020.

Smith, Don G. *Lon Chaney, Jr.: Horror Film Star, 1906–1973*.
    Jefferson, NC: McFarland, 1996.

Weaver, Tom, Michael Brunas, and John Brunas. *Universal Horrors:
    The Studios Classic Films, 1931–1946*, 2nd edn. Jefferson, NC
    and London: McFarland, 2007.

Young Frankenstein
1974 – 105 mins
Mel Brooks

With Buck Henry, comedian Mel Brooks created *Get Smart* (1965–1970), a spy parody television sitcom. Transitioning to cinema, Brooks continued down the same parodic path with *The Producers* (1967), *Blazing Saddles* (1974), *Young Frankenstein*, *Silent Movie* (1976), *High Anxiety* (1977), *History of the World: Part I* (1981), *Spaceballs* (1987), and *Robin Hood: Men in Tights* (1993), all box-office hits. *Blazing Saddles* and *Young Frankenstein*, released the same year, are the two most successful of these, both offering some degree of critique of the ideological elements of their generic target, the Western and the horror film, respectively.

DIRECTOR Mel Brooks
PRODUCER Michael Gruskoff
SCREENPLAY Mel Brooks, Gene Wilder
CINEMATOGRAPHY Gerald Hirschfeld
EDITOR John C. Howard
MUSIC John Morris
PRODUCTION COMPANY 20th Century Fox
MAIN CAST Gene Wilder, eter Boyle, Madeleine Kahn, Marty Feldman, Cloris Leachman, Gene Hackman, Terry Garr, Kenneth Mars

Young Frankenstein, one of the year's most commercially successful films, plays with the conventions of Universal's cycle of Frankenstein movies in a way that is affectionate yet analytical.

The plot involves Dr. Frederick Frankenstein (Wilder), grandson of the notorious Victor Frankenstein, who inherits his family's estate in Transylvania although he completely disavows the dubious heritage. Traveling there with his fiancé Elizabeth (Kahn) to settle the estate, he meets a hunchback servant Igor (Feldman), an assistant, Inga (Garr), and housekeeper Frau Blucher (Leachman). The film evokes the Universal Frankenstein movies throughout, beginning immediately in the opening title credit, in a stylised font recalling some of the advertising for the 1931 *Frankenstein*. The film also uses several optical techniques common in the 1930s such as irises, wipes, and spins, and even employs the old 1:85 aspect ratio. Some of the lab equipment were original props created by set designer and electrician Kenneth Strickfaden for the 1931 film.

Young Frankenstein makes numerous comic reference to the earlier films: Igor has a deformed spine, as does Ygor (Bela Lugosi), who survived a hanging, in *Son of Frankenstein* (1938). The same film also provides the model for Kenneth Mars' Inspector Kemp in Lionel Atwill's Inspector Krogh, both having a wooden arm as the result of a previous encounter with the monster – although Krogh's is never used as a battering ram to storm the castle! The scene with the blind man (Hackman) parodies a similar scene in *Bride of Frankenstein*** (1935), here played for slapstick rather than sentiment. And so on. The film's jocular appreciation of genre convention is shared with the audience when the creature (Boyle) comes upon the little girl by the well. In James Whale's 1931 film, he inadvertently drowns the girl when, delighted at the sight of flower petals floating on the water,

he innocently tosses her in too; in *Young Frankenstein*, when they run out of petals to float, the girl innocently asks, 'Oh dear, what shall we throw in now?' – after which the monster looks conspiratorially at the camera.

Yet for all the film's jokes (like Igor's migrating hunch) *Young Frankenstein* offers a rather radical interpretation of the Frankenstein story. If, classically, the monster, including the one created by Dr. Frankenstein, typically represents an aspect of his maker's psyche that is disavowed (as in the 1910* and 1931* adaptations of Shelley's novel), here Frederick Frankenstein comes to a satisfying acceptance of his own monstrous sexuality in the form of the monster. Even as the townspeople become the conventional mob bent on destroying the creature, Dr. Frankenstein saves him with a final experiment, willingly swapping some of his own intellect with the creature in return for some of his virility – often, the very human element that, monster movies tell us, has to be repressed for society to function. *Young Frankenstein* thus ends happily, with a double marriage, Elizabeth happily wed to the creature while Inga expresses delight ('Ah, sweet mystery of life') in the doctor's newly acquired capability.

Further Reading:

Friedman, Lester D., and Alison B. Kavey. *Monstrous Progeny: A History of the Frankenstein Narratives*. New Brunswick, NJ: Rutgers University Press, 2016.

McGilligan, Patrick. *Funny Man: Mel Brooks*. New York: HarperCollins, 2019.

Yacowar, Maurice. *Method in Madness: The Comic Art of Mel Brooks*. New York: St. Martin's Press, 1981.

Index

References in entries that are included in the book are indicated with an asterisk (*)
Bold numerals indicate location of main entries.

List of Illustrations

While considerable effort has been made to correctly identify the copyright holders, this has not been possible in all cases. We apologise for any apparent negligence, and any omissions or corrections brought to our attention will be remedied in any future editions.

The Addiction, © Fast Films Inc.; *American Psycho*, © Am Psycho Productions Inc.; *American Werewolf in London*, © American Werewolf Inc.; *The Avenging Conscience*, Reliance Majestic; *The Birds*, © Alfred J. Hitchcock Productions; *Blade*, © New Line Productions Inc.; *The Blair Witch Project*, © Haxan Films Inc.; *Brain Damage*, The Brain Damage Company; *Bram Stoker's Dracula*, © Columbia Pictures Industries Inc./American Zoetrope; *The Bride of Frankenstein*, © Universal Pictures Corporation; *Bubba Ho-Tep*, © Starway International Inc.; *Bud Abbott Lou Costello Meet Frankenstein*, Universal Pictures Company; *The Burrowers*, Lionsgate Films/Blue Star Entertainment; *Candyman*, © Candyman Films Inc./Propaganda Films; *Carnival of Souls*, Harcourt Productions; *Carrie*, Red Bank Films; *The Cat and the Canary*, Universal Pictures Corporation; *Cat People*, © RKO Radio Pictures; *Child's Play*, United Artists; *Colour Out of Space*, © Hot Pink Horror LLC; *Contagion*, © Warner Bros. Entertainment Inc.; *The Crazies*, © Pittsburgh Films/Cambist/The Latent Image; *Creature from the Black Lagoon*, © Universal Pictures Company; *The Dead Zone*, © Dino De Laurentiis Corporation; *The Devil's Rejects*, Cinelamda Internationale Filmproduktionsgesellschaft mbH & Co.; *Dr. Jekyll and Mr. Hyde*, © Paramount Publix Corporation; *Dracula*, © Universal Pictures Corporation; *Eraserhead*, © David Lynch; *The Evil Dead*, Renaissance Pictures; *The Exorcist*, © Warner Bros./Hoya Productions; *Fallen*, Turner Pictures/Atlas Entertainment; *The Fall of the House of Usher*, James Sibley Watson/Melville Webber; *Fatal Attraction*, Paramount Pictures Corporation; *The Fly*, Twentieth Century-Fox Film Corporation; *Frankenstein*, Edison; *Freaks*, Metro-Goldwyn-Mayer; *The Frighteners*, © Universal City Studios/Universal Pictures/Wingnut Films; *Funny Games U.S.*, © Celluloid Dreams/Halcyon Pictures/Tartan Films/X Filme International; *Ganja & Hess*, Kelly-Jordan Enterprises Inc.; *Get Out* (Jordan Peele, Universal Studios/Blumhouse Productions/QC Entertainment/Monkeypaw Productions/Universal Pictures/Dentsu/Fuji Television; *Gremlins*, © Warner Bros. Inc.; *Halloween*, © Falcon International Productions; *The Hellstrom Chronicle*, Wolper Productions; *Henry Portrait of a Serial Killer*, Maljack Films; *The Hills Have Eyes*, Blood Relations Company; *Hostel* (Eli Roth, © Screen Gems Inc./Lionsgate Films; *House of Wax*, © Warner Bros.; *The Hunger*, Richard Shepherd Company/MGM/UA Entertainment; *I Walked with a Zombie*, © RKO Radio Pictures; *I Was a Teenage Werewolf*, Sunset Productions; *In the Mouth of Madness*, © New Line Productions Inc.; *Interview with the Vampire: The Vampire Chronicles*, © The Geffen Film Company; *Invasion of the Body Snatchers*, © United Artists Corporation; *It's Alive*, © Larco Productions Inc.; *Jaws*, © Universal Pictures; *King Kong*, © RKO Radio Pictures; *The Last House on the Left*, © The Night Company; *Let Me In*, © Hammer Let Me In Productions LLC; *The Little Shop of Horrors*, Filmgroup; *The Lodger*, © Twentieth Century-Fox Film Corporation; *Mad Love* (Karl Freund, Metro-Goldwyn-Mayer Corporation; *The Magician* (Rex Ingram, Metro Goldwyn Corporation; *Martin*, Braddock Associates/Laurel Entertainment; *The Masque of the Red Death*, © Alta Vista Productions; *Midsommar*, © A24 Films LLC; *Misery*, Columbia Pictures Corporation/Castle Rock Entertainment; *The Mist*, © The Weinstein Company; *The Mummy*, © Universal Pictures Corporation; *Murders in the Rue Morgue*, Universal Pictures Corporation; *Near Dark*, Near Dark Joint Venture/F|M Entertainment; *Night of the Living Dead*, Image Ten; *Office Killer*, Good Fear/Good Machine/Kardana/Killer Films; *The Omen*, © Twentieth Century-Fox Film Corporation; *Paranormal Activity*, © Oren Peli d.b.a./Solana Films; *The Phantom of the Opera*, © Universal Pictures Corporation; *Phantom of the Paradise*, Pressman-Williams Enterprises/Harbor Productions Inc.; *Poltergeist*, © Metro-Goldwyn-Mayer/SLM Entertainment; *Psycho*, © Shamley Productions; *The Purge*, © Overlord Productions LLC; *Race with the Devil*, Saber Productions/Paul Maslansky Productions; *Ravenous*, © Twentieth Century-Fox Film Corporation; *Rosemary's Baby*, © Paramount Pictures Corporation/William Castle Enterprises; *Saw*, © Saw Productions Inc.; *Scream*, Dimension Films/Woods Entertainment; *The Shining*, © Warner Bros. Inc.; *The Silence of the Lambs*, © Orion Pictures Corporation; *Sisters*, Pressman-Williams Enterprises; *Targets*, Saticoy Productions; *The Texas Chainsaw Massacre*, Vortex; *The Tingler* © Columbia Pictures Corporation; *Twentynine Palms*, © 3B Production/Thoke+Moebius Film; *Two Thousand Maniacs!*, Friedman-Lewis Productions; *The Unknown*, © Metro-Goldwyn-Mayer Distributing Corporation; *Weird Woman*, Universal Pictures Company; *What Ever Happened to Baby Jane?*, © The Associates and Aldrich; *White Zombie*, Halperin; *The Wind*, Soapbox Films/Divide|Conquer/Mind Hive Films; *The Witch* (Robert Eggers, Parts & Labor/RT Features/Rooks Nest Entertainment/Maiden Voyage Pictures/Mott Street Pictures/Code Red Productions/Scythia Films/Pulse Films/Special Projects; *The Wolf Man*, © Universal Pictures Company; *Young Frankenstein*, © Twentieth Century-Fox Film Corporation.